PENGUIN BOOKS

Futebol Nation

David Goldblatt was born in London in 1965 and lives in Bristol. He shares his affections between Tottenham Hotspur and Bristol Rovers. In 2006 he published *The Ball is Round: A Global History of Football*. Since then he has made sport documentaries for BBC Radio, reviewed sports books for the *TLS* and the *Guardian*, taught the sociology of sport at Bristol University, the International Centre for Sports History and Culture, De Montfort University, Leicester and Pitzer College, Los Angeles, and gone swimming.

Futebol Nation

A Footballing History of Brazil

DAVID GOLDBLATT

PENGUIN BOOKS

PENGUIN BOOKS

Published by the Penguin Group
Penguin Books Ltd, 80 Strand, London WC2R ORL, England
Penguin Group (USA) Inc., 375 Hudson Street, New York, New York 10014, USA
Penguin Group (Canada), 90 Eglinton Avenue East, Suite 700, Toronto, Ontario,
Canada M4P 2Y3 (a division of Pearson Penguin Canada Inc.)
Penguin Ireland, 25 St Stephen's Green, Dublin 2, Ireland (a division of Penguin Books Ltd)
Penguin Group (Australia), 707 Collins Street, Melbourne, Victoria 3008, Australia
(a division of Pearson Australia Group Pty Ltd)
Penguin Books India Pvt Ltd, 11 Community Centre, Panchsheel Park, New Delhi – 110 017, India
Penguin Group (NZ), 67 Apollo Drive, Rosedale, Auckland 0632, New Zealand
(a division of Pearson New Zealand Ltd)
Penguin Books (South Africa) (Pty) Ltd, Block D, Rosebank Office Park,
181 Jan Smuts Avenue, Parktown North, Gauteng 2193, South Africa

Penguin Books Ltd, Registered Offices: 80 Strand, London WC2R ORL, England

www.penguin.com

First published 2014
001

ISBN: 978-0-241-96977-9

www.greenpenguin.co.uk

Contents

CONTENTS

Introduction

The Curious Rise of the Futebol Nation

'Football is played in the stadium? Football is played one the beach' – *Carlos Drummond de Andrade.*

The Futebol Nation: Ipanema Beach, Rio.

Brazil does not want us! It is sick and tired of us!
Our Brazil is in the afterworld. This is not Brazil.
There is no Brazil. By any chance, are there Brazilians?
Carlos Drummond de Andrade, 1934

Brazil is empty on a Sunday afternoon, right?
Look, sambão, here is the country of football.
Milton Nascimento and Fernando Brant, 1970

I

Brazil, by both area and population, is the fifth largest nation on earth. Its economy is perhaps the sixth or seventh largest and will soon surpass those of France and Britain. Yet this great continental state has barely registered its presence globally. In the complex flux of globalized popular cultures or the rarefied circuits of high culture and the sciences, Brazil is an undercurrent.[1] Brazilian cuisine, or rather its beef-heavy southern regional variant, can be found in the global cities of the north and the few urban enclaves where a recent Brazilian diaspora has emerged (like Massachusetts and London), but it is a small side order compared to the truly global reach of Chinese, Thai and Indian cooking. Even coffee, with which Brazil was once synonymous, has been culturally colonized in the global north by its Italian variant. The nation's once hegemonic position in coffee production has been eroded. Starbucks serves cappuccino not *cafezinho*. Brazil, at its height, supplied 70 per cent of the global market; now it supplies less than a third.

Music and carnival are, in their picture-postcard form, perhaps the most widespread if glib images of the nation. Denuded of their social and political context, they serve, alongside Copacabana and the other palm-fringed beaches of the Atlantic coast, as code for languid tropical hedonism, the brand identity of Brazil in the global tourist market. Alluring as these traditions might seem, the global popularity of samba and its valence for crossovers with other musical forms are dwarfed by that of salsa or Jamaican reggae, a now global musical genre from an island with 1 per cent of Brazil's population. In the late 1950s and early 1960s bossa nova found a small market niche and considerable critical acclaim in the United States, before it was tragically rendered down by the music industry into the staple saccharine groove of 1970s lift muzak. The complex constellation of MPB (*Música Popular Brasileira*) has given the world Chico Buarque, Gilberto Gil and Caetano Veloso, but the world music audience has vastly preferred the rhythms of the Caribbean and Africa. Capoeira, the nation's Afro-Brazilian martial art, has been gaining in global popularity since the 1970s and has established beachheads across the world, but it is almost a century behind the globalization of judo, and is still catching up with the post-war East Asian export drive led by karate, ju-jitsu and taekwondo.

We need not take the views of the Nobel Foundation and its

judges as the definitive word on the nation's sciences and the arts, but it is notable that not a single award has been made to a Brazilian. In the social sciences and humanities, Brazil's extensive university sector and wide arc of well-funded research foundations are primarily in conversation with themselves. On the global stage perhaps only the work of Roberto Unger, the political philosopher, has been widely recognized. The nation's literary traditions are unquestionably rich; a canon which includes the brilliant short stories of Machado de Assis and the widely translated novels of Jorge Amado is not marginal. Yet the global appeal and standing of Spanish-language writing from Latin America – a roster that includes Borges, Allende, Neruda, Márquez and Fuentes – exceed Brazil's.

Despite being an early adopter of celluloid technologies and creating, at times, a sustainable national film industry, Brazil's only cinematic movement of international note was the Cinema Novo of the late 1950s and early 1960s. Even then, outside the country it only registered with the small art-house audiences and cineastes of Western Europe. More recently, the very best of Brazilian movies, like *Bus 174*, have made the same journey, but only *City of God* has troubled the world's box offices. While Brazilian cinema has yielded most of its home market to Hollywood, the Brazilian television industry has proved a very different competitor. Dominant at home, technically polished, it may speak with a narrow range of political and social voices but they are unambiguously Brazilian. In the *telenovela* the sector has forged its own unique mass popular genre in parallel with the Anglo-Saxon soap opera rather than simply imitating the European version.

In the visual arts, Brazilian painting and conceptual art in the last century developed their own variants on the dominant movements of Europe and North America, but rarely made an impact in the auction houses and galleries of London or New York. The nation's single most famous sculpture, *Cristo Redentor* – standing, hands outstretched, on Corcovado above Rio's beaches – is the work of a Franco-Polish sculptor. Only the sinuous tropical modernism of Brazilian architecture has acquired a truly global profile, and even this rests overwhelmingly on the work of one architect – Oscar Niemeyer – and one complex – the federal government buildings in Brasília.

In one realm, however, Brazil is not only visible but ubiquitous, not merely competitive but the clear winner: football. Nike, whose commercial judgement on the value of global brands should be respected, have been prepared to pay more money than any other company for any other kit deal in pursuit of the yellow and green shirt. The Brazilian football authorities can charge more for the presence of the Seleção, as the national team is known, at an international friendly than anyone else. Since the 1970s, when film and television coverage of the team first reached Africa and Asia, the Brazilians have been supported across the global south, often alongside or even in preference to national teams. In the Gulf and South-East Asia, where the English Premier League and the Spanish duopoly of Real Madrid and Barcelona have made deep advances into the market for consumer loyalties, their respective national team shirts are a sideline. Brazil is the tribune of those football cultures that have never qualified for the World Cup. Except in Argentina and Uruguay, Brazil is almost everyone's second team when the tournament rolls around.

Rio hosted the United Nations' most important environmental conference in 1992, but for most of the twentieth century Brazil's contribution to international institutions was invisible. By contrast,

FIFA, although founded and run by Europeans for almost seventy years before the presidency of João Havelange, is now a global player built in the country's image. Primarily responsible for the massively increased media profile and economic worth of the World Cup, as well as the growing cultural capital of FIFA in the global political arena, Havelange brought to the institution the unique imprimatur of Brazil's ruling elite: imperious cordiality, ruthless clientelistic politics and a self-serving blurring of the public and private realms, institutional and personal benefit. Havelange stepped down almost two decades ago, but business at FIFA is still conducted in the mould which he cast, though without a fraction of his discretion or style.

In this realm Brazil's standing rests not merely on the value of the brand or the breadth of its support, but on the fact that Brazilian football has become, in the collective imagination if not the daily practice of professional football, the gold standard of the game. Since 1938, when Brazil dazzled Europe at the World Cup in France, the European and then the world's media have framed Brazilian football as exotic and other-worldly, musical and terpsichorean, a unique blend of the effective and the aesthetic. Cliché it may be, but very few Brazilian phrases have entered the global lingua franca like the phrase popularized by Pelé, *O Jogo Bonito* – the Beautiful Game.[2] Hugh McIlvanney's elegiac account of the 1970 final in Mexico City is among the best of simply thousands of similar paeans to Brazilian football that have secured its place in the global imagination:

> Other teams thrill us and make us respect them. The Brazilians at
> their finest gave us pleasure so natural and deep as to be a vivid

physical experience . . . the qualities that make football the most graceful and electric of team sports were being laid before us. Brazil are proud of their own unique abilities but it was not hard to believe that they were anxious to say something about the game as well as themselves. You cannot be the best in the world at a game without loving it and all of us who sat, flushed with excitement, in the stands of the Azteca sensed that we were seeing some kind of tribute.[3]

In the stands of British football Brazil's football pre-eminence is invoked as both praise and sardonic comment on incompetence when crowds sing, 'It's just like watching Brazil'. In Belgrade, the fearsomely nationalist Serbs of Red Star named their ground the Marakana in honour of Rio's great stadium. These tributes do not stand on mere invention or orientalist fantasy. The World Cup may only happen once every four years, just twenty occasions since its inception in 1930, and it may only be a football tournament, but for much of the twentieth century it has – alongside the Olympic Games – provided a rare and genuinely cosmopolitan cultural moment that reaches a global public like no other spectacle. Brazil is the only country to have participated in every one of them. It has won the World Cup five times and lost two finals. As well as being the most successful nation, Brazil's style of play and the manner of its victories and its disasters have been seared more deeply into global football culture than any other. As importantly, long before the rest of the world came to consider football the exemplar of Brazilian national identity, Brazil had done so itself.

||

It took less than four decades for Carlos Drummond de Andrade, Brazil's mid-century poet laureate, to get an answer to his question posed at the beginning of this Introduction. Milton Nascimento's much-recorded song 'Here is the Football Nation' replied, 'At the match'. It was, from the 1960s onwards, a commonplace of Brazilian culture that football was the national ritual. When the Seleção took the field at the World Cup and over 95 per cent of the population were watching them on television, Brazil existed in a more complete way than at any other moment. This was not just a symbolic practice; the demands of football could produce tangible material change too. The 1970 World Cup in Mexico was not only the occasion of Brazil's third, and most scintillating victory, but also, to ensure nationwide coverage of the games, the first time that a comprehensive north–south telecommunications infrastructure had been built; just one of the many ways in which the Brazilian state has tried to use football to create the nation.

The creation of a Brazilian nation-state and a living sense of the Brazilian nation or people has been a long and arduous process, for both tasks began with the most meagre of resources. Although the country notionally acquired independence from Portugal in 1822, it entered the post-colonial world without experiencing the defining break that characterized the emergence of nations in Spanish-speaking South America. First, the Portuguese court decamped en masse from Lisbon to Rio, fleeing Napoleon's invading armies. Settling in for almost two decades, the royal court ruled the Lusophone empire from Brazil. When, reluctantly, Dom

Pedro I returned to take up his throne in Europe, he left behind his son Dom Pedro II as emperor of a now independent Brazilian Empire. Thus Brazil's life as a nation rather than some unusual imperial specimen began only in 1889 when the army deposed the emperor in a brief bloodless coup and declared the first Brazilian Republic. Nation in name, the Brazilian republican state was a fragile creature. The nation's borders were only finally resolved in the early decades of the twentieth century and they remained, if geographically defined, virtually unpoliced. The federal state and the presidency, whatever their constitutional prerogatives, lacked the reach and power to govern a nation that stretched from the capital Rio over 500 miles south to the Uruguayan border and more than 2,000 miles to the depths of the Amazonian basin and the Caribbean coast of the far north. In effect, enormous autonomy was ceded to the states and their local elites.

At the turn of the twentieth century, economically and topographically Brazil might as well have been four or five nations. In the south an almost completely European population presided over rich cattle ranching; in the south-east, in the most important and populous states of São Paulo, Rio and Minas Gerais, a world-beating coffee plantation economy was at its peak. In what is now known as the centre west, the inland states of Mato Grosso and Goiás were still a refuge for indigenous Brazilians. A future inland capital had been located there on the maps, but the area was virtually uninhabited and unworked by Europeans. In the north-east, along the Atlantic coast, the remnants of the sugar plantation and slavery complex were combined with the vast, harsh-ranching latifundia of the dry interior, where the same families that had personally commanded these states for centuries remained firmly in control. In the north, but for Manaus, Belém and the short-lived rubber boom that created them, Brazil had barely scratched at the surface of the vast Amazonian rainforest. Moreover, until the advent of reasonably regular air transport in the late 1940s and 1950s, these regions were connected by the thinnest of threads. Coastal shipping remained the most reliable and the fastest way of communicating between the south and the north, roads were poor, and the country began the century with fewer railway tracks than Belgium.

Over the next half century or so Brazil would be transformed from an overwhelmingly rural to a predominantly urban society, and in Rio de Janeiro and São Paulo it acquired cities of truly metropolitan magnitude. Brazil's agrarian economies, while remaining significant, were now joined by a rapidly growing industrial sector centred on the south-east. Both of these processes were driven by migration, internal and external. With the end of slavery in 1888, a vast Afro-Brazilian population of landless peasants was created which, along with the many poor whites and mulattos of the north-east, began heading for the coastal cities of the country. Simultaneously, millions of Europeans – predominantly Italians, Portuguese and Germans – crossed the Atlantic and stayed in Brazil. Among the many social and cultural transformations wrought by these changes perhaps the most significant was the emergence of the urban working and middle classes and the slow spread of literacy down the social hierarchy. In an electoral system where literacy was the key qualification for voting, this began to produce a larger and more complex electorate.

Brazil's flimsy federal state and its antiquated military would eventually acquire significantly more power at the expense of individual states, making a national government a reality, but who and what was this geographically and socially fragmented nation?

In the century after independence, Brazil's tiny intelligentsia had looked to Europe for inspiration. Portugal itself proved as hopeless a source of cultural ideas as it had of both capital and labour, so the guiding compass for Brazilian high culture was France. The decorative architecture of the Parisian Belle Époque was reproduced with considerable flourish in Rio, and French novels and poetry were widely read. Auguste Comte, the founder of the discipline of sociology, provided the intellectual inspiration for the cabal of modernizing junior officers that drove the republican revolution. It is, after all, a Comtean notion of 'Order and Progress' that is spelt out on the Brazilian flag; a reminder of a time when it was thought that the European sciences could diagnose a nation's ills and produce rational and effective interventions to deal with them. Alongside this kind of absurdly optimistic positivism, Brazil drew upon European biological theories of race and eugenics. On the one hand, they provided an apparently legitimate scientific explanation of white European superiority. On the other, they made their Brazilian advocates worry about the declining demographic position and racial health of European Brazil, and advocate the whitening of the nation. What didn't make the journey across the South Atlantic were the more radical and democratic dimensions to the French Republic, the concept and indeed the practice of universal citizenship. This carefully edited cluster of ideas and imagery might have been enough to create a notion of upper-class, white European Brazilianness, albeit one constantly threatened by the demographic and racial realities of the country, but as an exercise in popular nationalism under conditions of rapid industrialization it was going nowhere.

The relentless demands of industrialized warfare have been a powerful catalyst for the creation of national state institutions and a collective sense of national identity, but Brazil never experienced this. Although its military was kept busy fighting a gruelling nineteenth-century war with its Paraguayan neighbours, suppressing independent ex-slave communities in the north-east, putting down a rash of mutinies, regional rebellions and revolts, and even sending a brigade to fight on the Allied side in Italy in the closing years of the Second World War, none of these conflicts could serve as a crucible of national myth, heroic triumph or collective fortitude. Given Brazil's calamitously low level of literacy, the creation of a national public sphere through a shared language and literature was not a plausible strategy either.

In this light, Carlos Drummond de Andrade's apparent flippancy belies a profound problem for Brazilian nationalists of the early twentieth century. At the most protean moment of Brazil's search to define itself, the answer could not simply be imposed from above on white, literate and elite terms. Brazil henceforth would have to incorporate some notion of its African demographics, its complex ethnicities, and the non-literate tastes and practices of its emerging urban popular classes. Brazil was, in actual fact, rich in precisely these cultural forms: popular music from *choro* to the samba and their accompanying dances and carnivals; *candomblé*, the generic term for African religious and spiritual practices forged from the hybrid of African cultures compressed under slavery; *umbanda*, the emerging urban form of *candomblé* that actively mixed African spirits and Catholic saints, pagan ritual and the Roman sacraments. Yet despite the various attempts made by Brazil's elite to appropriate these forms, and to integrate at some level the African contribution to Brazilian life, they did not carry a sense of modernity. On the contrary they remained rooted in deeply antiquated cultures. Brazilian nationalism required a cultural practice that could encompass the full spectrum of the nation's complex social and racial hierarchies, and that acknowledged the nation's past but set it on a course for the future. Football, especially in its initial association with Britain, the most modern nation of the time, provided just that. It was in this context that the game, as a physical bodily practice, as a collective ritual, as a carnivalesque spectacular and as a historical narrative, open to all Brazilians, acquired its status in the national pantheon; a position solidified by the global success and poetic acclaim of the national team.

Although football was introduced by the British in São Paulo, and initially played by a predominantly expatriate body of players, it is remarkable how swiftly and completely these influences were overtaken. By the end of the First World War, just twenty years after the first recorded games had been played in São Paulo, the British influence had dwindled to almost nothing. Portuguese vernacular rapidly replaced the remnants of English in the game's vocabulary. Corinthians, the team of working-class São Paulo, retained their Anglo-Hellenic name, but the gentlemanly, amateur ethos of elite British sports culture was on its last legs and by the end of the 1930s it had collapsed altogether. British football, represented by touring professional teams, was already seen as profoundly different from the emerging Brazilian style of play. Over the next half-century, as well as being the most popular participatory sport, with the biggest crowds and the overwhelming favourite of media audiences of all kinds, football would become a subject of inquiry and depiction in almost every form of Brazilian popular culture and high art.

Whereas the response of the visual arts in twentieth-century Britain to football can be boiled down to a single Lowry canvas, football has appeared in the oeuvre of dozens of Brazil's leading artists – from the nationalist surrealism of Cândido Portinari to the abstract geometries of Ivan Serpa to the pop art of Claudio Tozzi. Its writers and novelists have, again and again, found space for the game in their literary landscapes: from Mário de Andrade's *Macunaíma,* to José Lins do Rego's epic saga of life on Rio's periphery, *Água-mãe,* from the urbane and witty *crônicas* of Clarice Lispector to the sharp short stories of Edilberto Coutinho's *Maracanã, Adeus.* The game has also been a thread and connector across the many spheres of Brazilian life. João Cabral Melo Neto was a diplomat who wrote poetry and his poetry featured Pelé. Pelé, a footballer, has gone on to be a businessman, the minister of culture and a singer and composer. The composer Ary Barroso crossed over into football commentary and then to municipal politics. Politicians regularly seek the presidency of clubs, while club presidents try to make the transition to formal politics. The crowd can become musicians, while musicians have endlessly written and composed songs for players and clubs. Poets and dramatists commentate on football. Football commentators like Washington Rodrigues and João Saldanha have become coaches.

When Globo's leading commentator Galvão Bueno criticizes the Seleção's opponents for a fumble or misplaced pass, he says with a mixture of pity and contempt, 'They don't have the same intimacy with the ball.' It is a tone that assures you that he and his listeners are quite convinced that whatever its origins, whatever the competition, it is only in Brazil that football is truly at home, sunk deep into the web of meanings and memory that the nation has spun around it.

III

This kind of intimacy with the ball is a mixed blessing, or as musician and composer José Miguel Wisnik has more floridly described it in his 2008 book, *Veneno Remédio* – a poison remedy.[4] In part this is because football is an unpredictable game. All the statistical evidence reinforces the observation that on any given day the worst team can win, that favourites are more vulnerable than in other sports, that the place for the random, the chaotic and the unexpected is surprisingly large in football. To gauge if not the ultimate fate, then at least the spirit and feel of the nation by the performance of one's national football team is a risky choice for a culture, even one like Brazil with a preference for ritual over reason; but the trade-off between the instrumental logic of winning and the creative aesthetic of play has, as Roberto DaMatta makes clear, its own wisdom and logic:

> In futebol there is art, dignity, genius, bad luck, gods and demons, freedom and fate, flags, hymns and tears, and above all the discovery that although Brazil is bad at a lot of things, it is good with the ball. It is a football champion, which is very important. After all, it is better to be a champion in samba, carnival and football than in war or the sale of rockets.[5]

The real price of making football the avatar of the nation is that the game's deep connections to Brazil's social structures, economic institutions and political processes are also laid bare. For the most part these have made much less edifying viewing, for

Brazilians and foreign observers alike, than the game itself. The history of Brazilian football, like the history of the Brazilian nation, must reckon with some harsh sociological realities. First, Brazil's location in the global economy has, despite everything, remained as a supplier of raw materials, from soya beans to footballers, so that Brazil reaps only a fraction of the economic value of its fertility.

Second, Brazil's economy and social relations are marked by an almost unparalleled level of inequality, across region, class and race: the global north and the global south sit side by side in Brazil's biggest cities. Social hierarchies and patterns of authority established centuries ago still persist. This is both the engine room of Brazil's endless conveyor belt of footballing aspiration and talent, and the source of so many of the game's pathologies: its harsh and often unfair treatment of players and fans; its persistent racism and sexism; and the systematic advantage that accrues to the already powerful, be they clubs or players.

Third, Brazilian football operates in a political and administrative culture that has struggled to live up to the democratic aspirations of its constitutions. In part this has been a consequence of the role of the military in arbitrating political conflicts and their predilection for coups and periods of governmental authority. However, even in their absence, the Brazilian state has been riddled with corruption and nepotism, has a weak sense of the public good, and has a dismal record of transparency and accountability. Increasingly its clubs and its football federations have been run on this model. Brazil, of course, has no monopoly on such practices in the world of football, but it is an ugly, vicious and chaotic football polity nonetheless.

Fourth, Brazil is a violent society. This is nothing new. The limited reach of the rule of law, the prevalence of weapons, and the erratic probity of its multiple police forces and militias, together with the long shadow of the country's history of forced labour, have all left their mark. Over the last three decades, approaching two hundred people have died in football-related violence in Brazil and thousands have been injured. Fights between players, officials, police and fans at both the highest level and the most marginal grassroots of the game are tragically common.

This book is a short history of the many dimensions of Brazilian football: its brilliance, its magic, its style and its dash, and the fabulous myths and stories that have been constructed around it; its tragedies and its miseries, the light it shines on the economic and political injustices of Brazilian life; and, just occasionally, the example it offers of a society that might underline Brazil's conviviality and creativity rather than its brutality and conservatism.

1

Champagne Football: The Game of the Belle Époque, 1889–1922

Gentlemen and Players: Fluminense host the professionals of Exeter City, 1914.

The first bug fell in Campinas, miles away; it was a caterpillar. The second bug fell thereabouts too, it was a woolly bear; the leather ball fell in a field. It was thus that Mannape introduced the coffee bug, Jique the cotton boll weevil and Macunaíma the football; three of the main pests in the country today.

Mário de Andrade, 1928

Football is as important in Rio de Janeiro today as the theatre is in Paris.

João Carlos, 1919

I

Football as popular curse, football as high art; the magical invention of an indigenous Brazilian anti-hero or the centrepiece of the nation's distinctive tropical urban modernity; either way, as the account of football in Mário de Andrade's epic novel *Macunaíma* and this description of the game in a Rio newspaper *crônica* suggest, Brazil's elite were not merely playing and watching football in the first three decades of the twentieth century, but thinking and writing about it, asking it to stand for something important, even profound, about the emerging Brazilian nation.[1] Andrade's novel takes indigenous folklore as the backbone of his tale. Macunaíma, described as a 'hero without a character', a shape-shifter possessing more than one life and voice, is sent on a long journey from the rainforests of Amazonia to Rio de Janeiro and São Paulo in search of a lost amulet. Playful and surreal, the book was a bravura combination of ancient mythic narrative and fractured modernist prose, Latin magic realism before the term had been coined, its meanings and symbols as slippery as its characters. Football might be a curse, but it was a Brazilian curse, not an import. In fact, by the 1930s, Andrade was a quiet football fanatic, exclaiming of his favourite player, 'What a dancer!' and complaining of the 'three hundred and fifty reasons that keep me from the stadium'.[2]

He has not been alone in the impulse to invent a Brazilian football creation myth. Nationalist historians of physical education have tried to claim that indigenous ball games provided both context and example for the emergence of Brazil's distinctive modern sporting culture. In Carlos Diegues's film *Quilombo* (1984), set in the independent communities of north-eastern Brazil created by runaway slaves and paupers of all kinds, one scene depicts two boys practising capoeira. From off screen, from nowhere, a ball appears in the air and without breaking step the boys incorporate it into their wheeling and swerving. There is not a scintilla of truth in any of these claims, but that is hardly the point.

More prosaically there are scattered reports in the Brazilian press, as well as the memories of elite Brazilians recalling the 1870s and 1880s, which reveal that slaves, the urban poor and dockworkers attempted to improvise some version of the strange but magnetic ball game they saw played by British merchant seamen, while wealthy schoolboys tried to mimic their footballing peers encountered on visits to Europe.[3] There is no evidence, however, that they possessed a real football or a copy of the FA's Laws of the Game, first printed in 1863. For both of these objects, Brazil would await the return from his English public school education of Charles Miller, son of a Scottish émigré father and an Anglo-Brazilian mother, herself connected to a great São Paulo coffee dynasty. Disembarking in 1894, he carried with him in his kit bag two leather footballs and a copy of the rule book. Both would spread with the speed and self-replicating energy of the most lethal weevil or virulent bug.

At first glance imperial Brazil did not appear fertile soil for football or indeed sport of any kind. As it was a slave economy for over three centuries, all forms of physical labour and exertion carried a subaltern taint; the ruling elite disdained work and, given the epidemiology of the day, preferred to refrain from close contact with large gatherings of people. Luíz Edmundo, an early twentieth-century historian of Rio under the Empire, recalled, 'Until the end of the century we were, in fact, indifferent to the pleasures and benefits of sport.' The word 'sport' had actually appeared in Rio's newspapers between 1840 and 1860, but its meaning was closer to the idea of games or an entertainment, referring for the most part to the city's increasing interest in gambling, card games and bullfights.[4] From the 1870s onwards, spurred by visits to Europe as well as the tastes of a new wave of prosperous and professional European migrants to Rio, the city's elite loosened up and began playing. First, they started swimming, making the shift from therapeutic bathing to recreational paddling and eventually competitive swimming. A flotilla of bath houses was erected in the Baía de Guanabara at the end of the century and they were used by male and, for the first time, female swimmers. There were also new crazes for skating, cycling and athletics, and so by 1885 Rio possessed two skating rinks, a velodrome (as did São Paulo), swimming pools, gymnasiums and clubs where, in addition, gentlemen could fence, wrestle and play billiards. In the British-dominated clubs cricket flourished, but it made few converts. Established papers and magazines found more space for sports news, and new journals like *O Sport*, started in 1891, and *O Remo*, first published in 1900, wrote about nothing else. The pages of every publication began to carry adverts for sports-sponsored products and medicinal tonics.

Yet all of these games were dwarfed in popularity by Rio's favourites – rowing and horse racing – for here alone the athletic was made spectacular, and sport mixed most easily with socializing. The first organized horse racing took place in the 1810s, initiated by the colony of British merchants. By 1895 Rio possessed four racecourses, with tram routes adapted to their location and local press brimming on a daily basis with rumour, review and preview of the racing scene. While organizationally the sport was in the hands of the rich who owned the clubs, the course and the horses, attendance was for virtually everybody. As the *Gazeta* headline read in 1875, 'Let's go to the races! Rich and poor, men and old men, old women and young women.'[5] In addition to the prestigious Jockey and Derby clubs, whose facilities and architecture matched the wealth of their patrons, more basic tracks were available in the working-class neighbourhoods of Prado Guarani and São Cristóvão. Such was the fervour for the races that the rich were prepared to travel across town and slum it there; there was not only the frisson of downward social mobility available, but also illegal betting.

Horse racing, for all its pleasures, had an ineradicable rural and agrarian feel. It was the spectacle of the past. For a more modern edge, Rio turned first to rowing. Based in the now exclusive and multi-sport social clubs of the beaches of the Zona Sul, the craze for rowing marked a shift among young Cariocas (as the city's inhabitants are known) from merely watching sports to playing them as well. By the early 1880s up to 30,000 people would line the beaches and quays that overlooked Rio's bays to watch boats compete, and spend the day drinking and mingling before making the short walk to a beachside house party or the luxurious dining rooms of the rowing clubhouses. Indeed the sport was so popular that in 1903 the mayor of Rio, Pereira Passos, won plaudits and votes for spending public money on improved regatta facilities in Botafogo. It was to be rowing's high point. Just a year later, the organizers of one of Rio's biggest regattas wrote to the organizers of the city's football matches begging them not to hold their games on the same day as their event, for the crowds they were drawing so depleted theirs.

‖

Charles Miller, with the kind of sentimentality in his voice that suggested he had fully acculturated to Brazilian norms, recalled his return from England in October 1894 to Santos, the port city to the south of São Paulo:

On the quay . . . solemn, as if he were at a funeral, my father was waiting for me to disembark holding my degree certificate. But in fact I appeared in front of him with two footballs, one in each hand . . . The Old Man, surprised, enquired:

'What is this, Charles?'

'My degree,' I replied.

'What?'

'Yes, your son has graduated in football.'

The old man, in good spirits, laughed, I was off the hook . . .[6]

Miller had been educated at Banister Court in Hampshire, played football for his school, then the county and even a few games for the newly professionalized club Southampton. Whatever the real manner of his return, he was soon ensconced at the São Paulo Athletic Club playing cricket and trying to persuade the uninitiated to give football a go. In spring 1895 he and a few other club members made their way to the flat scrubland east of the old city centre where the mules that pulled the trams were left to graze. The mules were chased off and two hastily assembled teams created – the São Paulo Railway Team and the Gas Team – whose players were drawn from those heralds of urban modernity, the new electrical tram corporation and the municipal gas supply company. Opposition was not long in coming; the students of the elite school Mackenzie College took to the game and formed a team. Then, in 1897, a German immigrant called Hans Nobiling arrived in the city with his own German-language rule book and a few games under his belt back in Hamburg. Initially rebuffed by the almost exclusively English members of São Paulo AC, Nobiling helped form SC (Sporting Club) Internacional with players from many of the city's expatriate communities; though strangely he would quickly go on to create a breakaway club of exclusively Teutonic members called SC Germânia. With the arrival of distinct Brazilian elite clubs like CA Paulistano, whose president was the state government's minister of justice, and AA Palmeiras, a team exclusively comprised of engineering and legal students, the city now had six teams and, just a few years after Miller's arrival, a small but functioning championship.

São Paulo had started the football mania, but Rio was not far behind. In 1897 Oscar Cox, a fabulously wealthy Anglo-Swiss Brazilian, returned from his studies in Lausanne, where among other things he had learned to play football. Initially Cox persuaded the Rio Cricket and Athletic Association to try the game and they were joined by the equally English Paysandu Cricket Club and the Rio Cricket Club across the bay in Niterói. In 1901 he arranged the first game between representatives of Rio and São Paulo, played at São Paulo Athletic Club in October of that year. The local press purred over the calibre of the occasion: 'The crowd . . . besides being very select was very big, and prominent were the elegant women who lent a happy note to the festivities.'[7] The following year, after the final match of the São Paulo Championship, the match ball was bathed in champagne. Brazil's relationship with the game was set in a hedonistic and flamboyant cast.

Not everyone was convinced. One newspaper report of a very early match in Rio seemed to find the sport genuinely incomprehensible. 'In Bom Retiro,' it spluttered, 'a group of Englishmen, a bunch of maniacs as they all are, get together from time to time to kick around something that looks like a bull's bladder. It gives them great satisfaction or fills them with sorrow when this kind of yellowish bladder enters a rectangle formed by wooden posts.'[8]

In São Paulo, it was considered by some to be just a passing fad, while other papers thought it both uncivilized and dangerously foreign. One dismissed it as 'A blind and barmy battle of physical force without the intervention of our superior faculties.' The same author concluded that, 'Football is an English game and should only be played by the English.' A São Paulo Athletic Club player, making his way to the velodrome in full kit for a match, was stopped and arrested by a Brazilian police officer who considered him 'dressed for carnival, out of season, offensively showing his legs in public in the centre of the city'. But for most of the Brazilians who came into contact with the English game it was neither too violent nor too modern. It was irresistible. Charles Miller, in a 1904 letter to his school in England, described the new football mania that had spread beyond the tiny enclave of elite athletic clubs:

You will be surprised to hear that football is the game here. We have no less than sixty or seventy clubs in S. Paul's city alone . . . We always get two to three thousand people to a league match, but for the final we had 6,000 . . . A week ago I was asked to referee in a match of small boys, twenty a side. I told them that it was absurd to be playing twenty a side . . . but I found I was very much mistaken. They played over two and a half hours and I only had to give two hands . . . even for this match about 1,500 people turned up . . . No less than 2,000 footballs have been sold here within the last twelve months: nearly every village has a club here.[9]

The social and cultural consequences of this kind of rapid diffusion of football would only become clear in the 1920s. For the first two decades of the twentieth century Brazilian football remained set in its elite cast. Any doubt about the enthusiasms of the rich and powerful for football, any concerns that it might be too uncivilized were brushed away by the formation of Fluminense, the super-club for the super-rich in Laranjeiras in Rio. The club was founded by Oscar Cox and a cross-section of his chums from the Rio elite, unhappy with the lack of enthusiasm for football at the various cricket and rowing clubs they had frequented. Mário Filho later described the cast of characters in the dressing room and around their fabulous dining tables as 'chiefs of companies, sons of rich fathers, educated in Europe, used to spending money'. The season was a relentless round of games, dinners, parties and dances. Jack Hamilton, the English coach who had been employed at the equally louche CA Paulistano in 1907, found that his squad needed 'a lot of coaxing to train properly'.

By 1917 the Estádio das Laranjeiras had been built. Nestled next to the Palácio Guanabara – the former residence of the Emperor's daughter – Laranjeiras was a striking mix of the functional and the decorative, the popular and the elite; the pitch was entirely enclosed, access was via the gates in walls of repeating neo-Palladian arches which led out on to three stepped terraces for the general public; the best view was from a seated stand for club members whose woodwork and detailing suggested a beachside palace. Behind this sat the clubhouse which included a gilded ballroom big enough for 500 guests, as well as ample space for drinking and dining, socializing and networking. Indicative of the place of Fluminense within Brazil's power elites was the role of the Guinle brothers. Carlos and Guilherme held the presidency three times between them before the oldest brother, Arnaldo, took over in 1916 and held on to the position until the 1930s.

From an old and wealthy aristocratic clan, Guilherme started out as a civil engineer, founded a bank in Bahia and then in the 1930s moved to the very centre of economic decision-making in Getúlio Vargas's government, responsible for the creation of a nationalized steel industry and then for a short period became president of the Bank of Brazil. Carlos was a composer and a key patron of the arts in the city, while Arnaldo had time and money to devote himself to Fluminense. Alongside them Fluminense could boast among its roster the leading writers of the day, from the novelist Henrique Coelho Neto to the poet Olavo Bilac.

In Rio the foundation of Fluminense was quickly followed by the creation of football teams at the Botafogo rowing club which drew players from the elite schools nearby, the Colégio Alfredo Gomes and the Ginásio Nacional. The following year América was created by the sons of old north-eastern families, declining rural elites who had gravitated to the capital and now appeared to embrace its modern urban cultures. The Flamengo rowing club in the luxurious lakeside neighbourhood of Gávea, had initially resisted the pull of football, many of its oarsmen considering the new game a form of unmanly prancing, but when in 1911 a group of Fluminense footballers broke from the club they found a home at Flamengo. The situation in São Paulo was no different. Thomaz Mazzoni, the great chronicler of the city's game, surveyed over forty players in the decade before the First World War and found them to be: 'Engineers, building contractors, and merchants . . . with a scattering of accountants, doctors, bankers, army officers, professors, architects and one poet-schoolteacher'.[10]

In this era, teams would formally enter on to the pitch, line up in front of the main stand and offer a salute or a bow to the crowd, who responded with three rounds of hip-hip-hurrah, loud applause and cheering. It was a level of decorum that, at first, was maintained despite the fiercely competitive character of the game. São Paulo newspapers praised a Rio team and noted 'the correctness of their game . . . this was to be expected from boys who benefit from a polished and distinguished education'. Rio's *Gazeta*, reporting on a match between Botafogo and América in Rio in 1908, wrote: 'After the arguments and the matches, footballers are always friends. They are polite young men from our society and respect each other. They do not fight seriously.'[11] Crowds were described as jovial; supporters of each club would clap both teams almost indiscriminately. Dress in the stands was formal but stylish. For men it was light suits, straw boaters, walking canes and a simply extraordinary array of waistcoats and waxed moustaches. For the true in-crowd a striped band of the club's colours could be wrapped around their hats, a detail familiar to those who had attended English public schools.

However, the single most important fact about the crowd – and an indicator of the social function of football – was that the society ladies of Rio were present and in very large numbers. They came in the latest summer fashions, millinery inspired by Paris, veils and netting, carefully coiffed curls and flowers in their hair. At half-time players would take the chance to join friends and family in the stands, engage in conversation with a lady who had caught their eye on the wing or join the gaggle of girls draping themselves decorously on the carved wooden banisters of the clubhouse. One observer, when watching Paysandu against Fluminense in 1913, looked at the crowd and saw 'A formidable array of vividly beautiful girls who seem to want to leap up and chant the names of players, the ladies were pale from their enthusiasm.' As late as 1919 the same writer was claiming that of the fans 'the most empathetic, the most constant and the most numerous para-doxically were feminine'.[12] It wasn't just flirting either, there was a tangible sexual undercurrent. The celebrity football couple of the era, the poet Ana Amélia and the banker turned historian Marcos de Mendonça, met when she saw him play as Fluminense's goal-keeper. Her poem 'The Leap' leaves remarkably little to the imagination.

> When I saw you today,
> Executing your relaxed, daring and vigorous leap
> Like a figure from the *Iliad*
> I trembled in the most intimate part of my being
> Swept by a frenetic impulse as if I were before a Greek,
> The hero of an Olympiad.[13]

Perhaps, in 1910, it really did feel that ancient Greece was being reborn in the football stadiums of Rio, but by the end of the First World War it was beginning to look more like the rabble that attended Rome's Colosseum. Writing in 1916, João do Rio reflected, 'I've seen enormous crowds in many countries, great carnivals of health and fresh air, but never have I seen such fire, such enthusi-asm, of a crowd like that.'[14] Certainly the size of the crowds at football games had grown from a couple of thousand in the first decade of the century to figures nearer 10,000 in the second, and on occasion even more. Clubs had now built walls and gates, and sold tickets to the public, though the members continued to gain free access to games and a spot in the reserved seats in the best stand. For the rest of the public there were standing terraces and tickets were still cheap, certainly less than a trip to the theatre and closer to the cost of a cheap meal in a workmen's café in the city.

This was still beyond the means of the poorest and most peripheral who often watched Fluminense games from the surrounding hills, but for the lower middle classes, indeed anyone with regular employment, it was an affordable pleasure.

The crowds, transformed by the arrival of this new social stratum, appeared to be changing their behaviour too. They became more partisan and possessed an altogether more excitable attitude. In the press and vernacular speech they were now referred to as *torcida*, literally meaning 'the twisted'. It was a term that drew on the imagery of handkerchiefs being spun in the air by celebrating fans, and the turning of their guts as the tension mounted. In the gossip columns of the sports press it was rumoured that Fluminense fan Captain João Pereira had got so overwrought at a game that he had 'lost his moustache'.[15] Apparício de Brinkerhoff Torelly, who as the Barão de Itararé would go on to be the nation's leading humorist in the otherwise decidedly unfunny Vargas years, was cutting his satirical teeth on football in Rio. His poem 'Match de Foot-ball' contrasted the high social standing of the game's participants with the now distinctly low-rent crowds.

> And the mad crowd, brutish and rude,
> Booed the honourable head of a family.
> Another fell to the floor. People booed him.
> He got up furious, but fell again.
> All of this seemed, in my considered opinion,
> Twenty-two furies, pursuing the world.
> And after an hour and a half of fighting,
> The referee blew his whistle.
> The game was a draw.[16]

The lower classes may have been arriving in the cities of the Old Republic; they may, at the margins, have been making their presence felt, but football and above all Fluminense was still essentially an elite affair. An hour before the decisive game of the 1919 Carioca Championships, played between Fluminense and Flamengo, the newly expanded Laranjeiras stadium was full to its 18,000 capacity with 5,000 people locked outside without a ticket. A warm-up game entertained the crowd but half an hour after it had started President Pessoa, together with the First Lady and the minister of the navy, entered the directors' box and the game was paused for five minutes while the teams lined up in front of them and the navy band played the national anthem. Fluminense won the main attraction 4-0 after which players and fans descended on to the pitch and, marching with the navy band, conducted a great shambling victory parade. Fluminense's third consecutive title – the *tricampeonato* – was celebrated by both heraldic trumpets and a 21-gun salute. Mário Filho wrote that, henceforth, Fluminense fans would recite the names of this team: 'Mendonça, Lais, Oswaldo, Strong, Mano, Zezé . . .' as if they were an Olavo Bilac sonnet.

III

The tiny rarefied world of the Olavo Bilac sonnet, of the ball-rooms of Fluminense and the glitter and allure of football in Rio and São Paulo sat at the social apex of the Old Republic. Laranjeiras appeared an elite citadel, an aristocratic pleasure palace. But the solidity of the social and political arrangements on which this otherworldly glamour and privilege rested and which also kept the rest of society out was being slowly undermined. Two processes would profoundly disturb them: migration and urbanization.

Migration was both internal and external. The enduring poverty of the north-east saw poor blacks, mulattos and whites move to the coastal cities. Salvador and Recife both doubled their populations under the Old Republic. Simultaneously, migrants from Europe flooded in. From around 25,000 people a year in the last days of the Empire, the number of annual arrivals climbed as high as 165,000 in 1895 and continued at this high rate into the 1920s, by which time over 4 million people had arrived in the previous half century. Italians were the most numerous of the new arrivals, making up over a third of the total. They were followed by the Portuguese and then the Spanish and the Germans and a long mixed tail that included the Swiss, the French and the Russians. In the early twentieth century the demand for labour in the São Paulo coffee fields was so high that Brazil accepted over a million landless Japanese farmers, subsidized by their own government to make the transpacific crossing. Alongside them there was a steady flow of Britons, especially engineers, technicians in transport, electrical and manufacturing industries, as well as considerable numbers of Syrians, Lebanese and Jews. Overwhelmingly this wave of migrants headed for the south of the country and while many began in agricultural work they too moved to São Paulo and Rio, whose growth was truly astronomical. With just half a million inhabitants at the beginning of the Republic, Rio alone was home to 1.2 million by the early 1920s. São Paulo grew eight-fold over the same period to a population of over half a million and would, within a decade or so, surpass Rio itself.

Together these processes created new social classes and social forces right on the doorstep of Brazil's urban elites: a literate urban middle class, and a small but expanding working class, both of which consisted of a mix of blacks, mulattos and whites. These people could not be entirely excluded from the public life of the nation, but nor could they be easily assimilated into the elite's own sense of itself as a white European nation, concentrated in the two big cities of the south-eastern corner of the country. Football in the first two decades of the twentieth century provided an arena in which these geographical and sociological shifts could be registered. Clubs could blackball members, stadiums could have gates, but no one could stop people just playing. In 1914 the chairman of Exeter City while departing Rio from the docks saw a game in progress and remembered his surprise 'To discover that the match was between junior teams . . . They were all niggers, as black as your hat, and most of them playing in bare feet.'[17] In 1922 the Brazilian writer and journalist Lima Barreto wrote:

> Everyone in this good city of Rio, provided they're not leaden footed, or at least with their head full of lead, play the so-called British sport. There isn't a rich man or a poor man, old man or youth, white or black, street kid or posh boy who doesn't belong, at least informally, to a club destined to perfect men in the art of using their feet.[18]

Football, unlike most other emergent popular cultural forms, provided a public space for Brazil's male urban and working classes, as players, fans and organizers, and put them in contact with elite circles they would only otherwise encounter in the workplace. The São Cristóvão club, named after its working-class neighbourhood in the port zone of Rio, was emblematic of these processes. It was founded in 1909, crystallizing out of informal games and teams that had marked out a pitch in a patch of open public space. Such was the enthusiasm for the project that by 1910 they were playing in the Rio metropolitan league and holding a wide range of social events. From 1913 to 1916 the club built its own small Estádio Figueira de Melo in a piecemeal fashion, drawing on the skills and resources of its many members.

The inaugural game in 1917 saw them play Santos, who had travelled many hundreds of miles from São Paulo state, in front of a crowd of 6,000; though sadly the game only lasted fifteen minutes before the referee, complaining of the vicious intimidation coming from the home crowd, called it off. São Cristóvão's players, needless to say, did not live the life of Oscar Cox. Like most of the new clubs that were emerging at this time, they drew their players from the lower classes, of all racial categories, and received jobs, housing and food from the club's directors. A similarly excluded group were the Portuguese bourgeoisie of northern Rio, who as recent arrivals and despite their wealth found themselves shut out of the leading clubs and facing a wider economic and political decline in the changing demography of Rio. In 1898 they created Vasco da Gama as a rowing and social club and fielded their first football team in 1915, using the same recruitment methods as São Cristóvão. By 1922 they had reached the same league as the elite teams.

These initiatives from below were matched by experiments from above as a rash of factory teams emerged in Rio in the first decade of the century. The first and most notable of these was Bangu AC, created in 1904 by the British managers and technicians of the textile firm Companhia Progresso Industrial do Brasil, located on the distant edge of Rio's Zona Norte. Initially the team was made up just of English and Scottish technicians and managers, but they soon gave way to Italians and then Brazilian mulatto and black players. There was a similar mix in the crowd which, unlike those of the downtown teams, could mingle freely in any part of the ground. Bangu were the most successful of the factory teams, gained promotion to the top division in Rio and became far more widely known than the factory and company that had given birth to the club. Players were increasingly recruited from outside the firm and then received one of the less strenuous jobs in the factory leaving them time and energy to train. This kind of corporate paternalism proved attractive to many other Brazilian companies who were grappling with the problems thrown up by Brazil's first wave of real trade union organization. The country's first workers' congress was held in 1906, and a national labour movement was established in 1908 and, fortified by the arrival of Mediterranean anarchists and syndicalists in the great wave of migration, conducted a decade of strikes and agitation. Andaraí in northern Rio grew out of a textile firm and in 1908, eighty miles down the rail tracks from the city, SC Pau Grande was founded by the América Fabril company.

In São Paulo the first challenge to the status quo came from the working classes. In emulation of the English team Corinthians who had visited the city, in 1910 a group of railway workers and painters met in the north-eastern corner of the city to found SC Corinthians who rapidly attracted members and supporters from the city's growing multiracial working class. Italians in São Paulo had, hitherto, occupied a middling position in the racial spectrum of Brazil's elites: white and therefore above people of colour, yet below those of northern European descent and worryingly proletarian. For the most part they had begun as agricultural workers but on the eve of the First World War they had created significant Italian neighbourhoods in central São Paulo, possessed over a hundred cultural and social institutions of their own including an Italian-language newspaper, *Fanfulla*, made up perhaps 10 to 15 per cent of the city's population and in Francesco Matarazzo acquired an Italo-Brazilian millionaire of considerable standing among the city's business community. After the Italian clubs Pro Vercelli and Torino had toured São Paulo in 1912, *Fanfulla* wrote: 'In São Paulo we have . . . the football club of the Germans, of the English, of the Portuguese, of the international and even of the Catholics and the Protestants, but a club that might be composed exclusively of Italian "sportsmen", and our colony [is] the largest in the state, [yet] still nothing has been tried!'[19]

Palestra Itália was founded the following year and its football team played in the Paulista Championships. Others followed their lead and over the next decade the foundation of clubs like Syrio, Hespanha and Portuguesa gave a public face to the mosaic of ethnic groups that the city had acquired. As with Rio, these new clubs, unable to draw upon a stock of university students and young professionals with time, energy and money to burn, found themselves paying in kind and in cash for players.

Beyond the Rio–São Paulo axis, football clubs and football mania first thrived in the big cities of the next most important and powerful states, Rio Grande do Sul and Minas Gerais, creating clubs that endure to this day. In the main city of the south, Porto Alegre, the considerable German-Brazilian community founded Grêmio in 1903. Apocryphally, the main mover, Cândido Dias, had gone to see an exhibition game between teams from São Paulo during which the match ball had burst. He lent his own ball to the teams so the game could be completed and, thus advertised as a football player and enthusiast, founded the club over drinks with a few dozen others that evening. Grêmio was an unambiguously German club, by language and membership, and intended to keep things that way, rebuffing players and members from other ethnic groups. In 1909 it acquired a rival, when those football enthusiasts of Spanish and Portuguese descent, especially among the city's students, formed the consciously cosmopolitan Internacional.

Belo Horizonte, the new capital of Minas Gerais, had been planned and built from scratch in the late nineteenth century as the garden city of the Belle Époque; but for all its municipal splendour there was precious little to do in the way of entertainment. In 1904 Vitor Serpa, a university student from Rio who had played football in Switzerland, and a small group of civil servants, shop workers and traders formed the city's first team, SC Football. Within a year they were joined by pop-up sides of students and clerks with a taste for the historical, calling their sides Pliny FC, Columbus and Vespucci, while the local press started publishing championship league tables. The resumption of the university term and the devastating rains of the autumn meant the fixture list was never completed. A few years of park football followed before a new rash of clubs were formed: Atlético Mineiro in 1908, the team of the local but liberal elites; the Yale Athletic Club in 1910, an exclusively Italian society which would become Palestra Itália in the 1920s; and América, who accepted only the most connected and conservative among the local grandees.

By the outbreak of the First World War state championships of some kind or another had been established in Bahia, Pará and Amazonas. By 1920 they had been joined by Paraná and Rio Grande do Sul in the south and by the cluster of small north-eastern states including Pernambuco, Paraíba, Ceará, Rio Grande do Norte and even the backwaters of Piauí and Maranhão. Here the state championships, like almost everything else, were overwhelmingly concentrated in the coastal state capitals, where the old elites gathered and the new migrants poured in. The former took to football once the elites of Rio had given it their seal of legitimacy. The urban masses, where they could, followed suit.

Thus in Salvador, the capital of Bahia, football emerged from the Anglophile and aristocratic Vitória cricket club. In Recife, the capital of Pernambuco, Náutico was founded in 1901 as a rowing and sailing club for the Anglo-German businessmen of the city; for the Brazilian elite, unable initially to gain entry, Sport Club Recife was founded in 1905 by Guilherme de Aquino Fonseca, an engineering graduate of Cambridge University, where he had played football. Less than a decade later, Santa Cruz, immediately the team of the poor, was created by a group of teenagers who met and played in a churchyard. The distance of this moment, geographically and socially, from Fluminense is a measure of just how far and how fast football mania had caught on in the growing provincial cities of Brazil.

IV

As the verses of Ana Amélia and Appárício Torelly make clear, football had found its way into Brazilian poetry and letters. In the world of the visual arts the first paintings of footballers began to appear, including Rodolfo Chambelland's *Boy with Ball* in 1914 and Ismael Nery's *Goal* in 1917. Carlos Oswald, who would later contribute to the design of the *Cristo Redentor* statue and painted panels for the walls and ceiling of Botafogo's clubhouse that depicted footballers as semi-divine Hellenic beings. The first recorded song with a football connection was released in 1913. 'Foot-Ball' was one of a series of polkas and waltzes featuring a saxophone, flute, ukulele and guitar, released on 78s by Grupo Lima Vieira. However, for the small world of Brazil's literate urban public, the newspapers were the place where football was most regularly examined and argued over. The overwhelming majority of the comment was positive. Three of the leading figures in Brazilian intellectual life, all members of the prestigious Academy of Letters, Afrânio Peixoto, Henrique Coelho Neto and Olavo Bilac, wrote in the game's favour.

Henrique Coelho Neto was an exuberantly mustachioed mestizo from the northern state of Maranhão, son of a white Brazilian father and an indigenous Indian mother. He rose to prominence in Rio at the end of the nineteenth century as a furiously productive and endlessly florid journalist, poet, novelist and playwright. He was also a Fluminense obsessive. The game first appeared in his literary work in the 1908 novel *Sphinx*, which featured an Englishman in Rio, James Marain, who mysteriously disappears on Sunday afternoons, it transpires, to watch the football. Coelho Neto himself was a regular spectator, reporting that he would see up to four games in a single day as he watched some of his fourteen children play in Fluminense youth sides. One of them, João, would go on to a long and varied athletic career under the name of Preguinho, playing football for Fluminense and Brazil, captaining the side at the 1930 World Cup as well as dabbling in water polo, volleyball and athletics. Coelho Neto is said to have led the first pitch invasion in Brazilian football when contesting the

23

decision of a referee at a Fluminense–Flamengo derby game and he certainly did write a hymn for the club, improbably to the tune of 'It's a Long Way to Tipperary':

> Fluminense is the crucible where our energy is forged,
> In the air, in the bright sun.
> The joy of the fair fight,
> Our efforts are focused on the manly ideal.
> Invigorating our race, our Brazil.

Like many of his class and generation, Coelho Neto had absorbed the biological models of race and the eugenic action plans of European scientific racism. If European Brazil was going to prosper as a nation it needed to get outdoors and get fit. Coelho Neto argued that '. . . a new breed will leave behind their dismal cultural heritage . . .'[20] Footballers were the sporting and eugenic missionaries of the new Brazil, and for those who didn't play football he was an endless advocate of walks in the fresh air, Baden-Powell-style scouting and swimming.

Afrânio Peixoto is best known in Brazil as a doctor and was the leading figure in the modernizing of public health and the mental health reforms of the early twentieth century. In 1918 he revealed himself as a fan of the game. While Coelho Neto had based his enthusiasm for football on biological theories of race, precepts which Peixoto by and large shared, it was the scientist and medic in him that saw football's contribution to nation-making as more cultural and educational. 'This game of football, this sport that makes us strong and healthy,' he asserted. 'It teaches discipline and order, demands cooperation and solidarity . . . it is a great school that is remaking the character of Brazil.'[21] But individual character was not enough. The point of football, at least the way the English and Germans seemed to play it, was that it gave individuals a powerful sense of the common good.

> The Latins who came here, were like all Latins, unattached from each other, incapable of surrendering their independence to the greater numbers, which added together, give a people its strength, a nation its victory. The . . . Anglo-Saxons are disciplined by education. A man is only worth something as a fraction of society; a player doesn't exist, but only as part of a 'team'. And this long collaboration, in their race and in the individual, always ensures eventual success, in all their enterprises. In sport, just as in life . . .[22]

Some critics of the game, like Carlos Sussekind de Mendonça, a Rio magistrate and journalist, were still operating in the same intellectual universe as these nationalists, but worked the logic of the argument differently. Football, rather than being a way of improving the nation's stock, was the route to decline and degeneracy. In his 1919 book *Sport and the Decline of Brazilian Youth*, the author argued that it is impossible to claim that sport in general, and football in particular, nurtures reason and the intellect. On the contrary, its passion and furies diminish them. Football was a 'microbe that spreads imbecility'.[23] Lima Barreto and Graciliano Ramos, both critics of the game, stood outside of this framework, however, and were all the more acute in their observations for that.

Barreto was the leading satirist of his day. Born a mulatto into a middle-class but hardly wealthy Rio household, he made his living as a novelist and chronicler of city life, with a sharp eye for the injustices and inequalities of Rio rather than just its grandeur and gossip. His sarcasm was directed at the sclerotic character of the Old Republic, its elite's secret shame over the mulatto nature of its people. He attacked their obsequiousness to foreignness and, uniquely for the time, peppered his text with vernacular language. His wariness of European influences on Brazil saw him decry the game, 'brought into our midst by arrogant and ruddy English clerks'. He deplored the use of public money to support elite clubs and football tournaments when so many social needs were ignored. Above all, he thought the game brutish and the emotions it generated in the crowd equally so. 'Football is a school for violence and brutality and doesn't deserve protection by the public authorities, unless these want to teach us how to kill.' A year after writing this, in 1920, when describing a game between a Rio XI and a São Paulo XI, he would record the first gunfire at a football match in Brazil. Drawing on the support of other medical and social critics of the game, in 1919 he launched the League against Football, arguing:

> It's impossible not to mention the sport they call British. Every hour of the day, it fills our papers with news of violent acts and, more than this, murders. It's impossible that the police authorities can't see this type of thing. Rio de Janeiro is a civilized city and can't be delivered into the hands of a certain type of ruffian posing as a sportsman. Those betting in cock fights behave better. Among them, there are no questions, nor arguments. The bets are held in peace and the police don't have to get involved. But the so-called footballers every Sunday are involved in arguments and fisticuffs and the police give them a pat on the head.[24]

Barreto also noted that football seemed to be coarsening the considerable female presence at games. Remarking on the women fans at one match, he wrote, 'What is most worthy of appreciation is their language. Rich in slang, vehement and colourful, their turn of phrase only has any equivalence among those pulling carts on the quayside.'

Graciliano Ramos was born in the north-eastern state of Alagoas, and though he would live for two long periods in Rio, it was the culture of his home region that shaped his writing and thinking. Ramos, who would later join the Communist Party and be imprisoned under the Vargas regime, certainly objected to the game's elitism, but it was from his position as a north-easterner that he launched his most trenchant attacks. In a *crônica* published in 1921, he expressed the opinion that such a foreign and urban game could never catch on in the north-east:

But why football? Wouldn't it perhaps be better for the youth of the nation to take its exercise by practising national sports, without any foreign mixture, the fisticuffs, the cudgel, the flick knife, for example? It's not that I'm repelled by the introduction of exotic things among us, but I like to check whether we can assimilate them or not.

Even then why should the culture of the whole country take on a foreign hue? Why should everything about the new, modern Brazil be established in the cities of the south?

Rehabilitate the regional sports out there that have been abandoned: the truncheon, the smack round the chops, arm wrestling, running, so useful for the citizen dedicated to the risky activity of stealing chickens, seizing the bull's horns, jumping, horse riding and, best of all, foot tripping. Tripping up! Now that is the national sport par excellence![25]

Ramos barely wrote on football again. Barreto died tragically young in 1922. Brazilian football lost its best and most acute critics. It would be all the poorer for it.

V

Visits by Argentinian clubs in 1907 and 1912, and later by the Italians Pro Vercelli and Torino, were warmly received but these matches never functioned in the minds of the participants or in the popular imagination as international games. In 1910 invitations were issued by the Argentine FA for a representative Brazilian team to attend its celebration of the centenary of the May Revolution which had begun the process of secession from the Spanish Empire, but no national Brazilian team was sent.

The visits of the English amateur team Corinthians – a collection of aristocratic sporting troubadours – in 1910 and 1913 to both Rio and São Paulo came closer to the mark, as select Brazil XIs were among the sides to take them on. Moreover, observers began to note a distinct difference in the style of play, the English appearing consistently more physical and organized. In 1914 the English professionals of Exeter City, on a South American tour, stopped off at Rio and played three games in the city. Their 2–0 defeat by a Select XI was deemed the first international match and the first victory for a Brazilian side.

The newly founded national football association, the Confederação Brasileira de Desportos (CBD, predecessor of the CBF), sent the same team to play in Argentina later that year in the General Julio Roca Cup. Roca had twice been President of Argentina and had been the man in charge of the country's near-genocidal expulsion of indigenous Indians from the pampas. Yet this cup, he said, was 'to encourage the young people who play such a noble sport and to cultivate good relations between our two countries'. Brazil won the third game of the three-match series by a single goal by striker Arthur Friedenreich. In itself this was unremarkable – except for the fact that he was a mulatto.[26]

Friedenreich was the son of a second-generation German-Brazilian father and an Afro-Brazilian mother, a dual inheritance that allowed him, as a child, to play in the free-form street football of the city as well as benefit from training and facilities at the elite SC Germânia where his father was a member. As an adult he played mainly for the elite side CA Paulistano and was, without question, the highest scoring striker of his day and the darling of the press, who nicknamed him *El Tigre* ('The Tiger') in Uruguay and 'Golden Foot' in Brazil. The fact that a visibly mulatto player could turn out for São Paulo's leading side demonstrates that Brazil's racial divisions were not insurmountable and that talent and social class could trump, on occasion, skin tone.

Not everyone was treated so well though. Carlos Alberto was the mulatto son of a Rio photographer who, in 1916, was playing for América's second team. He was called up to play in the first team of Fluminense and, of course, took his opportunity. Mário Filho recounted the story a decade or so later as a kind of morality tale. He described the player arriving late for the line-up with his teammates in front of the crowd, delayed in the dressing room because he was applying rice powder to his face in an effort to lighten it. When he turned out for Fluminense against his old club América the crowd chanted '*Pó de arroz*' (white powder) at him, a name that Fluminense fans have since adopted themselves.

Argentinian fans and writers were no less strident in their

racism. Their press described the Brazilian team at the 1916 South American Championship (later called the Copa América) as 'monkeys'. More of this was a prospect so acutely embarrassing to the Brazilian football authorities that they sent an all-white team to Buenos Aires for the following year's tournament. Lima Barreto, caustic as ever, wrote, 'The Holy College of Football has met to decide whether they could send to Buenos Aires champions that had in the veins a little black blood . . . Our vengeance is that the Argentinians don't distinguish the colours in us. For them, we're all monkeys.'[27]

Thus by 1919, when Brazil hosted its first South American Championship, football had become an arena in which Brazilians had begun to decide what the nation actually was. The tournament was testament to the depth of Rio's football mania as well as the national symbolism of the sport, with almost 200,000 people attending the seven games played at Estádio das Laranjeiras. For the final between Brazil and Uruguay an unbelievable 25,000 spectators crowded into a stadium built for barely 18,000, another 5,000 clung to the hills and trees that surrounded the ground, and more were left outside. Many thousands of people gathered in Rio's squares and on some of its broadest avenues where loudspeakers had been set up to relay news of the game. Banks and government offices closed early, by presidential order. It took four periods of extra time to break the nil–nil deadlock. Then Arthur Friedenreich scored the winning goal, and the crowd broke into wave after wave of 'Viva o Brasil!' President Epitácio Pessoa, present for the occasion, said of the team, 'I salute you in the name of the nation.'

It was a Brazilian triumph made by a footballer of European and African ancestry, and it was celebrated most memorably by the great black flautist, saxophonist and composer, Pixinguinha. His song, 'Um Zero' ('One Nil'), and indeed all the music composed and played by his great band of the time, *Os Oito Batutas* ('The Eight Amazing Players'), was a complex and original mix of Afro-Brazilian rhythms, American jazz influences, and European waltzes and polkas. This kind of hybrid was surely the future of the Brazilian nation and Brazilian football too, but it would take another decade of struggle and the collapse of the Old Republic to begin to make it a reality.

2

Modern Times? Football and the Death of the Old Republic, 1922–1932

'A formidable array of vividly beautiful girls' – Fluminense vs Paulistano, Estádio das Laranjeiras, 1920.

The noise of an engine celebrated the victory.
The field was emptying like a water tank.
Miquelina wilted inside her sadness.

Antônio de Alcântara Machado, 1927

I

Just a decade earlier Brazil's poets had been composing hymns to
the eugenic power of football, casting players as the new Hellenic
gods of the South. By 1927, when Antônio Machado published
his short story/prose poem, 'Corinthians (2) vs Palestra (1)', it
was being described with the metaphors of the machine age – of
engines and water tanks, the game of an industrial city told in
oblique fragments rather than orotund epics. Modernity, in the
form of industrializing cities and its cultural correlative, Modernism, had arrived and was reshaping Brazilian football. Virginia
Woolf, in her 1923 essay 'Mr Bennett and Mrs Brown', expressed
the thought that 'In or about December 1910, human character
changed.' D. H. Lawrence dated the end of the pre-modern era
slightly later, writing, 'It was in 1915 the old world ended.' Ezra
Pound, high priest of Atlantic Modernism, had insisted that

modernity had arrived in 1922 or Year One of the new era as he referred to it, before opting for Mussolini's new Fascist calendar. Given its decidedly pre-modern plantation economy and peripheral geography, Brazil might have been expected to lag some way behind this. However, in its most advanced zones – Rio de Janeiro and increasingly São Paulo – Brazil showed a remarkable technological and cultural precocity.[1]

Cinematic techniques and equipment had arrived from France at the turn of the century, just a few years after the Lumière brothers' first experiments. The take-up and spread of radio broadcasting were in advance of many European states. In 1922 São Paulo could claim an important place in an emerging global avant-garde when the Modern Art Week was staged at the city's Municipal Theatre. It was the single most important event in Brazil's literary and artistic world in the century since independence; it was also just the first of a whole series of events that year which announced the modernization of Brazilian society and demonstrated the limits of the political and cultural structures of the Old Republic.

Modern Art Week had been conceived, at least in part, as a deliberate riposte to the Independence Centenary International Exposition to be held in Rio from September 1922. This government-initiated city spectacular, part fair, part cultural festival, part urban-development programme, would attempt to cast Brazil in a nostalgic, exclusively European light. The artistic radicals of São Paulo wanted to offer something very different. But before Brazil could make the comparison it would endure another six months of change and upheaval. In April the old order seemed secure when the candidate favoured by the previous incumbent and the dominant coffee interests, Artur da Silva Bernardes, easily defeated his republican opponent, Nilo Peçanha, in the presidential election. However, the opposition put the victory down to electoral manipulation, further discrediting federal politics and the presidency. Bernardes, despite his electoral majority, would be forced to rule much of the next four years with the help of the army, imposing martial law in Rio, and establishing Amazonian internment camps for his opponents. Less than 5 per cent of the adult population had actually turned out to vote in the election and neither candidate had sought to represent or engage with the interest of Brazil's new urban masses.

In 1922 there were three separate attempts to do precisely that. First, the Brazilian Communist Party (PCB) was founded in Niterói, across the bay from Rio de Janeiro, and, despite its small size and periods of illegality, it would be an important force in destabilizing the Republic. Second, the Brazilian Catholic Church, long accustomed to ministering to the needs of the rich alone, began its flirtation with more radical theology and attempted to establish a physical and spiritual presence in industrial Brazil with the formation of Catholic workers' social clubs and social programmes. Finally, in July, the simmering discontent inside the junior ranks of the army, where a whole variety of ultra-nationalist and hyper-modernizing aspirations for Brazil had been taking hold, boiled over into open rebellion. Troops in the fortress of Copacabana in Rio briefly raised the standard of a modernizing revolt before being gunned down in the street. There was more of this to come.

Nineteen twenty-two was a high-water mark for global Modernism, when bath *Ulysses* and *The Waste Land* were published. São Paulo Modern Art Week, held in mid-February that year at the city's Municipal Theatre, was part of this global movement, but offered its own distinctive take on Modernism and challenged its

Eurocentrism. Its principal organizers were the painter Emiliano di Cavalcanti and mulatto polymath Mário de Andrade, but they were closely connected to a wide circle of São Paulo-based artists, musicians, sculptors and poets who would form the core of the country's intellectual elite over the next couple of decades. Key members of this circle had made the journey to Europe and brought some part of the Modernist movement back with them: Oswald de Andrade imbibed the wild manifestos and machine freakery of Italian Futurism, while the painter Anita Malfatti introduced Brazil to the techniques and styles of German Expressionism and then of Cubism. To this kind of avant-garde cosmopolitanism Andrade, di Calvacanti and others brought often radical forms of nationalism and a deep concern with finding Brazilian rather than European sources of artistic inspiration. Andrade had already begun his lifelong compilation of Brazil's indigenous folklore and music; composer Heitor Villa-Lobos would try to incorporate this into modern classical music; poet Menotti del Picchia called polemically for the 'Brazilianization of Brazil', and most acknowledged the enormous but often hidden African contribution to Brazilian culture. The week consisted of readings, exhibitions, lectures and concerts. Many of the more conservative members of the audience were shocked, some booed, and others stormed out. The old guard in Rio were so appalled that Graça Aranha, the only member of the Brazilian Academy to attend, was shunned by his conservative colleagues.

While these artists drew upon the new repertoire of techniques developed by European Modernism, they were self-consciously attempting to deploy them in a Brazilian context for their own ends. Two themes stand out. First, that the proper subject of Brazilian art must, henceforth, include the life and language of the city and every strand of society within it. Second, the idea of Brazil as a cannibal culture developed by Oswald de Andrade. In more of a rhetorical flourish than a coherent anthropological theory, Oswald argued that Brazilian culture was the product of absorption and digestion, eating and then transforming the flesh of European, African and indigenous cultures. If football was not, initially, an obvious candidate for the Modernist epitome of Brazilian culture – too foreign in their eyes in 1922 – it was the perfect subject matter for their writings. Authentic Brazilian art would need to get out of the drawing room and on to the street and reflect something of the real life of the urban popular classes. It would certainly include the vernacular vocabulary of its cities and the peculiar cadence and fragments of reported speech. Both of these promises were delivered in the poetic work of Mário de Andrade and Oswald de Andrade – they were not related – where football is an unremarkable feature of the urban landscape. In his long poem *Pauličéia Desvairada* ('Hallucinated City'), Mário de Andrade spliced together tiny slices of a match day in the city, flashes of the action on and off the pitch and snatches of football conversation, before wondering whether it amounts to anything at all:

> Who's playing today? Paulistano
> Of Jardín América, the garden of roses and kicks!
> Friedenreich scored a goal! Corner!
> That referee!
> Do I like Bianco? I love him.
> How about Barto . . .
> How about my marvellous namesake!
> Futility, civilization . . .[2]

In his novel *Memórias Sentimentais de João Miramar*, Oswald de Andrade made football an element of an urban dreamscape where trams are goals, the air is filled with football chants, and football matches take on the air of the dance hall.

> Streetcar goals
> *Aleguais!*
> Sleepwalkers of championship matches
> And dust.
> With afternoon entertainment
> Tennis girls unwrapped
> At Paulistano
> *Paso Doble*[3]

In time both Mário and Oswald de Andrade would shed their scepticism about football – indeed, both would recognize that the development of the game precisely fitted their prescription of a cannibalized culture in which Brazil would absorb, digest and remake European and African cultures. Mário would celebrate the game as both carnival and dance; Oswald, in his later writings, cast the game as a form of Modernist religion. Menotti del Picchia went so far as to write the script for Brazil's first fictional football movie, *Campeão de Futebol*, released in 1931 and starring Arthur Friedenreich and other players of the day. It was, needless to say, not Modernist verse but a simple-minded popular comedy reflecting the author's steady move towards the super-populist right wing of Brazilian political and cultural life. Perhaps the most significant literary work to engage with football was the short story/poem 'Corinthians (2) vs Palestra (1)' by Antônio de Alcântara Machado, who though not present at Modern Art Week was part of the same circle. Where de Andrade's novel had offered soundbites, Machado wrote the whole match report, capturing the action at Palestra's home ground, Parque Antárctica, and the complex social and emotional processes going on around it.

> The ball landed on the far left.
> The stand stood up.
> She held her breath. Sighed: Aaaah!
> Miquelina dug her nails into Iolanda's fat arm.
> Around the green rectangle twenty thousand people craved.
> Greedy eyes. Electric nerves.
> In black. White. Blue. Red.
> Football loathing in Parque Antárctica.[4]

In just a decade, in the imagination of its devotees, football's shape had shifted from Coelho Neto's carnival of fresh air into a kind of collective nervous breakdown.

II

The final of the South American Football Championship in 1919 had been interpreted as a victory for the whole nation. Yet despite the presence of the mulatto striker Arthur Friedenreich and his winning goal in the final, Brazil's football and political elites remained resistant to embracing the notion of an ethnically mixed nation. In 1920 King Albert of Belgium made a state visit to Brazil and among the many formal occasions held in his honour the most significant was the parade of sports clubs at the Estádio das Laranjeiras. Unlike the 1919 national team, this was the nation – but without either São Paulo or any of the rest of the country. The parade was headed by delegations from the over-whelmingly white clubs of the city – Fluminense, Flamengo, Botafogo and América – while the smaller, more working-class and even mixed-race clubs of the suburbs were given a much lower profile. In the photographic record of the day the football and rowing teams of the leading clubs line up in club colours in front of the King and much of the Brazilian cabinet, oars held to attention: an all-white, all-male nation bursting with European vitality. The following year, on the eve of the 1921 Copa América due to be held in Buenos Aires, Brazil's President Epitácio Pessoa decreed that the national team would not field a black player in the tournament lest the nation be embarrassed by its African and mulatto elements.

It was a similar impulse, to display to the world the improving health of Brazil's racial stock and to raise the profile of the nation in the world, which animated the plans for the 1922 Independence Centenary International Exposition. In a remarkable anticipation of the political coalitions and interests that have informed Brazil's twenty-first-century hosting of sporting mega-events, the exhibition was closely linked to grandiose plans for the transformation of the urban environment. When the exhibition was first announced in 1917 the *New York Times* reported that the organizers intended to make 'satisfactory plans for the material and aesthetic transformation of the city of Rio de Janeiro with a special view to the probabilities of its development'.[5]

Rio had already undergone a major period of change in the early years of the century initiated by the activist mayor Pereira Passos. In an attempt to rid the city of the threat of contagious diseases and to build a capital that matched the elite's ambitions,

Rio was reshaped. Tunnels were dug through the mountains opening up the hitherto inaccessible beaches of Copacabana and beyond; coastal parades were decorated with the city's signature black-and-white mosaic pavements; in the old centre, large areas of lower-class housing and narrow eighteenth-century lanes were swept aside, Haussmann-like, to create public squares and grand boulevards adorned with magnificent municipal buildings. The plans for the 1922 exhibition, which was to be located in the south-east corner of the central area, were not dissimilar. The Morro do Castelo, a hill close to the shoreline, was levelled and with it a long-established favela of self-built housing was removed – just one of a number of forced relocations at the time of a kind that has since become the hallmark of such mega-events. Suitably cleansed, Rio would appear to the world as a modern European capital, a safe and healthy destination for investors and tourists rather than a dangerous and disease-ridden tropical port.

For the first time in Brazil's history we have cinematic evidence of this transformation and of the place of football within it. The country's early embrace of the cinema meant that many short films had been made in the first twenty years of the new century, including footage of over a dozen football matches. In 1922 Brazilian cinema made the leap to longer and more structured documentaries. Among the leading figures in this process was the cinematographer Silvino Santos who was commissioned by government agencies to make films about his home city of Manaus in Amazonas and about the centenary exhibition. His Rio movie was called *Terra Encantada* ('Enchanted Land'). It was both ambitious and innovative. Unlike the one- or two-reel shorts of the past, it was put on general release in Brazil at two hours long. Urban scenes were shot from a moving vehicle, use was made of fade-ins and fade-outs, and the camera seemed to search out the relentless motion of the new city. Only thirteen minutes of the original film have survived, but even in this reduced version football appears as a natural component of the urban canvas. Alongside bustling boulevards, fashionable cafés, long white beaches and decorative architecture, Santos included a game at Estádio das Laranjeiras. We see the gentlemen of Fluminense raising their flag to a large and seemingly vocal crowd. The written titles announce: 'Fluminense Football Club is in Rio, a prodigious human endeavour'.[6]

The footage of the exhibition itself includes most of the domestic and foreign pavilions, nearly all of which were built in the well-worn style of Portuguese neocolonial mansions or as French Belle Époque confections. Whereas world's fairs in Europe and North America had heavily featured experiments in modern architecture, industrial products, machinery and technological and consumer innovations, Rio was dominated by food processing and exporters. The seaplane *Santa Cruz* aside, the most technologically advanced elements of the exhibition were the roller coaster and the roundabouts at the amusement park. The organizers' best energies were reserved for the themes of health, hygiene and sanitation, with exhibits and lectures pointing to the successes of Rio's recent period of rebuilding and, in keeping with the eugenic positivism of the Republic, looking forward to the development of a healthy nation through the creation of a physical culture. These points were driven home by staging a host of South American sporting championships alongside the fair: basketball, swimming, water polo, athletics, boxing and sailing. In a rare concession to the notion that indigenous Brazil might have something to contribute to the nation's culture, a group of Pareci Indians were brought to Rio, as part of the same thinking. First encountered by a Brazilian army officer in 1915, the Pareci had developed their own ball game, *zinucati*. It was a version of head tennis meets keepy-uppy using an inflated rubber ball. Dressed in Fluminense kits, with their hair heavily waxed and styled in a European – even Edwardian British – coiffure, they performed at the Estádio das Laranjeiras to the perplexity of most who attended.

However, none of these events had the drawing power or acquired the wider significance accorded to the South American Football Championship which was held as part of the show in late 1922. In anticipation of the kinds of crowds that had attended the 1919 tournament, the Estádio das Laranjeiras was expanded to accommodate 25,000 people, though even this was exceeded by the huge crowd that attended the final march; an estimated 35,000 people squeezed inside, with thousands of others in the streets or precariously perched on the hills around the stadium. As before, banks and shops closed early, and speakers were put up for the crowds that gathered on the city's main avenues and squares. The tournament proved to be a more boisterous and controversial affair than that of 1919, with some of Brazil's games experiencing minor pitch invasions, and during the game against Uruguay what were described by the press as 'scenes of real vandalism'. The Rio police department resorted to putting notices in the papers warning the public that they would use their full legal authority to control the crowds.

The five-team tournament produced a three-way tie after the completion of all the games – Brazil, Uruguay and Paraguay all on five points. The Uruguayans, who had bitterly contested what they perceived to be biased refereeing by a Brazilian in their game against Paraguay, refused to take any further part. Brazil went on to crush Paraguay 3–0 in the final game and claim the mantle for the Brazilian nation in the eyes of both politicians and the football public. The absence of Arthur Friedenreich from the final (though he had played in earlier games), indeed of any of the other players of African descent who were emerging in Brazilian football, made it an incomplete avatar. Yet players were drawn this time from both Rio and São Paulo, and as the surnames of the winning squad – Kuntz, Palamone, Domingues, Barto – suggest, Brazil's German, Italian, Spanish and Portuguese strains were all present. Certainly *O Imparcial* thought it a universal triumph, leading with the headline, 'All Brazil rejoices at this time with a deserved victory'. *Gazeta*, celebrating the country's victories in water polo and sailing as well, wrote, 'Brazil – Champion of land and sea'. Senator Benjamin Barroso proposed that the squad should split the gate money from the Paraguay game, over $50,000, and while this was no fortune for the fifteen players it was still perhaps twenty times what a labourer might earn in a week. The proposal was approved in the Brazilian Congress despite widespread press criticism and its contravention of the CBD's hitherto strict amateurism. One cartoon offered a defence of the payments, showing four members of the team, all bruised, bandaged and on crutches, telling the female embodiment of the Republic: 'And now what we want is a life pension, because, after all, we were wounded in the "defence of the country".'[7]

Others worried about the impact of the game on international relations and its overimportance in political life. The rancour and the violence of the games with Uruguay, in particular, alarmed some, and given Brazil's diplomatic efforts to secure a seat at the League of Nations in preference to its small neighbour, the clashes took on a distinctly political quality. Federal Deputy

Carlos Garcia actually proposed stopping international games altogether. Meanwhile, in a cartoon entitled 'The New Ministries', President Pessoa was shown in his office where a note announced that he would be 'offside' during lunch hours. His litter bin was hung with a sign reading 'goal'. A footballer standing in his office asks: 'Why doesn't the government create a ministry of football? Wouldn't it be more useful than any other?'[8]

Such a ministry, such dilemmas would have been a pleasing diversion for Pessoa's presidential successors Artur Bernardes and Washington Luís, who tried to hold the nation together over the next eight years as they dealt with persistent military mutinies. The most serious was a revolt in São Paulo which saw another group of ultra-nationalist junior officers take the city before retreating into the jungle where they eluded loyal federal troops for three years. The status quo was creaking; the polity of the elites was under attack. Amateur football would be next.

III

One indicator of the intensity of football mania in Brazil's biggest cities in the 1920s was the ever-growing space devoted to the sport in the press. It had steadily expanded from perhaps half or a single page to six or seven in many newspapers, often making the front page as well as the back page and forming the subject of innumerable comments, *crônicas* and cartoons. In keeping with the increasing popularity of the game among the urban working and middle classes, the language of the press began to change too, with many English phrases and words transmuting into Brazilian Portuguese. Most obviously football or foot-ball was becoming *futebol*; shoot mutated into *chutar*, backs became *beques*, rough translation turned corners into *escanterios* and forwards into *atacantes*. But in time Brazilian Portuguese would develop its own rich and complex idioms: Didi's free kicks that dropped sharply from the peak of their trajectory became a *folha seca* – dry leaf.

Brazil's first radio transmission was broadcast during the 1922 centenary exhibition by engineers of the American firm Westinghouse. Over the next four years radio stations were established in Rio and São Paulo broadcasting an eclectic mix of opera, classical music and educational talks. It was only a matter of time before the new technology was swept up by the country's football mania. In 1931 Nicolau Tuma of São Paulo's Rádio Educadora Paulista broadcast the first live commentary of a football match, from Campo da Floresta. With a voice like a master of ceremonies at an exclusive dinner, Tuma welcomed the ladies and gentlemen of radioland to the game, describing in some detail, and for many for the first time, the actual laws of football.

The expansion of the sports pages and the arrival of radio were themselves products of the rising interest of paying crowds at football, which began regularly to reach 10,000 and more for the big local derbies. Crowds like this meant money, and money and competition inevitably led to teams paying their squads to train and play. The elite clubs in São Paulo were wise to this as early as 1913, when they broke away from the Liga Paulista and created their own competition, unwilling to mix it with the proletarians and new immigrants of Corinthians and Palestra Itália. Indeed they were hard-line enough to expel fellow secessionists Scottish Wanderers in 1916, who were openly paying their players. The city reverted to a single league in 1917, but after another few years of turning a blind eye to the hidden professionalism of the game there was, in 1924, a final effort by the leading elite team, CA Paulistano, to run a real amateur league. It lasted five years, but the crowds and the players had moved on. In 1929 the league fell apart and CA Paulistano, among the founders of football in the city, withdrew from playing the sport altogether.

Professionalism remained illegal and, for those at the summit of Rio football, immoral. Rivadavia Meyer, the president of Flamengo and the Metropolitan Athletic Sports Association (AMEA) league, spoke for many of his class. Reflecting on Brazil's defeat in the 1923 Copa América, with a team made up only of Rio amateurs, he said that it was better to have lost than 'taken the Paulista mercenaries who only run after the ball for money'. Later in the decade, faced by a rising tide of professionalism in the game, he verged on the splenetic. A professional was, he said, 'a gigolo who exploits a prostitute. The club gives him all the material necessary to play football and enjoy himself with the game and he wants to earn money as well? I will not allow this in Flamengo. Professionalism degrades the man.'

Amateurism also retained the virtue of excluding poor Brazilians, including non-whites, from the inner sanctum of elite football, a prospect that was both socially and sportingly unappealing. Rivadavia and his ilk preferred not to mix with them, but above all not to lose to them either, and both became increasingly likely as the decade wore on. The key moment came in 1923 when Vasco da Gama fielded the best black players, played the best football, drew the biggest crowds, and won the league in Rio. The team's stars were its four black players: Ceci, Nicolino, Bolão and Nelson da Conceição.

Vasco were not the only club in Rio prepared to field black players and to pay them, but they were always the most likely to

47

make it work. Founded by the small businessmen and merchants of the Portuguese community, they and their sons were eager to play sport but would never have had the free time available to the aristocrats and university students who turned out for the clubs of the Zona Sul. They had therefore always recruited players from beyond their social circle. The Portuguese community was right in the heart of the city's burgeoning industrial sector, where Vasco's stadium was also situated. At the ground, in the workplace and on the street, Vasco's members rubbed shoulders with the poor. Given the intensely commercial character of their working lives, they saw no moral barrier to paying players. And with the community's desire to make its mark on the city, they were ready to invest. From the lowest levels of the Rio league in the years after the First World War, Vasco were promoted to the top division and then won it.

Shocked, humiliated and threatened, the grander clubs withdrew from the league, deploring the hidden professionalism of Vasco, and created their own AMEA league in 1924. However, crowds and takings were down without Vasco as the public flocked to them and the league that they had joined. América, Bangu, Botafogo, Flamengo and Fluminense were forced back to the negotiating table and asked Vasco and two of the other leading popular clubs, São Cristóvão and Andaraí, to join them. The price of re-inclusion was the introduction of the AMEA card – a document that had to be completed by hand and under supervision by every player before every game, detailing name, address, date and place of birth, as well as addresses of place of work and study. The league actually created a three-man commission to ensure the process was implemented. It was, like the operation of the Brazilian electoral franchise, a crude instrument to try and exclude the illiterate and thus in effect to exclude the poor and black semi-professionals. Vasco responded by sending theirs to night school.

The league then started investigating players' finances and employment status but Vasco's directors outflanked them by giving all their stars ghost jobs and real salaries in their businesses. Vasco's fans bought up every lottery ticket they could in a competition for a new car, all in the name of one of their star players, who ended up with the wheels. Vasco won the title again in 1929 and the authorities relented, abolishing the card but keeping professionalism hidden.

Black players were not welcome in all clubs: São Paulo informally excluded them until the late 1920s. Independent black teams and leagues were reported in the city as early as 1914, but the first black versus white game was not held until 1927, when a series of matches were played on the day celebrating the abolition of slavery. Grêmio in Porto Alegre remained resolutely all-white; América in Rio saw its membership completely split over the fielding of the club's first black player, Manteiga. Fausto was loved at Vasco, but the press would still frame him as a hungry black man when he went for the ball 'as if it were a plate of food'.[9]

The real measure of Vasco's rise was its new stadium. The Estádio São Januário, designed by the Portuguese émigré architect Ricardo Severo, was built in just ten months, opening in April 1927. At a stroke, the centre of gravity of the city's football moved from Fluminense's Laranjeiras to the north. São Januário was the biggest and most modern arena in the country, with a capacity of 50,000. The stands themselves were a horseshoe of terraces with a single seated area on one side for the club's directors and paying members (*sócios*). The clean and simple lines of both stands and the roof contrasted with the main external façade: it was a riot of neocolonial detailing, gables, balconies, finials and Maltese crosses, stained-glass windows and ornamental blue tiling – a suitable juxtaposition of Brazil's European colonial past and its urban modernity. Vasco's standing was underlined by the presence at the stadium's opening of representatives of state, church and celebrity, including President Washington Luís and five cabinet ministers. Having recently lifted the state of siege under which Rio had been run for the previous four years, the politicians received a three-minute ovation. The stadium was blessed by Cardinal Leme, the Archbishop of Rio, and the Portuguese aviator Sarmento de Beires, who had recently flown the first night-time air crossing of the South Atlantic between Lisbon and Rio, cut a symbolic ribbon before the kick-off between Vasco and Santos. Santos won a wild game 5–3, and Waldenyr Caldas reports their centre forward claiming, 'They build a ballroom. We put on a show!'[10]

IV

National politics, like Brazilian football, had reached an impasse by the early 1930s. The elite clubs maintained their rule over the game, still arguing that the ideology of amateurism, born in the early days of the Republic, was morally intact and that the forces of commercialism and the social challenge from below were resistible. In national politics the old order seemed to be functioning as ever when in March 1930 Júlio Prestes, the establishment candidate for the presidency, was elected and planned to spend what little public money he had shoring up the coffee oligarchs as they struggled with a fall in global prices rather than attend to the economic pain elsewhere. Since the Wall Street crash of the previous year Brazil's economy had shrunk by almost 5 per cent, as it would again the following year. Despite mobilizing a broad coalition of the south and the north-east against São Paulo, the challenger Getúlio Vargas, governor of Rio Grande do Sul, found that the coffee lobby's control of the presidency was immovable.

In the immediate aftermath of the election, the Brazilian national team, supported by government money, made the journey in July 1930 to Montevideo to play in the inaugural World Cup. Once again it was an all-white team representing Brazil and they were shocked by an opening defeat to Yugoslavia. Brazil did thrash the Bolivians 3–0 but they went home from the tournament empty handed.

Vargas and his allies had been expecting defeat in the election, and had ceased to place any legitimacy on the now notoriously corrupt electoral system. Vargas was not alone in thinking this. The nation's jurists, lawyers, artists and intellectuals had, for the most part, abandoned any defence of the polity, increasingly rejecting its implausible sense of national identity, and had set about exposing its many limitations. As the succession of military revolts and mutinies demonstrated, the very institution which had created the Republic in the first place now had enlisted men who would not fight for it and officers who were no longer convinced of its value. The Old Republic stood on increasingly unstable foundations.

Vargas had contemplated organizing a coup immediately after the election but had chosen to wait his moment. When his running mate, Pessoa, was assassinated, in what was in actual fact the consequence of a romantic entanglement, Vargas took his chance along with a number of sympathetic state governors who mobilized their militias and persuaded some federal army units to join them. They marched on Rio in October 1930. Incumbent president Washington Luís was persuaded to stand down by the high command of the military units in Rio. They held the city for a few days and even imagined themselves the government for one or two of them, but on Vargas's arrival they handed the presidency to him. Over the next two years Vargas began the process of centralizing and concentrating power in the Brazilian federal state that would characterize the next decade and a half of his rule. He dissolved Congress, retired lukewarm supporters and regionalists from the upper echelons of the army, ruled for the most part using emergency law and removed all but one elected state governor, replacing them with administrators whose first loyalties lay with him.

The Old Republic fell for three key reasons: the external economic pressures exerted by a changing global economy; the destruction of any shred of ideological coherence or legitimacy; and finally a decisive set of reforming actions from a new group of elites. The fall of amateurism and the end of Brazilian elite football can be traced to a similar mix of circumstances. The global pressure came in the form of competition for players from increasingly wealthy and openly commercial foreign football cultures. The process began in 1925 when Enrico Marone Cinzano, the Italian industrialist and owner of the Cinzano drinks company and Torino football club, went on a business trip to Buenos Aires. While there he saw striker Julio Libonatti play for Newell's Old Boys and signed him on the spot. In 1928 the all-South American final of the Amsterdam Olympic football tournament made the depth of talent on that continent apparent across Europe: offers of signing-on fees, cars, flats and fabulous salaries proved irresistible. Players of Italian descent were particularly welcomed by both the clubs and the Italian Fascist authorities who intended that they represent the mother country. In 1930 Amílcar, the great striker at Palestra Itália, and the Fantoni brothers had left São Paulo to play for Lazio in Rome. In 1931 Italian agents came looking again in Brazil and in particular to São Paulo, where the vast majority of Italian immigrants had settled. In one sweep they took nine of the best players from Corinthians and Palestra Itália. For some it was about more than money, it was about pride and respect. One of the players, Rizetti, argued, 'Aren't theatre artists esteemed and applauded? Well, I'll also be an artist of the feet.' Amílcar was in no doubt what he was going to do and why:

> I'm off to Italy, I'm tired of being an amateur in football when such a condition has stopped existing a long time ago, masked by a hypocritical system of tips which clubs give to their players while keeping most of the income for themselves. For 20 years I have offered my modest services to Brazilian football. What has happened? The clubs got rich and I have nothing. I am going to the country that knows how to pay for the players' skill.[11]

The São Paulo press was generally sympathetic to their position, one writer arguing that the public should not be concerned about the views of 'half a dozen football magnates, who live almost exclusively from the exertions of these players'.[12]

No Italian club came knocking at the door of the new generation of black Brazilian stars, but they found their way to the money anyway. When Vasco da Gama went on a tour of Iberia in 1930, Fausto and Jaguaré got off the bus at Barcelona and on to the payroll. The threat from Italian clubs had forced the pace of commercialism in both Uruguay and Argentina, and as legal professionalism inevitably approached, the wage rates available to the best began to climb. In 1932 the two leading Brazilian black players of the day, Leônidas da Silva and Domingos da Guia, headed for Uruguay to rivals Peñarol and Nacional respectively. Ideological and moral appeals were useless; not only was the model of elite amateurism impossible to sustain, but it was common knowledge that all the old elite clubs were now in on the act themselves. Antônio Gomes de Avelar, president of América in Rio, broke the silence in 1932 by admitting that he paid their players. He called for everyone else to come clean and go professional. In 1933 both the Carioca and the Paulista Championships were openly professional; they would soon be followed by the emerging regional football centres of Minas Gerais, Paraná and Rio Grande do Sul.

The decisive break with the Old Republic in politics would require more than just external pressure and coming clean. Opposition to the centralizing and authoritarian nationalism of Vargas's coalition was strongest in São Paulo, and in July 1932 the state was in armed rebellion against the government in Rio. São Paulo mobilized for war, built its own ramshackle arms industry and sent Arthur Friedenreich and a hundred other football players to the front. Nicolau Tuma, the pioneer football commentator on the city's radio stations, swapped the press box for a foxhole and reported on the battle for the city; it barely made it to half-time. São Paulo was outgunned and outnumbered, and surrendered to Vargas, who was as generous a victor as he was ruthless an opponent. He disarmed the city but did not destroy it. So gentle was the occupation that the Paulista Championship, rudely interrupted by this short-lived conflict, was resumed and concluded before Christmas. Better still, in the opening game of the following season, the first openly professional game in Brazilian football's history, Friedenreich helped São Paulo beat Santos 5–1 at the grand old age of thirty-eight.

3

Brasilidade: Football and the New Order, 1932–1950

Brazilian dreamtime: the nationalist surrealism of Cândido Portinari's Futebol.

Flamengo's *Tricampeonato* is more important to the people of
Brazil than the battle of Stalingrad.

José Lins do Rego, 1943

I

José Lins do Rego, one of the leading Brazilian novelists of the
1940s, was prone to controversy in his newspaper writings, but in
the early months of 1943 as the Carioca Championship headed
towards its conclusion, few in Brazil would have disagreed with
him. Secluded from the firestorm, by distance and neutrality, for
the first four years of the Second World War, and barely touched
by it for the few years in which it was part of the grand alliance,
Brazil spent much of the 1930s and 1940s tending to itself. These
were two decades during which the unfinished business of the
Old Republic could be settled: the incorporation of the new
popular classes into politics, and the creation of a sense of Brazilian national identity more plausible than the narrow European
elite model of the early twentieth century. Football would play a
key role in both of these.

Getúlio Vargas, who had come to power in the coup of

1930 and won the short civil war with São Paulo in 1932, ruled for
another two years by endlessly extending the duration of the
country's emergency laws while a constitutional convention drew
up a new plan for the polity. In 1933 it completed its work. The
constitution was agreed, women acquired the vote and Congress
made Vargas president for the next four years, after which elections would be held.

Having dealt with the regionalist threat to the Brazilian
nation-state, Vargas now saw off challenges from the left and the
right. For three years the communists and their allies in the Aliança
Nacional Libertadora fought a propaganda war and street battles
with Brazil's very own uniformed fascist party, the Ação Integral-
ista Brasileira (AIB) led by Plínio Salgado, and both looked to
directly challenge the federal government. In 1935 Communist
Party cells in the army launched a revolt in three barracks, all of
which were sharply put down. Vargas took the opportunity to ban
the party. Then, in 1937, with the prospect of elections in
1938 which Vargas was constitutionally debarred from contesting,
he and his military allies launched a pre-emptive coup. Loyal troops
surrounded the Congress building and Vargas announced on the
radio the establishment of the Estado Novo – the New State.
There was remarkably little organized resistance to the move. The
following spring Plínio Salgado and a small group of his armed
supporters launched an assault on Vargas and the presidential palace in Catete but were easily defeated. Salgado's movement, like
the communists, was dissolved. Civil rights were curtailed and political parties were banned. Federal officials publicly burned the
flags of every state in Brazil before consigning their ashes to an
urn at the Museu Histórico. Elected state governors and city

mayors were all replaced by *interventores* ('inspectors') appointed and controlled from Rio. Centralized executive power was fused with a semi-corporatist model of society that owed much to Mussolini's early attempts to control working-class power through state-sponsored unions.

Coercion was the foundation of Vargas's Estado Novo, but it relied most of the time on surveillance and co-option. Serious political opponents went into exile or retired from public life, and all were kept under close watch. Under the beady eyes of the DIP, the Departamento de Imprensa e Propaganda, control of the press was very close and reporting of Vargas himself generous to the point of obsequious. Politically, Vargas left the north-east and the countryside to their own devices on condition of total loyalty from the local oligarchs. In the cities he sought to build a new popular coalition of the federal state and the new working class. This unlikely combination of social forces was held together by the quiet but brilliantly effective negotiating skills of Vargas and a diffuse but palpable sense of Brazilian nationalism. In the realm of economic policy this took the form of protectionism and tariff barriers to encourage domestic growth; state-led industrialization through the creation of nationalized companies (like steel and petrochemicals) and government-funded infrastructural development; and a package of social welfare reforms that included the minimum wage in exchange for government control of workers and their unions. In cultural policy, given that Vargas was not the material out of which any kind of personality cult could be fashioned, the Estado Novo searched for expressions of *Brasilidade* – the Brazilian way – and thus attempted to mobilize and shape the nation's popular cultures for nationalistic ends. This was a task made easier by the active participation of the country's intelligent-sia and artistic communities in precisely this debate.

Portuguese was made compulsory in the press and the radio; schools that taught in a foreign language either shifted or were closed down. New federal agencies were created which actively censored and subtly manipulated key areas of cultural production: the Instituto Nacional do Livro regulated publishing, while the Instituto Nacional do Cinema Educativo both controlled the film industry and sought to shape its agenda. Music was a special concern of the DIP; no sheet music could be published or record released without its stamp and its censors paid careful attention to their lyrical content. In all of these areas, the blunt tools of control were married with subtle strategies of incorporation. All of these ministries offered artists, publishing houses and film and record companies a mixture of sponsorship, subsidies, prizes and, for the music business, access to the airwaves.

In a country where still less than half the population could read, and cinemas were rare outside the big cities, radio was the single most important means of communication of the Vargas era. The small, virtually amateur radio stations that had popped up in the 1920s disappeared. The federal government permitted advertising and sponsorship, and nurtured the emergence of a nationwide network of private radio stations, all of which owed their existence to the government. The compulsory broadcasting of *Hora do Brasil* – a centrally produced hour-long mix of news, music and educationally improving talks – was the closest that Brazil came to a national conversation. To ensure that everyone could listen in, the regime erected speakers in the public spaces of the small towns in the interior of the country where domestic radio sets were few and far between.

The control and use of football fell into a similar pattern. The universal imposition of Portuguese, and – once Brazil had joined the Allies in the Second World War – the new opprobrium in which Germany and Italy were held, saw an end to the old ethnically identifiable clubs – or their names at any rate. In São Paulo, Palestra Itália became Palmeiras and SC Germânia became Pinheiros; Palestra's namesake in Belo Horizonte became Cruzeiro, the 'southern star'; and Curitiba FC took the Portuguese spelling Coritiba. Clubs that still used the language of their homeland in internal documents desisted.

In 1941 the federal government reorganized the CBD and created a National Sports Council. This body was staffed by three handpicked civilians, a general and an air force marshal, and given the authority to determine policy in all areas of Brazilian sport. This included stamping out any lingering conflicts between the sports federations of the large states which had plagued Brazilian football in the 1920s and early 1930s; and banning women's football on the grounds that it was morally, physically and eugenically damaging to the nation's health. The CBD had long been run by Vargas's placeman, Luiz Aranha. A director of Botafogo and active supporter of Vargas during the 1930 coup, Aranha had been made CBD president in 1936. It probably helped that his brother Oswaldo was Vargas's finance minister and that another brother, Citro, was the president of Vasco da Gama; all three came from Vargas's home state of Rio Grande do Sul. As with so many facets of the Estado Novo, a tiny group of very conservative men, connected by familial and personal networks, ruled in alliance with the military and the upper reaches of the state civil service.

Alongside these administrative changes, the regime began to

use football stadiums as stages, even crucibles of *Brasilidade* – the nation's new culture. In 1935 Brazil's First National Congress of Education was held at the São Januário with Gustavo Capanema, the minister of education, and President Vargas in attendance alongside thousands of teachers and students. Billed as a discussion about the direction of national education, it was light on detail and big on showpieces, more a social-policy spectacular than an earnest colloquium. The great composer Heitor Villa-Lobos, one of the participants at São Paulo's Modern Art Week, devoted much of the 1930s to a nationwide musical-education programme, staging huge popular concerts with schoolchildren and local choirs. In 1940, on Independence Day, the São Januário hosted his largest concert yet, with 40,000 students and over 1,000 musicians performing a variety of works, including his own melding of European classical and indigenous Brazilian music. The poet Carlos Drummond de Andrade was moved to write:

> It was so beautiful and overwhelming, that for many there was no choice but to weep tears of pure joy. Through the curtain of tears emerged the foggy figure of the conductor, who had captured the musical essence of our people, Indians, blacks, workers, mestizos, seresteiros, the suburbs, who joined the echoes and hints of rivers, hills, caves, crops, kids' games, whistles and laughter.[1]

If football stadiums could serve as the stage for state spectaculars and the crucible of collective national experiences, they could also be used to corral and control popular energies. Rio's carnival and the samba schools of the city were subject to the regime's wider politics of cultural regulation. In 1943 and 1945 the samba parade was redirected to the São Januário. Here, the First Lady, Darcy Vargas, presided over a decidedly more regimented version of carnival's street samba than usual, its themes and motifs, like 'Glorious Brazil', set by the state.

The Vargas regime cultivated nationalist educators and musicians, but its main political constituency in the cities was the workers. The Estádio São Januário served as the primary theatre of Vargas's Brazilian version of corporatism. In a move designed to undercut and exclude the remnants of the radical left and free trade unions, Labour Day on 1 May became the key symbolic moment conjoining the regime, its unions and the urban working classes. In 1940 free public transport helped ensure that more than 40,000 packed into the São Januário to watch Vargas arrive and circle the football pitch in a magnificent open-topped car, announcing to the crowd the latest consolidation of the regime's labour laws. Radio star Carlos Galhardo sang a specially composed 'workers' song' and then the president signed the decree that would establish a minimum wage. Labour Day in 1941 was similar except that this time the establishment of the new labour courts was being celebrated. Matters began with a parade of worker-athletes, organized by occupation, dressed in a mix of sports and working clothes; then there were athletic displays by military units and a patriotic dance performance from the Municipal Theatre. The day concluded with two Rio select XIs playing an exhibition game, the Zona Sul beating the Zona Norte 6–5.

Until this point, the Zona Sul had held on to the national team, with their games being played at Fluminense's Laranjeiras or Flamengo's Gávea stadium, but from 1939 the national team played its games at the São Januário, including the 1945 Copa Roca (an irregularly contested clash with Argentina) and the 1949 Copa

América, both of which Brazil won. While none of these tournaments had quite the nation-building impact of the South American Championships of the previous decades, they did serve to cement the relationship between football and the nation, and suggested that in the new Brazil the centre of gravity of both had switched, in Rio at any rate, from south to north, from the oceanside mansions to the dusty suburbs. However, São Januário was just one stadium, Vasco was just one club and Rio just one city. If football was to serve the truly nationalist agenda of the Estado Novo it would need to include others, and for that it would turn to Flamengo and build the Estádio do Pacaembu in São Paulo.

||

The truly national ambitions of Vargas's regime sat uneasily with the idea that only one stadium in one city could embody the nation or host its Labour Day parades. Something had to be done in São Paulo, but its club stadiums were all small. So in the mid-1930s the local municipality began to plan a new stadium for what was fast becoming Brazil's biggest city. In keeping with the generous peace terms after the 1932 civil war, when the federal government had assumed half of São Paulo's war debt, the city was allowed to create its first public university, and its stadium project now received significant government support.

Work on the Estádio do Pacaembu began in 1936. It was situated in a long hollow between gently rolling hills on what were then the outskirts of the city. The complex was approached by an open, ceremonial space, more oblong than square – Praça Charles Miller – at the end of which sat the rounded end of a vast horseshoe of stands. The Pacaembu was almost double the size of Vasco's São Januário. Whereas the São Januário was ornate and baroque, the façade of the Pacaembu was clean and simple and geometrically proportioned, its detailing reflecting the lines of the era's sleek ships, touring cars and aeroplanes. Its signage employed sans serif fonts that were elegant, uncluttered and modern. More than just a stadium, the complex also incorporated a gymnasium and facilities for many other sports, open to the public.

The scale of the opening day festivities in late 1940 was also a good measure of the political meaning that had come to be invested in the new stadium. To the sound of a blast of trumpets, a special police detail entered the ground carrying an Olympic flag brought from the Rio club Fluminense. It was a rather heavy-handed symbol but made clear that the locus of Brazilian national sport, and perhaps national identity too, had moved from the private and elite surroundings of Laranjeiras to the municipal and demotic Pacaembu. There followed a parade of over 12,000 athletes from the city's sporting institutions, all of whom were instructed to make sure that they wore only white shoes, official club colours and no head coverings of any kind. While the athletes' parade that had greeted King Albert of Belgium in 1920 in Laranjeiras had been headed by the elite clubs of Rio, the Pacaembu's parade began with the teams of the masses: Corinthians and Palestra Itália. However, it was São Paulo FC who got the biggest cheers. This was surprising given that the club had been formed only five years beforehand from the remnants of elite clubs CA Paulistano and AA Palmeiras, who had turned their backs on professional football. São Paulo was now a fully professional side, but it retained its identity as the team of the city's elites. However, its name and badge offered the opportunity to the crowd to make their Paulista identity public. Indeed, it seemed clear to observers that the acclaim with which the club's colours were met was directed at President Vargas, a public reminder of the city's pride and desire for autonomy.

In the best seats in the house sat the majority of the country's most important politicians: São Paulo's mayor, Prestes Maia, his counterpart from Rio and the *interventores* of the states of São Paulo, Rio and Minas Gerais, together with Vargas, his wife and his daughter. The mayor's speech was typical of the era. Oleaginous, circuitous, at times obsequious, he was, when not just lauding Vargas, almost grovelling. He praised Vargas, the regime and the navy, and indulged in a nationalist eugenic fantasy so intense that he envisaged 'every citizen mimicking the legendary Hercules', able to 'take Brazil on their shoulders'. He also suggested that the president's spirit was the key to making the project work and asked His Excellency if he would kindly do all present the honour of opening the stadium. In reply Vargas was rather less florid and made, in his sidelong manner, two key political points: first, that the stadium was about more than sport, for sport had to serve other ends:

> These clean lines, this beautiful imposing mass of concrete and steel, will be just an architectural symbol unless it affirms and supports the efforts of our new regime to implement its programme . . . this monumental sporting playground is for a healthy patriotism, for the purposes of physical education and civic education.[2]

And second, that this wasn't just São Paulo's show, this was Brazil's, and they had better not forget that:

> The Pacaembu stadium is a matter for you, made by your contri-
> bution and efforts . . . and yet you understand that this monument
> marks the greatness of São Paulo in the service of Brazil.[3]

The following day the stadium saw swimming, boxing and fencing
competitions before a capacity crowd watched a double header of
São Paulo teams against clubs from other states – Palestra Itália vs
Coritiba, and Corinthians vs Atlético Mineiro – still a rarity in
Brazil where competitive club football was organized at state
rather than national level.

In 1942 the Pacaembu was fully integrated into the Estado
Novo's national pantheon when it hosted Labour Day. Some
70,000 people watched the scouts, the police and the fire brigade
and swooned at the low-flying aircraft putting on a display over-
head. From the stands of the most modern stadium in South
America the crowd cheered the workers of Volta Redonda – the
new city rising on the banks of the Paraíba do Sul in Rio state,
where Brazil would build its, and South America's, first steel plant.

When in 1927 Flamengo won their last Carioca Championship
of the amateur era they were, like their neighbours and rivals
Fluminense, an elite sports and social club whose members overwhelmingly came from Rio's upper classes. The club's president,
Rivadavia Meyer, was among the most vocal opponents of professionalism, revolted by the prospect of mixing it on the pitch
with the people. By the late 1940s, the team was, without question, the most popular in Brazil – not just in Rio but, uniquely for
the time, with a truly national following. Flamengo could fill stadiums in north-eastern cities like Recife and Natal, as well as at

home. While other clubs might claim to be popular clubs, Flamengo claimed it was the people's.

This remarkable shift was led by José Bastos Padilha, the wealthy owner of a printing company, and president of the club between 1936 and 1939. Padilha is an example of the ways in which practical and ideological initiatives emerging from civil society gave real content to the regime's notion of *Brasilidade*. Having made the club's peace with professionalism, Padilha recognized that, under the new economic circumstances of professionalism and mass paying audiences, success would only come from having a bigger membership and bigger attendance and that in turn would require a better team and better headlines in the press that football fans were consuming in increasing amounts. To these ends he raised the money to build a new stadium, the Gávea, on what was a lakeside quagmire in the Zona Sul. Membership qualifications were eased, a recruitment drive was conducted and over a decade the club added another 10,000 *sócios* to its roster. The club bought into the newspaper *Jornal dos Sports* where they teamed up with the editor, Mário Filho. Together they began to crank up the level of Flamengo news and hype, and Filho would, in time, turn their history into pure golden myth. If you couldn't get the people to Flamengo, Flamengo would go to them. A combination of nationwide coverage of the team on radio and national tours by the squad saw it establish a considerable body of support in almost every city in the country.

Back in Rio crowds grew as Padilha invested money in a new team. First, he bought Argentinians, who at one point comprised almost half the starting eleven. He added the tactical innovations of the Hungarian coach Dori Kürschner, who brought the new thinking of Danubian football to Rio. Then, in a populist master-stroke, he hired the three leading black players of the day, Fausto, Domingos da Guia and Leônidas da Silva. No clearer statement of the new Flamengo could have been made. When Fluminense fans began to chant '*Pó de carvão*' ('coal dust') at them, Flamengo fans took it up themselves as a celebration of the club's openness to poor, black Brazilians.

Alongside the commercial sporting spectacle, Padilha had an ideological agenda. For him, the youth of Brazil, whom he referred to as Generation Flamengo, were going to be remade as healthy, socialized patriots through their love of sport and their love of club. Flamengo began to set up a range of educational and sporting programmes for working-class children. As Padilha himself put it:

> We made the courses completely free to all the boys and girls of the city up to fifteen years old, poor or rich, white or coloured[;] it was a campaign for the broader democratization of sport . . . aimed at the improvement of the breed by training and the enhancement of the motherland.[4]

Jornal dos Sports was both gushing and creepy: 'Miracles of belief and enthusiasm are the hallmark of Flamengo . . . Beings barely awakened to life have let themselves get carried away by these two beautiful emotions: paternal love and an interest in physical culture.'[5] The club and the press ran a competition asking children to submit the best sentence that they could including the words Flamengo and Brazil. The winners included 'Flamengo teaches you to love all things about Brazil' and 'Flamengo: Brazil's sentinel'.

Although Padilha had made the key structural changes that would turn Flamengo into the people's champion, he was not able to bring a championship to the club, nor in the end was there much room for the people. The club accepted their ticket money, but it remained an operation entirely controlled from above. Both of these deficits were remedied over the next decade. The key figure in this case came from the other end of the social spectrum. Jaime Rodrigues de Carvalho was born in 1911 in Salvador and, as part of the great internal shift of the poor north-east to the growing cities of the south, arrived on a boat in Rio in 1927. His first experience of football in the city was watching Fluminense but when he returned to the club to see the team train he found his way barred. Down the road Flamengo's squad trained in the open and, thus drawn to them, he never left. For five years he climbed the stadium's walls, begged for money for tickets and asked players for spares until he landed a lowly but steady clerical job in the Ministry of Justice. It was precisely this kind of state employment that drew immigrants to the cities, and for the few that could get a job it transformed their lives. Carvalho, a poor provincial mulatto immigrant, was now able to become a Flamengo *sócio*, marry a Portuguese woman and buy his ticket to watch the club, and not just the football: he attended all of Flamengo's rowing regattas until the late 1940s as well.

Carvalho first came to public attention in 1942. On the eve of the final and decisive game of that year's Carioca Championship he personally raised Flamengo's flag over their clubhouse and stayed up all night with a giant roll of calico and red and black dye making a huge flag for the next day. On it were emblazoned the words '*Avante Flamengo!*' He arrived at the stadium, not only with the flag, but with a band of over a dozen other fans equipped with a trombone, trumpets and drums. Initial reactions were mixed. The crowd and the club officials seemed to like them, but Ary Barroso commentating on the radio thought the band unspeakable and nicknamed them the *charanga* – the out-of-tune band. Undeterred, the *charanga* made their own Flamengo shirts and placed hand-stitched harps on them as their club badge. They also began to attend away games and use the open space of the *geral* – the standing zones around the pitch – to get close to their opponents and distract them with their music. After Flamengo scored a fourth goal against São Cristóvão under these conditions the referee banned the *charanga* from the ground. The case went to court, but the football authorities were supportive, with both Mário Filho and Vargas Neto, head of the Rio Football Federation, arguing that football needed this kind of spontaneous spectacle from the crowd.

It might not have been the *charanga*, but something was working . At last, in 1942, Flamengo won the Carioca title and went on to win the next two, their own *tricampeonato*. The final victory of the three was recorded in Mário Filho's short story, 'Carnaval na Primavera', in which he claimed that the game began with a bang so loud that police on duty had fallen to the ground. It wasn't quite like that but the game did see plenty of pyrotechnics. For some time TOV (*Torcida Organizada do Vasco*), the new fan group created at Vasco da Gama (and emulators of the Flamengo *charanga*), had been putting on the best firework displays before matches. With Flamengo facing Vasco in the key game of that season, Jaime de Carvalho decided to upstage them by taking a home-made bomb to the game. It didn't blow anyone off the field but it completely filled the stadium with smoke and set a precedent for their use. When, at the end of the match, Flamengo emerged as champions again, the band and thousands of supporters took to the streets to celebrate. While this kind of behaviour might have panicked some ruling elites and led perhaps to a ban on fan groups or fireworks, Brazil's chose to co-opt these new energies. Equipped with club endorsement and commercial sponsorship, and the blessing of the football authorities, Jaime de Carvalho was made the official cheerleader for the Brazilian team at the 1950 World Cup, completing his journey from penniless Salvadorian immigrant to the nation's leading fan. As we shall see, such an office was a mixed blessing.

III

The Estado Novo may have engaged with Brazilian popular culture, even publicly celebrated it, but it was not, in its elite and conservative heart, entirely happy with its content and meanings. The attitude of many of the regime's most senior functionaries is encapsulated by this civil servant's thoughts on the regime's policy towards samba: 'We recognize that all the rude illiterate louts who live in our cities are frequently linked to civilization through music.'[6] This kind of attitude certainly shaped the treatment of carnival by the Estado Novo and its predecessors.

Rio's first carnival was held in 1641, decreed by the colonial government to commemorate the restoration of the Portuguese monarchy. It became a wild and unpredictable affair combining Afro-Brazilian dance and music with hordes of wild Portuguese young men on a rampage through the town. By 1900 the Rio authorities had excluded the rampages and required participants in carnival to register, policing the event to keep the popular carnival clear of the private parties and masked balls of the wealthy. The emergence in the early twentieth century of the *Escolas de Samba* – grassroots but organized samba bands and dance clubs – ensured an enduring presence for the poor at carnival. Under Vargas, in return for subsidies and cash payments to cover floats and costumes, the *Escolas* were required to toe the patriotic line; the theme had to be tame enough that the regime could use a sanitized carnival as one of its main attractions to foreign tourists.

Thus the Estado Novo's attitude to carnival and samba was double-edged. On the one hand it welcomed them as powerful examples of a distinct Brazilian culture that had safely absorbed its African cultural heritage. On the other hand they were a zone of danger, immorality and potential disorder that required co-option and control. A similar ambivalence can be detected in the regime's attitude to football. For all the celebrations of the game as the route to the nation's demographic renewal, and footballers' roles as missionaries of hygiene and good healthy patriotism, it was clear to all that in an era of professionalism this was no longer, if it ever had been, the case. The rise of star players whose popularity and wealth rested on their footballing skills rather than their moral probity was a persistent challenge to the regime's version of football. Leônidas and Fausto were the most famous players who failed to conform to the authorities' austere norms of humility and obedience, but they were hardly alone. Fausto was, in the end, consumed by high living and low drinking. Leônidas, although occasionally corralled by the regime into supporting its labour laws, lived a life diametrically opposed to the sober patriotic workers the Estado Novo hoped to mould. He was a high-flying celebrity and hard-nosed businessman,

73

excruciatingly handsome, powerfully photogenic, showing off the latest threads, parading on Rio Branco on the day after a game to take the public's acclaim. What bothered the authorities was not only the dissolute bohemian lifestyles of the stars, but the deeper linkages that were being made between Brazilian football and the lifestyle and culture of the *malandro*. The *malandro* was a stock figure of Brazilian culture – the hustler, the street smart, an urban warrior living on his wits and his charm. Leônidas walked, talked and seemed to play with the same improvisational spontaneity and street cunning, his signature move the balletic bicycle kick.

This tension between the regime's conservatism and the new ideas and forces it could never fully control can be seen in three key areas of popular culture: football on the radio, and football as a subject of music and cinema.

Radio was the main way in which football was actually consumed by most Brazilians in the 1930s and 1940s. It provided a welcome addition to the otherwise rather limited output of the stations, which were heavily reliant on operatic music and the occasional drama. Commentators were therefore pivotal in shaping how football was received and understood. In the early 1930s, Nicolau Tuma and Armando Pamplona were the leading figures. Pamplona was always the slightly stuffy master of ceremonies, while Tuma's delivery began to speed up and acquire a staccato rhythm that saw him nicknamed 'Speaker Metralhadora' – the Machine Gun. Gagliano Neto was the safe pair of hands during the late Vargas era. Advertised to the public as a 'Speaker Esportivo Perfeito', he was the man who covered Brazil's progress, live, at the 1938 World Cup in France.

While all three commentators stayed within the bounds of the regime's sanitized and patriotic model of football, the late 1930s and 1940s did see the emergence of a much more partisan and exuberant coverage of the game, typified by Ary Barroso. Barroso rose to fame in the newly fashionable Copacabana area primarily as a composer, but also as a writer, painter, local councillor and fanatical Flamengo fan. His commentary was witty, fantastical and deeply partisan. In an effort to be heard above the crowds he bought a harmonica from a toyshop and took to signalling goals with a sprightly trill. When the opposition scored he emitted a rasping screech or a doleful dropping note. Some opponents considered his presence and his partisanship so disturbing that he was refused entrance to their stadiums and forced to commentate from the rooftops of nearby houses with a view of the ground. Apocryphally he was said to have descended to the touchline during a match in Buenos Aires to commentate on a close game between Brazil and Argentina, and was so vocally partisan that he ended up being attacked by Argentinian fans and officials.

Rebello Junior began his commentating career in the maniacal, breathless context of horse racing, and brought the intensity of that to his coverage of football. He is credited, in the early 1940s, with the first extended, orgasmic goal celebrations, the '*goooooooooooooooolll!!!!!*' that has become the cliché of Latin American commentary. At the time there was a school of thought that considered it excessive. Nicolau Tuma argued, 'I think the long-form announcement of a goal is a waste of time. When an announcer says "*goooooooooool*" and it takes twenty seconds, the listener just wants to know who it was that scored.' However, Brazilian radio was a competitive and innovative business with a huge popular market; restraint was never going to be its strong suit. Thus, not content with just one commentator, radio stations began to have two in the stands and at least one somewhere on the touchline. Jorge Curi and Antônio Cordeiro pioneered the radio football double act, while the later role was exemplified by the jocular Geraldo Blota. Blota began by calling offsides from the touchline but soon graduated to disturbing goalkeepers from behind their net, interviewing players and coaches during the game, and as increasingly happened in Brazilian club football, stepping on to the pitch during a match to talk to someone. In 1949, in a brilliantly executed hoax, Geraldo de Almeida called a game between São Paulo and a European opponent. São Paulo lost 7–0, until it was revealed the next day, 2 April, that it had all been invented. It was not a feature that would have made it to the *Hora do Brasil*.

The many living musical cultures of the country, combined with the new radio industry and the spread of gramophones in the 1930s and 1940s, created a burgeoning Brazilian recorded music industry. Although a variety of styles and genres existed – European polkas and waltzes, the mulatto sound of *choro*, which mixed these dances with Afro-Brazilian rhythms, and regional variants from the north-east and Bahia – the dominant popular music of the era was samba. The genre grew out of the musical cultures of Rio's poorest and blackest neighbourhoods at the turn of the twentieth century. It took *choro*'s mix of influences, emphasized African rhythms, and added call-and-response singing and some European instrumentation. In the 1920s there was a popular genre of samba, as well as a more refined version for white and middle-class consumption. Under the Estado Novo samba was also divided between those who toed the line – regime samba – and those who didn't. Regime samba could be crude propaganda, as in Luís Menezes's paean to the Vargas revolution: 'Slavery has ended. Long live the 1930 Revolution which was our salvation.' In the hands of composers like Ary Barroso, samba drew on a stock of imagery that depicted Brazil as a peaceful tropical paradise, a newly found Eden.

The first recorded football songs stood to one side of these mainstream compostions: 'Fluminense', by Américo Jacomino, for example, was an instrumental combination of classical guitar and tango rhythms. In the early 1930s humorous ditties and joke songs were the norm, like 'Futebol' by the backwoodsmen double act of Alvarenga and Ranchinho and comic impresario Capiao Furtado. However, as the 1930s progressed football came to occupy a distinct place in popular samba and dance music. Eduardo Souto's 1936 hit 'É Sopa, 17 a 3' recounted the politics of the 1930 presidential election and the subsequent coup led by Vargas as if it had been a football match. *É sopa*, literally 'it's soup', translates best as 'it's easy'. Catete Football Club was the presidential palace, Team A was led by Tonico, who was Antônio Carlos Ribeiro de Andrada, governor of Minas Gerais; Team B's captain was Julinho Prestes, the governor of São Paulo. The referee, Dr Macaé, was the outgoing president Washington Luís, and the man who found it all so easy was Getúlio Vargas, the gaucho who with his Mineiro and Paraíba allies eventually triumphed.

> Go for the big game, winning the Catete Football Club cup.
> Team A's Captain: Your Tonico.
> Team B's Captain: Your Julinho.
> The Judge: Doctor Macaé.
> The very worthy president of the Catete Football Club
> To win Brazil.
> Getulinho says: 'It's easy, easy, easy.'
> A Paraíba with a gaucho and Mineiro.

Football as a playful political metaphor was fine, but football as the natural habitat of the *malandro* was harder to stomach. Noel Rosa, whose hugely popular samba lyrics of the 1930s stood outside of the cosy and regulated imagery of the regime, never made it on to the radio. He often placed football in his songs as a feature of everyday life, and of special interest to the urban hustlers he liked to portray. In 'Conversa de Botequim' he imagines his man taking advantage of a waiter in a restaurant:

> If you don't stay and clean the table
> I won't get up or pay the bill.
> Go ask your boss for a pen, an inkwell,
> An envelope and a card . . .
> And a cigarette to scare the mosquitoes.
> Go tell your man to lend me some magazines,
> A lighter and an ashtray.

And of course, what the *malandro* really wants to know, once he's settled at the table, is what was the score? Rosa sang, 'Waiter feel free to quickly bring me piping-hot bread . . . Go ask your customers, what happened in the football.'[7]

The regime responded to this kind of depiction of football fans with the release of 'O Bonde São Januário' – 'the São Januário Tram' – performed by Ataulfo Alves. This was a samba which paradoxically hailed the new sober urban worker, who preferred getting to work on time than going to the Estádio São Januário and the louche life of drinking and football that bohemians and slackers indulged in: 'The São Januário tram/It carries a worker/I am going to work.' More than that, the model worker was turning his back on football: 'I never used to have a clue/But I decided to look after my future/You see I'm happy, I live well/Laziness doesn't put clothes on anyone's back.'

In the 1940s, as government control eased on musicians and composers, it was the street-level voice of Rosa rather than the official tones of Alves that lived on in football samba. Wilson Batista's 'E o Juiz Apitou' ('And the Ref Blew his Whistle') cast the football fan as an obsessive who tries to rest on Sunday but is compelled to attend the game, 'ninety minutes of suffering'. More than that, he is not interested in fair play, only in getting the right result. Lourival Ramos celebrated the Brazilian national team in his song 'Copa Roca'. Lamartine Babo, in a stunt sponsored by local radio, wrote the lyrics of a new hymn for every one of Rio's eleven biggest clubs in a single day.[8] They were all realized on record, a testament to the size of the market and the now immense popularity of football in Rio.

The political turmoil and difficult economic conditions of the early 1930s saw few films of any kind get produced and nothing that featured football since the clowning and comedy of *Campeão de Futebol*, released in 1931. But at the end of the decade two films were made that depicted football in terms that the Estado Novo could feel comfortable with. *Alma e Corpo de uma Raça* ('The Body and Soul of a Race') received its premiere in Rio which was attended by the directors of Flamengo, the education minister Gustavo Capanema and President Vargas himself. The film was made with the support of Flamengo, who provided sets and players, as well as money from government agencies. The main melodrama was mixed with semi-documentary footage of the new social programmes and enthusiastic youths of Padilha's patriotic Flamengo. The film's chief character is Louis, a relatively

poor Flamengo player and medical student, who hopes to emu-
late his dead father, who had been the star striker at Flamengo.
Life is perked up but complicated by the return from Europe of
his childhood sweetheart, Maria Helena. Maria is still game but
the family would prefer her to marry Rubens, also a Flamengo
player and a medical student, but from a very rich family. Maria
declares that she will marry whoever scores the most goals for
Flamengo that season. Everyone's moral blushes are saved when
Rubens realizes he cannot win her heart, and concedes Maria and
Flamengo's goal-scoring opportunities to Louis; and Louis successfully completes his medical thesis, thus ensuring his upward
class mobility.

Futebol em Família featured a conservative doctor, ironically
named Professor Leônidas Jau (his namesake was the era's ultimate bohemian player), whose lectures sharply criticize football. He
claims that the game deforms the mind and the body, and declares
his loathing for star striker Arthur Friedenreich. His son, inevitably, is a football player and a medical student, loves Friedenreich
and is eventually called up to play for Fluminense. The professor
forbids this, which gives the film the rest of its storyline. The conflict is happily resolved as the son successfully combines football
and study, and the professor, against his inclinations, becomes a
devoted football fan.

With the fall of Vargas and the Estado Novo, Brazilian cinema
was in theory released from this combination of officially sanc-
tioned melodrama, clowning, excruciating sentimentality and
lamentable plotting, but for the most part that's where the medium
stayed. José Carlos Burle's first football movie of the era, *O Gol da
Vitória* ('The Winning Goal'), made in 1945, remained true to
these formats, but his second, *O Craque* ('The Star'), released in

1953, broke with some of these conventions, suggesting that the attempts to impose eugenic and moral frameworks on to football were waning. *O Gol da Vitória* centred on a star striker, Laurindo, modelled on Leônidas da Silva, and played by the leading black comic of the era, Grande Otelo. *O Craque* was set in São Paulo where Julinho, a Corinthians player, struggles with his injured knee and his sweetheart's father. Elisa loves Julinho, but as ever the father wants her to marry a doctor instead. The film ends with a game between Corinthians and the fictional Uruguayan club Carrasco Montevideo (played by the Paraguayan side Olimpia) and in a fictional reversioning of the 1950 World Cup final, the Brazilians win 2–1. Julinho's knee holds up, he scores the winner and gets the girl, and for the first time the hero is not the doctor, nor does his ascent depend on passing exams or climbing the social hierarchy; scoring the winning goal is enough.

IV

In 1934 Brazil played a single game at the World Cup. They were defeated by Spain and went home. Few had taken much note and the most significant response in Brazil was the damage inflicted on the clubhouse of Palestra Itália in São Paulo; not because the club had fielded Spaniards, but because so many of the best Italo-Brazilian players from the club were representing Italy rather than Brazil. In 1938 the nation was actually listening in as Brazil's games were broadcast live on the radio from France. This time Brazil were the only South American side at the tournament and the two undisputed stars of the squad were black: striker Leôni-das da Silva – the Black Diamond – and central defender

81

Domingos da Guia. In their opening game against Poland the Brazilians found themselves 3–1 up at half time, 4–4 at 90 minutes and, thanks to a Leônidas hat-trick, the winners of a pulsating match 6-5 after extra time. In the second round they showed they could mix it with the physical Europeans. During their very rough 1-1 draw two Czechs had to leave the field with broken bones and one Brazilian was sent off. Brazil won the replay and headed for Marseilles where they met world champions Italy in the semi-final. Italy proved to be too good, winning 2-1, but the Brazilians regrouped and thrashed the Swedes in a play-off to finish third overall.

The team's progress was heard live on the radio, followed avidly in the press, and watched a few days later in the cinemas of the big cities after precious reels of film had been flown home. It was a national triumph, but what did it mean? The most influential interpretation, and one that continues to shape perceptions of Brazilian football today, was given by Gilberto Freyre, one of the country's leading social scientists and commentators:

Our style of football seems to contrast with the European style because of a set of characteristics such as surprise, craftiness, shrewdness, readiness and I shall say individual brilliance and spontaneity, all of which express our 'mulattoism' ... Our passes ... our tricks ... that something which is related to dance, to capoeira, mark the Brazilian style of football, which rounds and sweetens the game the British invented, the game which they and the other Europeans play in such an acute and angular way – all this seems to express ... the flamboyant and at the same time shrewd mulattoism, which today can be detected in every true affirmation of Brazil.[9]

Freyre had made his name in 1933 when he published *Casa-Grande e Senzala* ('The Masters and the Slaves'), which described in extraordinary detail every aspect of life on a north-eastern sugar plantation, and every aspect of life seemed to lead back to sex.[10] While the sexual relationships between slave master and slaves in Protestant North America were largely nasty, brutish, short and shameful, in Catholic Brazil, where the demographics of colonialism were so much more heavily weighted against Europeans, miscegenation was a necessity and a virtue. It was an alluring notion, particularly at a moment when the country's elite was searching for a form of *Brasilidade* that could turn the nation's diversity from a source of shame to an advantage. As Peter Robb has written, 'It was immensely seductive, Freyre's tropical pastoral of the vanished worlds of the sugar estates, conjured in sensual and living detail. Most seductive of all was the idea that out of Brazil's sensual and promiscuous past a new society had grown where all races flourished and racism was extinguished.'[11]

Freyre's work has come under increasing attack in recent years, as detailed studies of economic and domestic relations under slavery have revealed a much harsher and more violent society, and of course the notion that Brazil effortlessly acquired a multiracial democracy without discrimination looks ever more laughable. But whatever the sociological truth of his thesis, Freyre left an ineradicable mark on Brazilian culture. Over the next forty years he would rework and republish the argument in a variety of ways. In the 1940s he coined the term *Futebol Arte*, and made the contrast between Brazilian and European football in terms of Apollinarian and Dionysian characteristics, Brazil, of course, representing the latter.

Freyre's arguments did not come out of thin air. For over two decades a small body of work on Afro-Brazilian culture and history had been emerging, and the São Paulo Modernists of 1922 had continued to look for hybrid forms of Brazilian culture. In 1939 Mário de Andrade wrote a noted *crônica* on a game between Brazil and Argentina played in Buenos Aires. In conversation with his Uruguayan companion he chews over the cannibalistic character of Brazilian football. But this was no nationalist rant. Brazil end up losing because they merely long for victory, whereas the Argentinians want it and act upon this desire. At least Mário seemed to enjoy the spectacle: 'Gorgeous! What a marvellous dance, the game of football! A hummingbird ballet!'[12]

In the visual arts, painters were increasingly turning to football as a component of the everyday landscapes of Brazil. Cândido Portinari, most famous perhaps for his depiction of life on the São Paulo coffee plantations of the era, also painted the extraordinary *Futebol* in 1935. It depicts a brown, parched, almost surreal environment in the bleak Serrano of the north-east. Among goats and stones and blasted stumps a group of boys, of all colours, strangely float around a ball in motion. In the distance is a graveyard and a garden they do not have access to. By the 1940s football was appearing in more playful landscapes, rural and urban, and was depicted as a more carefree, joyous game in the work of Carybé and Djanira da Motta e Silva.

Over time Freyre's argument also served to explain Brazil's cultures of music, dance and capoeira. *Ginga*, the basic hip-swivelling moves of the latter, became synonymous with the swerves and feints of footballers and sambistas alike. All, it was argued, could claim a cultural lineage that was not only Afro-Brazilian but retained the body of cultural and physical capital that was required to survive under conditions of brutal slavery – improvisation, quick-wittedness, the capacity for deception and illusion, spontaneity: taking your chance when it came. This was the same set of skills attributed to the *malandro*. Domingos da Guia, star of the 1938 World Cup, looked back on his youth forty years later in Freyrian terms:

> My older brother used to tell me: a *malandro* is a cat that always lands on his feet . . . I used to really be good at dancing and that helped me on the field. I swerved a lot. You know, I invented that short dribble imitating the *miudinho* – the 'little one' – that kind of samba.[13]

Domingos's words underline the final but most important factor in explaining Freyre's impact. His work was absorbed and adopted by Mário Filho, scion of a Rio publishing family, and Brazil's most influential football writer from the 1930s to the late 1950s. It was Filho that truly popularized these notions and created a language in which intellectuals, public and players alike could frame their shared understanding of Brazilian football. In his 1947 landmark book *O Negro no Futebol Brasileiro* he argued that Brazilian football's distinctiveness rested on its mulattoism and proceeded to illustrate, invent and mythologize this in a series of fabulous essays. Filho was more than a writer. An immense red-headed character, all linen suits and fat cigars, he was an editor and networker, an impresario and entrepreneur, inventing competitions for football fans and carnival floats. He set the intellectual framework in which Brazilian football was discussed for three decades and went on to recruit and publish some of the best football writing from some of the nation's best authors. These included his brother, the playwright Nelson Rodrigues, and the novelist José Lins do Rego.

Zé Lins, as he is known, was one of a group of writers – like novelist Rachel de Queiroz and poet Jorge de Lima – who had emerged out of the north-east of Brazil and made the desperate poverty and harsh lives of the region their subject matter. In his novels and journalism of the 1920s he had shown no interest in football, but all this changed when he moved to Rio in the 1930s and caught the bug. He joined Flamengo and became a director of the club. His 1941 novel *Água-mãe*, set in the salt flats outside Rio de Janeiro, is a multi-family saga with a ghost story that features a working-class football star and his inevitable decline. He was recruited by Mário Filho to write regular *crônicas* for *Jornal dos Sports*, where he coined the adjective Flamengista. He too absorbed Freyre's arguments and incorporated them into his writing on football and other matters. Indeed that cluster of ideas linking Freyre's idyllic model of Brazilian ethnicity with football, music and dance, and all in turn with spontaneity, trickery and artistry, became the common view of Brazilian nationalism and Brazilian football. Writing in 1942, but looking back to the mixed-race Brazilian team of 1932 that won the Copa Rio Branco in Uruguay, Zé Lins, like most of the country's intelligentsia, now saw the past and the future through Freyrian eyes:

> The young men that won in Montevideo were a portrait of social democracy, where Paulinho, the son of an important family, united with the black Leônidas, with the mulatto Oscarino, with the white Martins. All this done in the good Brazilian style, with the most sympathetic improvisation. Reading this book on

soccer, I believe in Brazil, in the eugenic qualities of our mestizos, in the energy and intelligence of the men that the Brazilian land forged with diverse bloods, giving them originality that one day will shock the world.[14]

V

Brazil's participation in the anti-fascist alliance of the Second World War made Vargas's own fascist affectations look absurd, and his continuing authoritarian hold over power unsustainable. He stepped down in October 1945, but got himself elected to the Senate and remade his network of power through the Brazilian Labour Party, which he had invented while still in office. The extent of his control over the Brazilian elite remained significant and he anointed the successful candidate in the 1945 presidential election – General Eurico Dutra. Early on in Dutra's presidency Brazil was confirmed as the host of the 1950 World Cup, and the plans and preparations for the tournament offered an interesting commentary on the broader political economy of the nation. Dutra maintained the football politics of the previous regime, donating a large piece of land to Flamengo. Vargas would later secure the club an interest-free loan that would allow them to build a major residential development on it. However, in the new and more democratic spaces of Brazilian politics, this kind of favouritism and largesse from above was for a short while challenged from the left.

Just as the war meant Vargas had to go and democratic elections had to be held, so too an alliance with the Soviet Union made it impossible to maintain the ban on the Brazilian

Communist Party. The party was legalized in 1945 and underwent a short boom, benefiting from pro-Soviet attitudes developed during the war and hopes for a more radical social policy. Intellectuals – from Graciliano Ramos to Oscar Niemeyer – and workers flooded into the party. Rather than just concentrating on industrial organization, the party, under the charismatic leadership of Luís Prestes, engaged with popular culture. The PCB supported and recruited among samba schools, held its own alternative carnival competitions and found backers among many musicians and artists. Similarly, the party took note of football, and, taking a leaf out of Vargas's book, began holding rallies in the country's major stadiums. Prestes's first significant engagement after being released from prison was to speak to a huge audience at Vasco's São Januário. Later in the year a fundraiser was held at the Pacaembu for the communist trade unions of São Paulo. The evening opened with two union teams playing and was followed by an exhibition match between Corinthians and Palmeiras. This rare coalition of football and the radical end of leftist politics in Brazil, however, had little time to develop. Emboldened by the direction of the new Cold War, and deeply distrustful of the communists, Dutra banned them again in 1947 – and this despite an electoral mandate that saw fourteen communist senators elected.

A more moderate but critical political voice could still be heard in Brazilian football, for the preparations for the World Cup under Dutra served as both a practical problem and a proxy debate about Brazil's economic development. Despite the advances of the Vargas era, Brazil suffered from a chronic lack of energy and transport infrastructure. Mário Filho led the charge of the football developmentalists who were calling for the construction of football's equivalent, a new stadium in Rio that would provide a proper stage for the World Cup and, in its scale and styling, speak to the country's footballing prowess and urban modernity: 'The stadium,' he said, 'will be a gift from this generation to the next, strengthening the human wealth of Brazil. This stadium will be a gift from all of us.' Critics argued that scarce capital should be spent on hospitals and schools, but Vargas Neto, president of the Rio Football Federation, responded in *Jornal dos Sports*: 'I'm not against your request! I'm in favour. But I want you to be in favour of stadiums. It could well be that hospitals will become less necessary.'[15]

The city council voted to build the stadium. The land, which had once housed the elite English Derby Club, was cleared for the construction of a popular sporting temple. Under municipal control the architects Galvão, Azevedo, Bastos, Carneiro, Feldman, Ramos and Valdetaro were appointed and building began. By the time of the World Cup it was barely finished, but it was magnificent. Brazil had built the largest and most elegantly modern stadium in the world. The Maracanã was an immense double-tiered white-concrete ellipse with an official capacity of over 160,000. Its concrete 360-degree flat roof, when viewed from above, gave the irresistible appearance of an alien spaceship that had chosen to park among the vacant lots on the poor fringes of the Zona Norte. The stadium from planet modernity was built with some of the first concrete actually manufactured in Brazil. The main entrances were dramatic stepped ramps leading right up to the top of the stands, supported by two lines of simple thin cylindrical pilotis, a touch of the city in the sky. There was no hint of a classical colonnade here. The hidden steel cantilevers in the roof were a bold statement of advanced engineering and minimalist design. The Maracanã's high internal arches and buttresses beneath the stands flanked great circular concourses that swept around the stadium and beneath the seating: a people's sporting boulevard. The newspaper *A Noite* wrote, 'Today Brazil has the biggest and most perfect stadium in the world, dignifying the competence of its people and its evolution in all branches of human activity.'[16] Mário Filho thought the country had acquired a new soul, the stadium prefiguring an awakening of the slumbering giant of Brazilian potential.

The Brazilian team's preparations were meticulous, cloistered as it was for months in a secluded out-of-town location. Rio prepared itself too. The carnival parade on Shrove Tuesday took the World Cup as its theme. The Jules Rimet trophy was put on view in a jeweller's shop on Avenida Rio Branco where thousands came to stare in awe. On the day of the first game the Korean War broke out but nobody in Brazil noticed. The huge crowd that assembled at the Maracanã saw 5,000 pigeons let loose and heard a 21-gun salute. English referee Arthur Ellis reported being showered by fine white plaster dust from the just-completed roof. Brazil sailed past Mexico 4–0, drew 2–2 with Switzerland in São Paulo and then secured their place in the final round robin by beating the Yugoslavs, one of whom had gashed his head on an exposed girder in the bowels of the unfinished stadium.

Two days later the final round robin of four teams commenced. The Rio local elections were in full swing and the squad's hotel, training camp and dressing room were all deluged with every last candidate of every party searching for a photo opportunity and the chance to make a speech. Despite the pressure of expectations Brazil seemed unleashed. Sweden were mown down 7–1. Spain were dispatched 6–1 in an atmosphere of euphoria. The crowd waved 100,000 handkerchiefs and wished the Spanish *adiós*. Jaime de Carvalho's official supporters' band struck up the insufferably jaunty carnival favourite 'Bullfight in Madrid', popularized at the time by Carmen Miranda's semi-official World Cup version, and the entire crowd responded in 'one of the largest collective demonstrations of singing ever known'.[17]

The last game loomed. Uruguay were the opponents and Brazil needed only to draw to win the World Cup. Over 200,000 people, perhaps a quarter of a million, 20 per cent of Rio's adult population, the largest crowd ever to assemble for a football game, made their way to the Maracanã. In the greatest act of sporting hubris ever the mayor of Rio spoke to the team over the stadium PA: 'You Brazilians, whom I consider victors of the tournament . . . you players who in less than a few hours will be acclaimed champions by millions of your compatriots . . . you who are superior to every other competitor . . . you whom I already salute as conquerors . . .'[18] You couldn't have scripted it. Brazil were one up at half-time, but lost the game 2–1. A terrible silence descended upon the stadium. When the final whistle came, players, officials and members of the crowd broke down. FIFA president Jules Rimet, uncertain what to do, thrust the cup into the hands of Uruguay's captain, Obdulio Varela, and made himself scarce.

Brazil had been spared the real slaughter of industrialized war, preferring news of Flamengo to the battle of Stalingrad. Now football was the metaphor for exploring the consequences of defeat and devastation. Pelé, then ten years old, recalled the mood of his small home town in Minas Gerais: 'There was a sadness so great, so profound that it seemed like the end of the war, with Brazil the loser and many people dead.' Nelson Rodrigues would come to see the game in apocalyptic terms: 'Everywhere has its irremediable national catastrophe, something like a Hiroshima. Our catastrophe, our Hiroshima, was the defeat to Uruguay in 1950.'[19] The search for *Brasilidade* had led the country to football and aligned it with the nation's fate. It was meant to reveal its strengths, which it had. Now would come the reckoning with its weaknesses.

4

Brasília and the Ball: Inventing the Beautiful Game, 1950–1964

'The Brazilian style of football, which rounds and sweetens the game the . . .
Europeans play in such an acute and angular way' – Gilberto Freyre.

Making Brazilian Modernity: Niemeyer's national cathedral under construction.
Brasília c.1964.

It is not the right angle that attracts me, nor the straight line, hard and inflexible, created by man. What attracts me is the free and sensual curve; the curve that I find in the mountains of my country, in the sinuous course of its rivers, in the body of the beloved woman.

Oscar Niemeyer

I

After the *Maracanazo* ('The Maracanã Disaster') Brazil was sombre. The electorate looked for nostalgia and safety and elected Getúlio Vargas, for the first time, as president of Brazil. The national team didn't play another game until 1952 and permanently abandoned the white shirts they had lost in. They kept away from the Maracanã until 1954. Investigation and recrimination followed and the main scapegoats were defenders Bigode and Juvenal, and goalkeeper Barbosa. All were condemned in the press as cowards, lacking fibre and discipline. All three were black.

Barbosa was singled out for special treatment until his miserable poverty-stricken death fifty years later. He recalled walking into a bar where a woman said to her son, 'Look, there is the man who made all Brazil cry.' In 1994 he was turned away from the Seleção's training camp in Teresópolis lest he should curse them before the World Cup. Brazil did not field another black goal-keeper until Dida in 1995. The multiracial, confident Brazil that Freyre and Filho had conjured from football was dissolved in an acid bath of racism, self-doubt and self-loathing. Footballers in general, and black footballers in particular, were cast as psycho-logically dysfunctional and over-emotional, lacking the self-discipline required to perform at their best.

At the 1954 World Cup in Switzerland Brazil were beaten 4–2 in the quarter-final by the Hungarians, a game remembered for its rising tide of violence and known ever since as the Battle of Berne. Hungary's Bozsik and Brazil's Nilton Santos were sent off for fighting, followed by Humberto, as scuffles broke out all over the pitch. Didi had to be restrained on the touchline. As the team left the pitch, a free-for-all began which continued into the tunnel and the dressing rooms. While the popular press celebrated the hard men of the team who had defended the nation's pride, the official report continued to cast the problem in terms of miscegenation: 'The Brazilian players lacked what is lacking for the Brazilian people in general . . . The ills are deeper than the game's tactical system . . . They go back to genetics itself.'

The Brazilian squad returned from their bruising encounter to a nation whose rancour was every bit as bad as the fist fight in the players' tunnel. Since 1950 President Vargas had pursued an increasingly populist economic course and in so doing had suffi-ciently unnerved enough of Brazil's generals and key industrialists and bankers to produce an air of mutiny. By summer 1954 the plotters were ready to strike. One of Vargas's most fearsome opponents was the right-wing newspaper editor Carlos Lacerda, who feared for his own life enough to employ an air force body-guard. In late August the bodyguard was shot and killed in an attack on Lacerda and the trail led back to Vargas's own body-guard. Knowing that the end of his political career had finally arrived, Vargas shot himself through the heart in the presidential palace. In the outpouring of national grief and confusion that followed this most political act of suicide the threat of a coup receded and Brazil limped along with a series of makeshift governments until late 1955. Vargas's legacy was a nation sufficiently developed that it stood poised between tropical agrarian lassitude and urban industrial dynamism. With the election of Juscelino Kubitschek as president in 1955 Brazil decisively opted for the latter, and with that the many pieces of Brazil's football culture fell into place.

Kubitschek was a hard-headed politician moulded by the pork-barrel pragmatism of Minas Gerais, but he brought with him an aura of dynamism animated by his personal charisma and his unwavering commitment to super-heated economic growth. He offered Brazil 'Fifty years' progress in five' and almost accomplished it. Riding the post-Korean War boom in the global economy, Brazil's economy grew by up to 10 per cent a year and its leading industrial sectors even faster. The military were neutralized with salary and budget increases, foreign multinationals were invited to invest in the country, and in the defining act of his presidency Kubitschek initiated the building of a new federal capital on a designated but still undeveloped bare plateau deep in the country's interior – Brasília.

The first constitution of the Old Republic, written in 1891, had stipulated the creation of a new capital and in 1893 the site for the city was selected in an attempt to move the government away from the coast and in so doing accelerate the process of internal colonization that remained so incomplete. Kubitschek finally made it happen. Planned by Lúcio Costa and furnished with the spectacular public buildings of Oscar Niemeyer, the city captured the imagination at home and abroad. It remains the most well-known architectural signifier of the nation, announcing a distinctive Brazilian modernity: the linearity and geometric simplicity of European Modernism, bent and rolled into the sinuous curves of *Brasilidade*.

However, the city was not alone in this. In the late 1950s and early 1960s, Brazilian football matched Brasília's global impact and paralleled its hybrid aesthetics. Niemeyer's own account of his curvaceous Modernism uses precisely the same formulation that Freyre had used to contrast the angularity of European football with the rounded sweetness of Brazil's. The architecture of the Maracanã had already established the link between urban modernity, economic progress and football, but the 1950 World Cup had left a terrible sense of doubt over the real scale of Brazil's achievements. It had built the most modern stadium in the world, but it had failed at the final and most important hurdle. Now the promise of those years would be realized. In a few short years, Brazil won the World Cup twice and did so with the spellbinding talents of the two most cherished players of the century: Pelé and Garrincha. Any ambivalence that the country might have had about hitching the nation's identity to football after the horror of the *Maracanazo* was abandoned.

Four factors explain the ascent of Brazilian football, its global

97

successes, and now its unambiguous place at the heart of the nation's sense of self. First, Brazil's uneven economic dynamism produced concentrated centres of wealth and organization that could mobilize the production line of talent that continued to emerge from among its poor and very poor. Second, the partial settlement of issues of ethnicity and nationhood achieved under Vargas opened the way for a flood of talent from every corner of Brazilian society whose diversity was now the guarantor of its Brazilian authenticity rather than a betrayal. Global success meant that 'football as eugenics' was finally finished as an argument. To this was added a third ingredient – a thriving urban civil society in which football clubs developed as successful social and sporting institutions, and in which the rich mix of popular cultures in Brazil's cities could cross-fertilize, bringing dance, music, poetry, art and football into close orbit with each other. And the fourth factor was that the prosperity of the era opened up the economic and psychological space for more popular forms of urban play and leisure: Rio's beaches embraced foot volley and beach soccer, with football fans increasingly turning games into their own pyrotechnic spectaculars. These changes also created the space for the emergence of a more critical and reflective response to football than hitherto, particularly in the the Cinema Novo movement.

However, serious play requires serious money and serious organization. In 1958 Brazil acquired the last of these in the tall, imperious shape of João Havelange, president of the CBF and the chair of the technical commission organizing Brazil's campaign at the 1958 World Cup in Sweden.

II

The 1958 World Cup campaign was funded by a significant sub-vention from Kubitschek's federal government and a paying tour of Italy before the tournament. Organization was provided by João Havelange, a Rio businessman and Fluminense insider, a masterly politician and legendary networker, who had just won the presidency of the CBF by 185 votes to 19. Alongside him, representing São Paulo's interests was a man cast in a similar mould: Paulo Machado de Carvalho, patron of São Paulo FC and owner of the city's leading TV and radio stations. The two appointed the corpulent Vicente Feola as coach and relieved him of all responsibilities but coaching as the CBF took on psychologists and cooks, dentists, doctors, fixers and spies. A few veterans from 1954 were called up – like Nilton Santos and Didi – but for the most part the players in the squad had come of age in the boom – Joel, Zito, Pepe and Vavá, and two others who were initially on the fringes: the mercurial Botafogo winger Garrincha and the teenage sensation from Santos, Pelé. The squad underwent extensive medical checks at Rio's leading hospitals, which revealed an extraordinary catalogue of disease and long-term malnutrition. Almost the entire squad had intestinal parasites, some had syphilis, others were anaemic. Over 300 teeth were extracted from the players' mouths. Epidemiologically, Brazil '58 was a team of the people. Planning for Sweden was meticulous, with twenty-five locations scouted before they settled on a base. Even then the Brazilians went as far as to insist that the hotel's management replace female staff with men.

Brazil started slowly and stiffly in the tournament, beating Austria and drawing with England. Garrincha and Pelé now came into the side, a move opposed by the team's psychologist on the grounds of their alleged low IQ and immaturity respectively. How wrong can you be? Brazil started to move in a new way, beating the Soviet Union with some verve and then sweeping aside Wales and France in the quarter- and semi-finals, a trio of games crowned by a hat-trick from Pelé as Brazil put five past the French. In the final they faced hosts Sweden and though Brazil went a goal down early in the game, they gave an untroubled, commanding performance of attacking and inventive football that saw them win 5–2. As *The Times* wrote, 'They showed football as a different conception; they killed the white skidding ball as if it were a lump of cotton wool.'[1] Pelé, who scored the best and final goal in the dying minutes of the match, passed out, was revived and broke down in tears. The King of Sweden actually came down to the pitch to join the celebratory melee. The Swedish crowd, who had cheered Brazil's performance as they played, now cheered their lap of honour. The Seleção reciprocated by carrying a giant Swedish flag between them. The team returned, via London and Lisbon, to Recife where receptions, plaudits, politicians and crowds awaited. In Rio a gigantic crowd had gathered at the airport to meet them. The squad piled on to a municipal fire engine that slowly wound its way from the airport to the vast multi-laned Avenida Brasil, heading for the presidential palace.

The bulk of this side went to Chile four years later when preparations were equally rigorous – high-altitude training was added to the repertoire and the CBF technical commission approved the Chilean government's licensed brothels near the team's hotel. Pelé's injury in an early game against the Czechs gave the spotlight to Garrincha who seemed to soar, scoring twice against England and gifting a third to Vavá as his shot rebounded off the bar and down to his teammate's feet. In the semi-final he was the chief architect of Brazil's 4-2 victory over hosts Chile despite the endless attention of Chilean defender Eladio Rojas. Garrincha snapped in the 85th minute, kicked his tormentor and was sent off. He was only allowed to play in the final after the Brazilian diplomatic machine went into overdrive: at the suggestion of the Brazilians, the Peruvian president got his ambassador to Chile to speak to the Peruvian referee. The referee rescinded his decision. Garrincha played, and though Brazil went 1–0 down to the Czechs in the final they never looked worried. Three goals later they were champions again. Garrincha could be seen repeatedly standing with his foot poised atop the ball, daring the Czechs to take it off him.

It is hard to underestimate the importance of these two footballing triumphs. Of course, there were phenomenal celebrations in the streets, and gigantic crowds gathered in the main cities to see the team parade the cup. Both victories were followed by presidential receptions and speeches; a torrent of memorabilia; photographic specials in the magazines; and the release of celebratory sambas and orchestral marches. But these moments left a deeper legacy. Sérgio Leite Lopes, then ten years old, recalled listening to one of the finals on the radio: 'It was so intense. I don't think I was ever more moved by a few minutes of football in all my life. It was football's turning point.'[2] This was the point when football became the national ritual, the barometer of the nation's health, and the crowning achievement of an unambiguously mulatto Brazil. As Nelson Rodrigues pithily put it, 1958 meant that Brazil could kick its 'mongrel dog complex' for ever. Brazil had won, not once but twice; not just a cup but the World Cup; and they didn't just win, they won in their own style. Brazil was the futebol nation.

The matter of what kind of nation Brazil is, has often turned on the comparative biographies and standing of its two greatest footballing sons, Pelé and Garrincha. Pelé, then Edson Arantes do Nascimento, was born poor in 1940 in the tiny town of Três Corações, deep in the back country of Minas Gerais. His father had played semi-professionally and encouraged his son, who played more than he studied and joined his first organized team when the family moved to the city of Bauru, São Paulo state. He was spotted by the coach of the local team AC Bauru, Waldemar de Brito, who was a veteran of the 1938 World Cup. He took Pelé to Santos, where he scored his first goal at sixteen and embarked on an unbelievable run of over 1,200 games for the club in seventeen years.

Santos were a club on the rise, based in the port city of São Paulo state. The city had prospered and then declined with the rhythms of the coffee industry. Now it was serving as the gateway for São Paulo's industrial might; in the 1950s it began to boom, the team began to win and then in 1955 they claimed their first Paulista Championship for twenty years. More domestic honours followed, then in 1962 they won their first international trophy – the Copa Libertadores, in an epic three-game marathon against Uruguayan club Peñarol. Their reward was a chance to measure themselves against the champions of Europe in the Intercontinental Cup. Santos beat Benfica at home 3–2 and then, with another Pelé hat-trick, beat them 5–2 in Lisbon. The government declared the next day a national holiday. This golden era continued when the following year they saw off Boca Juniors in the final of the Libertadores as well as retaining the national league title.

Pelé's coach at Santos, Lula, made the case for his greatness like this:

> Pelé can no longer be compared to anyone else because he possesses all the qualities of the ideal football player. He is fast on the ground and in the air, he has the kick, the physique, the ball control, the ability to dictate play, a feeling for the manoeuvre, he is unselfish, good natured and modest. I think he is the only forward in the world who always aims the ball at a precise point in the opposition's net at the moment of scoring a goal.[3]

Garrincha was born Manuel Francisco dos Santos into a mestizo Indian-European family in the small industrial town of Pau Grande beyond the edge of the Rio periphery, where the local textile company had been supporting a football team since before the First World War. As a baby it was clear that his left leg curved outwards and his right curved inwards, a condition that, while it never altered, seemed to make no difference to his movement, indeed it may have made his dribbling even more elusive. As a diminutive teenager Garrincha – 'the Wren', a nickname given him by his sister – played for the factory team, did light chores in the factory, drank, danced and larked about. He was unconcerned about his talent, and it required his friends to drag him to professional trials in Rio. At Botafogo he was put up against the commanding left back Nilton Santos and destroyed him. He was signed immediately and spent the majority of his career and all his best years with the club of the new bohemian middle classes of the Zona Sul. He was carefree, socially unambitious, ignorant and sheltered to the point of otherworldliness when in the company of his social superiors. His approach to playing football was equally unformed and unstructured. Primarily a winger of some brilliance, he would drift and fade only to reappear and score goals from everywhere. He never knew who he was marking and was allowed to abandon team talks for the ping-pong table. Yet it was for Garrincha that the *olé* chant of the toreador was transferred to football. If he had a trademark it was this – to find any way, sublime, crafty, cunning or brazen, to get the ball round an opponent. Sometimes, he would enjoy it so much that he would go back and do it all again a second time.

Pelé lived a model professional life; Garrincha ate and drank like the most dissolute factory worker. While Pelé, even through his teenage shyness, was a talker, there is barely an interview of any substance with Garrincha. Pelé, ambitious, knew the value of his talent and though he lost money on a number of occasions to unscrupulous business partners, he always managed to extract something of value. Garrincha had a pathological lack of ambition, neither knowing nor caring how much money he had made or where it might be going. In the unspoken but obvious racial hierarchies of Brazil, Pelé, a black man with a white partner, had married up. Garrincha married down. Pelé planned for the future. Garrincha lived for the moment. Pelé trained. Garrincha slept. Both players would acquire another nickname – an essential suffix. Pelé was *O Rei* – 'the King', honoured but ultimately distant, of another world. Garrincha was *A Alegria do Povo* – 'the Joy of the People', of this imperfect world, disabled, drunk and fragile, and in the end broken. The King was and continued to be revered but Garrincha was loved. Over the next two decades their careers and fortunes would wildly diverge, but for these few short years, the futebol nation, on the pitch and in the collective imagination, could accommodate both stories and both talents.

III

While the success of the Seleção and the brilliance of Pelé and Garrincha provided the core narrative of Brazilian football history in the 1950s and early 1960s, their triumphs rested on a thriving domestic club culture. From the early 1950s through to the early 1970s, Brazilian football clubs constituted one of the most active elements of urban civil society, drawing social classes together and providing somewhere that popular and high cultures could mix. Football was a place where poetry, dance and music continued to take and offer inspiration. In an otherwise highly unequal and immobile society, it offered routes to fame, material comfort and occasionally fortunes for a new generation of activist fans and professional players.

At the apex remained the directors of the clubs. Nearly all were self-made businessmen, though there were routes to the top via politics and public office. The posts were unpaid and one incumbent went so far as to argue that it was a form of 'public service – just like waving the flag'.[4] There were, however, hidden benefits to the position. Most importantly it put one inside the interlacing network of urban elites, connecting business people, leading figures in the media, civil servants, politicians and developers; a sine qua non of operating successfully in Brazil's highly personalized and clientelistic economic and political life. Janet Lever reported one Flamengo director describing how 'he was eventually elected a vice-president even though he had no wealth. During his term in office he made so many friends and contacts that his small business boomed and he made a fortune.'[5] The post also opened the door to a whole raft of sinecures in the state and national football authorities and provided an opportunity to bestow patronage and largesse, from which influence and votes could then be reaped: two state governors of Minas Gerais, Juscelino Kubitschek and Antônio Magalhães, were instrumental in getting the Estádio Mineirão in Belo Horizonte built. In return directors were expected to cover clubs' debts, pay for at least some of the votes that got them elected and, for the richest and most ambitious, a club presidency could be won on the promise of paying for the arrival of the latest star: coffee magnate Amadeu Rodrigues Sequeira won the top seat at Vasco da Gama by promising and then delivering Tostão to the club.

Football, however, was just one element of club life in the 1950s and 1960s. In fact, one could argue that the social and recreational life that centred on the clubs was at its strongest in this era – clubs really were clubs, providing not just facilities and parties but a tangible sense of community and identity. In the 1930s Flamengo had become in effect a mass-membership club, with fees that were within reach of the city's lower middle classes if not its workers or the poor. By the 1950s all the biggest clubs in Rio and São Paulo counted their members in the tens of thousands. In addition to using their now expanded sporting and social facilities – including ballrooms, dining rooms, swimming pools, tennis courts and gyms – the clubs offered 'dinners, dances, theatre, movies, fashion shows and picnics to their members. Women and girls [were] very active in the clubs' yoga lessons, bridge tournaments and other recreational and social events.'[6] Smaller clubs fared less well. Teams like São Cristóvão and Bonsucesso in Rio's Zona Norte had just a fraction of the grand clubs' wealth and members, and the gap widened in the 1960s. New migrants to the cities invariably chose the big sides over an affiliation to their new neighbourhoods. Bangu's victory in the 1966 Carioca Championship was the last time a team from outside the big four (Flamengo, Fluminense, Vasco and Botafogo) would win the title.

The position of players at the clubs had barely changed since the formalization of professionalism in the late 1930s. Players' pay in the early 1950s, while better than that available to most urban workers, didn't match that of professionals in other fields. Players were tied to the clubs that they originally signed for. If the club didn't want you to play elsewhere, then you couldn't play anywhere. In the absence of an exit option, player power inside the clubs was strictly limited. While many did struggle against the authority of directors and coaches, there remained a pervasive culture of deference, made all the more effective by the absence of a players' union, indeed of any kind of formal organization to represent them. Advisers, agents and managers of the era seemed to be better at looking after their own interests than their players'. By the late 1950s and early 1960s, as the economy boomed and the clubs became better at capitalizing on sponsorship and advertising opportunities, some footballers' wages did begin to rise. Outside Rio and São Paulo they remained pitiful, but at the big clubs in the big cities the leading players were now comfortable and the stars well heeled. That said, insurance, health care and a pension were not part of a player's contract. A long and often penurious post-game career awaited many of them.

Finally there were the fans, whose tickets not only paid for the football, but often subsidized the social side of the club too. Despite the presence of the *torcidas organizadas*, numbering around 3–4,000 at most games, the rest of the crowd was more fickle. Few held season tickets and attendances were notoriously

variable. In Rio and São Paulo, games against small teams from
the suburbs might attract less than half the turnout for a game
against a big city rival. On the other hand, for derbies and finals,
demand was huge. The 1963 Fla–Flu, the decisive game of the
championship, drew almost 200,000 people to the Maracanã. Flamengo played five similar games in the late 1950s and early 1960s
with attendances of 150,000 or more. Whatever the precise numbers, it is clear that Brazilian fans had created a popular spectacle
second to none in world football. Jacques de Ryswick, visiting in
1954, saw Brazil's last qualification game for the World Cup in
Switzerland later that year.

> As soon as the Brazilian team had won its ticket to Switzerland, a
> single, formidable cry rang out from the masses '*Vamos Suiça,
> Vamos Suiça*'. Thousands of shirts were torn off, set alight and
> waved about like triumphal torches. For me the game here had
> always been an accessory to the spectacle . . . I had the impression
> that it was no more than a pretext, an excuse for the extraordinary
> striving of the people: a sort of safety valve invented to allow the
> superabundant life of the people, their exuberance and need to
> escape.[7]

The emergence of organized groups of *torcidas*, the creation
of bands or *charangas* and the use of fireworks and smoke bombs
all dated back to the late 1940s. In the 1950s and 1960s these
groups would grow and dominate the atmosphere in the stadium.
The *Jornal dos Sports*, which had supported the phenomenon in the
1930s and 1940s, sought to encourage it now, as it had with carnival, by making it competitive: the paper started awarding points
on the basis of the power and beauty of the displays, their

originality and the quality of their costumes. The spectacle was impressive. *Torcidas* came early and claimed a key spot in the stands. They brought an increasingly large range of home-made flags, banners and icons. *Charangas* and itinerant musicians helped direct the singing, chanting and whistling. The arrival of the players on the pitch was accompanied by fusillades of flares, firecrackers, fireworks and smoke bombs. From the upper levels a great storm of streamers and newspaper confetti rained down. A newspaper could be rolled into a tight cone and lit as a statement of victory or a curse on defeat.

Jaime de Carvalho remained the most public face of organized fandom, financed by sponsorship and government, to be in the stands for Brazil's games at the 1954 Copa América, for which his wife sewed the then largest known Brazilian flag – ten metres by eight. He also attended the 1954, 1962 and 1970 World Cups. By the mid-1950s equivalent groups of *torcidas* and *charangas* had emerged at the other clubs in Rio and beyond. In 1967, to honour the silver jubilee of the formation of the Flamengo *charanga*, all the leading figures in Rio's other *torcidas* gathered to present him with an American electric megaphone. Flamengo eventually made him a shareholding member of the club, a level of upward social mobility that he was unlikely to have experienced in any other sphere. At Vasco TOV (*Torcida Organizada do Vasco*) were led, unusually, by a woman, Dulce Rosalina – who won the *Jornal dos Sports* Best Fan in the City award; at Fluminense it was Paulista; and at Botafogo the key figure was Tarzan.

Born Otacílio Batista do Nascimento in Minas Gerais in 1927, Tarzan acquired his nickname and a reputation as a troublemaker before he walked the 300 miles to Rio in his twenties. As with a lot of migrants of that era, football was his way into Carioca society.

He first went to see the team in 1953, and by 1957 he was bringing home-made flags and fireworks to the ground. By the early 1960s he was running a wig shop in the centre of Rio as well as the *torcida organizada* at Botafogo. Tarzan was a gift to the press, ready to offer his opinion at some length, to stand as a tribune of the fans and to rail against players and directors who, he thought, were not serving the best interests of the club. It might not have looked like the public sphere as imagined in European political theory, but in a society where self-organization was rare, and the confidence necessary to speak truth to power was rarer still, it looked like democratic progress.

IV

In the big cities of Brazil, beyond the stands themselves, football had become a multi-media experience.

> An ordinary football match in the Rio Championships . . . is listened to in the streets, cafés and public squares by hundreds of thousands of people . . . The principal newspaper column is a football column . . . The biggest circulation of all papers in Brazil is a sports daily, the *Gazeta Esportiva de São Paulo*.[8]

Writing in 1963, the author could have added television to the list. Pioneering TV stations in São Paulo began to film football matches and then broadcast them as early as the mid-1950s. However, very few households had a set and the medium would become widespread only in the late 1960s. In any case, some were positively against television. Nelson Rodrigues, appalled by its capacity to take the mystery and uncertainty out of the game, exclaimed: 'If the videotape shows it's a penalty then all the worse for the video-tape. The videotape is stupid.'[9]

Television's time would come, but until the 1970s radio remained the most popular way in which football was consumed. In fact, as almost the entire nation came within reach of a radio with the advent of the new transistor radio, the audience for football grew. Listening to the football on a portable radio was so ubiquitous that it appears as a well-worn gag in Amácio Mazza-ropi's 1966 comedy *O Corintiano*. Sitting in full evening dress in a fancy theatre, Mazzaropi's character has a small radio in his lap to listen to the Corinthians game. He sees a police officer stalking the aisles and guiltily hides it beneath his jacket. The officer leans over conspiratorially and asks, 'So what is the score?' Films of crowds from the era show many fans with small earphones or a set jammed against the side of their head.

The new stars of the medium brought wit and warmth to the game. Fiori Gigliotti, who was the key commentator for the 1962 World Cup final, announced kick-off with, 'The curtains are open, it's the start of the show,' and mordantly noted of a team chasing a game, 'Time goes by . . .' The final minutes of the drama were the 'twilight hour'; conceding a goal evoked stern sympathy, 'Now there's no use crying'; while a winner was met with '*Uma beleeeeza de gol!*' ('A beeeeautiful goal!') and '*Um beijo no seu coração*' ('A kiss in your heart'). Pedro Luiz approached new records of exasperation and words per minute in the maniacal school of commentary while Waldir Amaral, who meandered through the game well into the 1970s, had a gift for catchphrases and nick-names: when a team looked like scoring, the goal was smoking; when they had scored, there was a fish in the net.

Literacy rates began to rise in the 1940s and 1950s, creating a real mass market for the printed press in general and sports publications in particular. The tradition of football writing established in the 1940s by Mário Filho and his collaborators was consolidated. It was a genre which crossed the boundaries of the public and the private, popular and high culture, journalism and literature, and for three decades it would flourish. Filho had something of the air of the twinkle-eyed uncle spinning you a yarn, offering a homely and uncontroversial Freyrian reading of Brazilian football as a bountiful multi-ethnic melting pot. Nelson Rodrigues, his brother, was cut from very different cloth. Playwright, critic and polemicist, his prose was by turns witty, barbed and scandalous. Alongside football his work explored Rio in search of perversion, infidelity and hysteria; fuelled by a cocktail of caffeine, nicotine and alcohol, he cut a frenetic arc across the cityscape. His partiality was more extreme than Ary Barroso's: 'I'm Fluminense. I always was Fluminense. I'd say I was Fluminense in a past life.' His penchant for the mysterious and the conspiratorial led him to personify the role of chance in football in the character of *Sobrenatural de Almeida* – the ghost of a medieval madman living in a northern suburb of Rio whose life was devoted to the creation of flukes and upsets.

Filho and Rodrigues, though continuing to write into the 1960s and 1970s respectively, gave way to a new generation of Freyrian commentators like Armando Nogueira and João Saldanha. And as the São Paulo Modernists of the 1920s and the north-eastern writers of the 1940s aged and died, their place was taken by a new generation of poets and artists engaged with football. Carlos Drummond de Andrade wrote a series of *crônicas* for *Folha de São Paulo* for every World Cup between 1958 and 1986. Informed and playful, he slyly suggested that the 1962 World Cup-winning squad would make a better and more unified ministerial team than President Goulart's turbulent executive. In dry sparse lines of poetry he compared football's place in Brazilian culture to that of an informal ludic cult, a zone of playful fantasy and joy:

> Football is played in the stadium?
> Football is played on the beach,
> Football is played on the street.
> Football is played in the soul.
> The ball is the same: a religious order
> for superstars and stilt-walkers.
> The same pleasure of playing
> An imagined World Cup,
> A game on a dusty hill.

João Cabral de Melo Neto, the diplomat-poet from Recife, had played for his local club Santa Cruz as a teenager and fiercely supported another Recife side, América. In a letter to his cousin he wrote of one victory, 'What more could one ask of life?'[10] His works include poems about fans of América, the defensive midfielder Ademir da Guia, and a dialogue between a Brazilian player and a Spanish coach that reworked the old Freyrian notions of Brazilian and European football. His description of Ademir's capacity for wearing down players is almost sultry: 'He sends him where he wants, rotting him. The rhythm of walking on warm sand ... numbing and tying down the most relentless opponent.' Even Clarice Lispector, the brilliant but enigmatic Ukrainian-Brazilian author, was lured into writing football *crônicas*. One of her short stories featured someone having a nervous breakdown in the concourses of the Maracanã, which perhaps explains why she, unlike earlier generations of writers, watched the games almost entirely from the comfort of her armchair.

To the small canon of football painting produced in the Vargas era, the 1950s and 1960s added considerably more and in a variety of styles: Ivan Serpa's cool, geometrically composed players; the gaunt football figurines of Aldemir Martins and their comic, elastic counterparts in the work of Roberto Magalhães; Claudio Tozzi's pop-art football shirts; and Rubens Gerchman's large playful canvases of crowded football stands. For the most part these were celebratory works, but in the football paintings of José Aguilar we can also see the emergence of a more critical position. His canvas of the Seleção, painted just after the military coup of 1964, had all their faces obscured by white paint, a haunting and hollow depiction of the futebol nation.

The link that had been established between music and football, metaphorically and literally, in the 1930s and 1940s was even stronger in the following two decades. The 1958 and 1962 World Cups alone saw over thirty-five football-related tunes released on to the market. The range of performers, composers and genres drew on the rich brew of contemporary Brazilian music and expressed a confidence that had hitherto been very rare in Brazilian culture. The breezily patriotic and massively popular march 'A Taça do Mundo é Nossa' ('The World Cup is Ours') exemplified this: 'That Brazilian abroad/Showed how football really is/ He won the World Cup / Sambando with the ball at his feet/ Goool!' Straight-ahead sambas like the song 'Aquarela da Vitória' ('A Victory in Watercolours') were plentiful. Old stars like Jackson do Pandeiro sang 'O Rei Pelé'. A new star, Jair Rodrigues, sang 'Brasil Sensacional'. Comic actor Ronald Golias cut a disc, while the back-country rhythms of *catarete* got a football workout from São Paulo guitar duo Tonico e Tinoco with 'The Big Brazilian Squad'.

Radio, music and literature all played their parts in creating Brazil's distinctive football culture of the 1950s and 1960s, celebrating and explaining its new brilliance and global victories. However, the most interesting art form of the era, and certainly the medium that offered the sharpest insights into football's problems, was film. For the mass audience there were more of the kinds of football films produced in the 1930s: the 1953 melodrama *O Craque* set at Corinthians in São Paulo was followed by *O Preço da Vitória*, Oswaldo Sampaio's bizarre adventure movie, half faux documentary, half fiction, that told the story of the 1958 World Cup. In the mid-1960s the strong demand for slapstick saw two football comedies released, *The Man Who Stole the World Cup* in 1963 and the aforementioned *O Corintiano* in 1966. The former was a shambling detective caper, the latter a more chaotic but illuminating family comedy from Amácio Mazzaropi, the undisputed star of Brazilian cinematic clowning. Mazzaropi plays a Corinthians-obsessed barber who fights with his Palmeiras-supporting neighbours, buys up every copy of the paper at the local stall on the days Corinthians lose, and ejects customers from his shop when they complain about the volume of football talk. In a fabulous reversal of the moral universe depicted in the football movies of the Vargas years, he deplores the thought that his son wants to become a doctor and his daughter a ballet dancer, suggesting that he should play for Corinthians and that she should marry the side's star – Rivelino. Not intentionally comic, but so sentimental and contrived that it was laughable, was the 1963 homily cum hagiography *O Rei Pelé*, which told the story of his life through a series of fictionalized flashbacks and edited footage from his playing career. It was based on a book by writer Ruy Barbosa, who went on to be one of the pioneering writers of Brazil's *telenovelas*. The football player, certainly a black one, was no longer a eugenic missionary, but he could be drenched in sentimentality, be cast as the humble hero, a model of hard work, personal discipline and deference.

Testament to the new creative energies of the time, this mixture of pantomime comedy and uncritical melodrama was challenged by the emergence of Cinema Novo, the collective product of a group of producers and directors working from the mid-1950s to the mid-1960s. It drew on Italian neorealism's use of street scenes and amateur actors, borrowed the documentary techniques of American *cinéma-vérité*, and infused both styles with a political and aesthetic agenda that would take the camera to Brazil's poorest and most troubled places. Among the earliest and most important Cinema Novo films, predating the term itself, was *Rio 40 Graus* ('Rio 40 Degrees') of 1955, directed by Nelson Pereira dos Santos. The film is made up of a series of interconnecting short stories of life in the favela of São Sebastião in Rio de Janeiro. These tales are linked by the journeys of five kids selling peanuts on the city's streets and at its famous landmarks – Sugar Loaf Mountain and a Sunday game at the Maracanã. It was shot entirely on location and with many of the cast drawn from local amateurs. This was groundbreaking – the first Brazilian film located among the poor where football was an everyday part of life – and disturbing enough to conservative Brazil for Rio's chief of police to seek to ban the film, on the fabulously pernickety grounds that Rio was never hotter than 39.6 degrees. Football also features in one of the stories in which an ageing star worries about his place in the team and an impending transfer to São Paulo; players are depicted, for the first time in a Brazilian film, as commodities to be bought and sold at another's whim. A decade later in *A Falecida* ('The Deceased'), a film based on a Nelson Rodrigues play, football was entwined with matrimonial strife in a poor neighbourhood in Rio's Zona Norte. The film tells the story of the unhappily married Zulmira and Toni. Zulmira, having a premonition of her own death, begins to plan an extravagant funeral. Toni shoots pool, drinks and worries about Vasco versus Fluminense. When Zulmira's premonition comes to pass and a bout of pneumonia takes her to her deathbed she sends Toni to see an old friend, Pimentel, who will pay the funeral expenses. Pimentel, it turns out, is an ex-player and an ex-lover of Zulmira. Toni threatens to blackmail the old boy, and leaves with the money. He spends a fraction of it on the cheapest funeral he can manage. The final scenes of the film show Toni watching Vasco at the Maracanã, crying and ranting to the crowd as he lets the money go. Football, supposedly an escape valve and a solace, does not actually offer joy or happiness, but just enough abandon to feel grief.

Cinema Novo went on to produce two important football documentaries in the early 1960s: *Subterrâneos do Futebol* and *Garrincha: Alegria do Povo*. *Subterrâneos do Futebol* ('Underground Football') was one part of a quartet of documentaries titled *Brasil Verdade* trying to get under the surface of the country that were produced by the great photographer Thomas Farkas. Directed by Maurice Capovilla, the film weaves together the lives and thoughts of three players at different phases of their careers at Santos. The film begins with Pelé, the established star, but its heart is with Luís Carlos Freitas, a young man just starting his career in professional football, and Zózimo, who is nearing the end of his. In scenes of training sessions, medicals and interviews, the film depicts the narrow confines of the player's life, regimented and controlled by club directors, coaches and doctors, all of whom are white, while all three players are black. Zózimo, a member of two World Cup-winning squads, has fallen from grace. He is bitter, players are just slaves and his wife complains of the long tours that take him away from home. The film ends with scenes of violence on the pitch during the São Paulo Championship, and the drunken, chaotic behaviour in the stands. Military police and helmeted soldiers rush the crowd, blood drips from a player's head wounds.

The central thread of *Garrincha: Alegria do Povo* ('Joy of the People'), directed by Joaquim Pedro de Andrade, is a portrait of the player, his life on and off the field, and his place in Brazil's new mythic football history. A fragmented, non-linear montage, the film includes footage of the *Maracanazo*, Garrincha's brilliant performances at the 1958 and 1962 World Cups, and visually roots those stories in the football-playing cultures of the poor. Garrincha plays a game of five-a-side in the dirt, shirtless and shoeless, in his home town of Pau Grande before enjoying drinks and cigarettes and gossip. Kids play football on Copacabana beach, when it was still open enough for the poor to play, and in the streets when Rio's traffic was light compared to today's gridlock. Like *Subterrâneos do Futebol*, the film gives a clear sense of the fragility of players' bodies and the authoritarian, controlled environment in which they live and work – the camera often lingers on Garrincha's pet bird in its cage. But its finest moments are its depictions of Garrincha as a player and the game as a popular spectacular. Against sparse percussive samba, Andrade rapidly cuts between dramatic pictures of Garrincha in action, his fabulous low centre of gravity allowing him to bend and twist down and around his opponents. Slow-motion pictures, filmed from the touchline, reveal Garrincha's delicacy of touch as he guides and slides the ball past a defender, cleverly uncluttered frames show him stopping the ball dead, sending his opponents sprawling then spinning round to scoop the ball back up. Simultaneously, the camera roves around the stands of the Maracanã with the eye of the portraitist, brilliantly framing dozens of faces, revealing the real demographics of Brazilian football: black, mulatto and white, so many with missing teeth and scrawny frames, so many looks of expectation, anticipation, anxiety and hope. These elements of the film combine most powerfully in the sequences that intercut Garrincha's goals and the riotous celebrations of the crowd. The firecrackers and the yells of pleasure explode over Bach's 'Crown Him King of Kings', a filmic climax equivalent to Vinicius de Moraes's poetic evocation of the divine joy of these moments.

> One dribble, two dribbles ; the ball like a braid
> It's happy between your legs – you are one wind!
> A single moment, the crowd poised
> In the act of death, stands up and yells
> united, their song of hope.
> Garrincha , the angel, listens and answers: Goooool![11]

The Brazil of the late Vargas and the Kubitschek regimes that had proved so culturally fertile, which had both nurtured and embraced the nation's greatest footballing triumphs, was coming to a close sooner than many had imagined. In 1960 the unpredictable but electric Jânio Quadros, governor of São Paulo, was elected president on a right-wing anti-corruption, anti-inflation platform. After just seven months his nerve appeared to fail or a wild bluff was called as he suddenly offered his resignation to the Brazilian Congress, which accepted it. His replacement was the vice-president João Goulart, previously the ultra-populist minister of labour in the last Vargas cabinet. His three years in power grew increasingly turbulent. The massive spending programmes of the Kubitschek years and the tendency to print money saw inflation climbing from less than 10 per cent a year to over 100 per cent in 1964, a collapse in the value of the currency and a real foreign-exchange crisis. As the economy spiralled out of control, political opinion polarized. The left in Brazil, though fragmented and querulous, pressured the government from one side, calling for radical measures of redistribution and public control of the economy. On the right, the military in particular looked askance at the economic chaos and social ferment that Brazil's democracy had helped produce.

Brazil's football clubs, like every other institution, were desperate for foreign currency that would hold its value. Unlike most of its exports, football was massively in demand, burnished by the two World Cup victories. Brazilian football went on a global tour. Santos and Pelé were the biggest attractions, playing on every continent, but Fluminense went to Scandinavia and the Soviet Union, Vasco da Gama played in West Africa, and Botafogo toured in France and Morocco. A tiny team from Rio's lower divisions, Madureira, could make a living on a three-month tour of Central America and the Caribbean. They even played in Cuba, just a year after the Missile Crisis, and were pictured in the Brazilian press with a smiling Che Guevara – a photograph that must have raised a few eyebrows in the officers' common rooms of the Brazilian military, where a paranoid anti-communism, provoked by the successes of the Cuban revolution, was already at fever pitch.

In late 1963 and early 1964 Goulart, who had tried hitherto to hold a centrist position, opted for the left and announced a series of nationalizations and land reforms backed by major public demonstrations in the big cities. The right rallied with their own counter-marches. Then in spring 1964, with the tacit agreement of the US government, the military stepped in. Key government offices in Rio and Brasília were occupied, and major figures on the left were rounded up and imprisoned. The vice-president called for the people to fill the streets, but they remained deserted, while Goulart fled to Uruguay. In February and March Santos and Pelé had left Brazil, still a democratic state and with a vibrant and inventive culture, for a short tour of Argentina, Uruguay, Peru and Chile. They returned to a Brazil in which the generals were settling down to almost two decades of power. Then, as if nothing had changed, Santos went out and won the São Paulo State Championship again. There would be blood and fire to come, but for the moment the military had taken power with a minimum of resistance, bloodshed or drama. It would only become apparent in retrospect that Brazilian football and society would be profoundly deformed by their presence.

5

Playing the Hard Line: Football under the Dictatorship, 1964–1986

'I'm struggling for freedom, for respect for human beings, for equality, for ample and unrestricted discussions, for a professional democratization of unforeseen limits, and all of this as a soccer player, preserving the ludic, and the joyous and the pleasurable nature of this activity' – Sócrates.

Brazil's victory with the ball compares with the conquest of
the moon by the Americans.

Jornal do Brasil, 22 June 1970

In Brazil the way you win does not matter. A very violent
form of football is being practised.

Telê Santana, 1985

I

Jornal do Brasil, a sober publication not given to joking, was perfectly serious when it compared Brazil's 4–1 victory over Italy in
the final of the 1970 World Cup to the Americans' Apollo space
programme. As far as the paper was concerned, it was a comparison between pinnacles of national development. The Americans
had applied huge amounts of money, the immense power of their
scientific and industrial strength, diamond-hard instrumental
rationality and an ingenious capacity for problem-solving to the
task of putting a man on the Moon: the manifest destiny of the
nineteenth century remade for the space age. Brazil possessed

none of these resources but it had drawn on the complex ecology of its popular cultures and the short-lived democratic civil society of the 1950 and 1960s to produce a generation of exceptional footballers. They emerged from an economy poor enough to guarantee a steady flow of aspirational and gifted talent, schooled in street football, but rich enough to mobilize and organize that talent at the highest level.

More than that, Brazil had won the World Cup for the third time and done so in a manner that was considered, inside and outside the country, to be more than just an act of instrumental reason, more in fact than just winning. It had been an artistic performance; a celebration of the nation's music and dance and its aesthetic standards of rhythm, beauty and poise. Yet by 1985 Telê Santana, coach of the national team and passionate advocate of the old school of attacking football, looked at the Brazilian game and despaired of its crude instrumentalism and the violence of its play. What had happened? It had been the fabulous good luck of Brazil's generals that Mexico 1970 should happen on their watch. They took the opportunity and hitched their political project to the game. It was football's bad luck that their rule should endure for so long and that in attempting to shape the game in their own image, the main legacy of the dictatorship was to harden and coarsen it.

The Junta that came to power in 1964 was divided between advocates of the soft line and those of the hard line. The former argued that Brazil's woes could be traced to the instability of democracy, the ill-discipline of populist political parties, and the demagogues and demons of the left. A short military intervention would purge the polity of these destabilizing forces and instil some much-needed discipline and direction into economic policy-making, after which the military could withdraw from power. Advocates of the hard line were far more pessimistic and paranoid, arguing that a much more thorough transformation of Brazil's economy and society was needed, one that required a long occupation of the seats of power, the use of force against opponents and the censorship of the media.

In 1964 the soft line held and General Castelo Branco was appointed president by his military peers. Congress was purged of leftists and other opponents; the senior civil service received the same treatment. Political parties were permitted to stand at state-level elections in 1965, but the government's political supporters did so badly that the regime decided to dissolve all existing political parties and replace them with their own party, ARENA, and an ersatz opposition, the PMDB. While the military dealt with the polity, economics was handed over to a group of supportive technocrats and economists who began a price-stabilization programme that brought inflation under control. Football's only place on the government's agenda was as a source of unpaid taxes. In 1965 the newly empowered internal revenue service pursued stars like Didi, Mário Zagallo and Nilton Santos for their unpaid dues. Garrincha's finances were in such a state of chaos, and his tax bill so large, that João Havelange, president of the CBF, fearful that the player would be imprisoned and unable to go to the 1966 World Cup, stepped in and paid up.

Castelo Branco never revealed any personal interest in football, and in the early days of the Junta the CBF had felt it necessary to cancel a friendly at the Maracanã against the Soviet Union lest it should be seen as fraternizing with the enemy. However, once in power, the new regime realized football was impossible to ignore. Indeed, it might have its uses. Thus the following year Brazil did host the Soviet Union at the Maracanã. It certainly didn't do the Junta's anti-communist credentials any harm to see the Seleção outplay the visitors, albeit in a 2–2 draw, and all this in front of Bobby Kennedy, who was visiting the country at the time. The following year, the poor showing of the Brazilian national team at the 1966 World Cup, knocked out at the group stages, saw a congressional commission of inquiry established to probe the reasons for this debacle. By 1969, when Castelo Branco's successor as president, General Costa e Silva, was dying of a stroke the highest circles in government were pondering whether they should announce his illness to the crowd at the Maracanã prior to Brazil's last qualifying game for the 1970 World Cup, afraid as to how the news would affect both the political mood of the crowd and the performance of the team.

From 1968 until the mid-1970s the balance between doves and hawks in the military shifted towards the latter. An outbreak of protests that included workers' wild-cat strikes, student demonstrations in Rio, coded cultural critiques from film-makers and musicians, and a small campaign of armed resistance from tiny leftist guerrilla groups combined to provoke a massive backlash from the military. Censorship of the press, radio and television was intensified. The repressive machinery of government, both legal and institutional, was ramped up, with the national security services and police force arresting, harassing and torturing thousands of opponents. Congress was effectively closed down. The legitimacy of the regime came to rest on two pillars – supercharged economic growth and a grandiose nationalism that increasingly relied on football for its successes and its imagery.

In late 1969 General Emílio Médici became the military's third president. By inclination, and with the active support of the regime's propaganda departments, he closely aligned himself with football. Within days of assuming office he started making public appearances at Flamengo games, his presence announced over the stadium PA. He also took an active interest in the composition of the squad for the 1970 World Cup and its management. After Brazil's victory in the tournament he received the team at the presidential palace in Brasília and spoke to the nation:

I feel profound happiness at seeing the joy of the people in this highest form of patriotism. I identify this victory won in the brotherhood of good sportsmanship with the rise of faith in our fight for national development. I identify the success of our national team with intelligence bravery, perseverance and serenity in our technical ability, in physical preparation and moral being. Above all, our players won because they know how to . . . play for the collective good.[1]

Under Médici the military would use football as an exemplar of the unified and morally upstanding Brazil it convinced itself it was trying to create. The reality was often less edifying. Their own use of football was, at times, really no better than bread and circuses. In 1973 when a below-inflation rise in the minimum wage was to be announced, the Rio office of the Ministry of Labour made 15,000 free tickets available for a Flamengo–Fluminense match in Rio.

Médici's successor, General Ernesto Geisel, who was known to be a bookish and introverted man, never gave a domestic press conference during the six years of his presidency. Yet such was the significance of football to the regime's public face that his appointment was announced in the press like this: 'Gaucho from

Bento Gonçalves, 64 years old, fan of Internacional in Porto Alegre and Botafogo in Rio, brother of two generals, married, with one daughter, Ernesto Geisel will be the 23rd President of the Republic.'[2] It isn't clear if he had ever been to a game before becoming president, but once installed he was a regular presence at new stadium openings and official receptions for the national team. At one such event, held on the eve of the 1978 World Cup, Geisel was heard to admonish the striker Reinaldo, who had been quoted in the press criticizing the rule of the army and the role of the regime in running the team. 'You play football, don't talk about politics, we'll deal with the politics.'

João Figueiredo, the last of Brazil's generalissimos, held the presidency from 1979 to 1985. He was known to prefer jogging to football and horses to people, but it was widely touted that he was a supporter of Fluminense and Grêmio. Indeed, unlike any of his predecessors he was photographed in a football shirt while president – the blue, black and white stripes of Grêmio from the state of Rio Grande do Sul where he did his military training. His tenure as president was dominated by two issues: the return of hyperinflation in a rapidly declining Brazilian economy and the process of *abertura* – 'opening' – in which the military were steadily relinquishing power and engineering a transition to civilian rule that they could survive intact. In this context, the Junta's strategy of using football as a public spectacular that expressed both their grandiose model of economic development and the regimented unity of the nation they hoped to fashion, had reached the end of the line. When João Havelange, now president of FIFA, tried to persuade President Figueiredo that Brazil should host the 1986 World Cup, he replied, 'Havelange, you know the favelas in Rio? You know the dry north-east . . . You really think I am going to spend money on football stadiums?'[3] Partly it was a question of money, but it was also a question of politics. For football had ceased by now to be the passive instrument of the government and the authorities. In the late 1970s and early 1980s the game had undergone a widespread process of politicization, and become one among many sites of active resistance to the dictatorship. Players were challenging the authority of coaches and directors, stadiums were hosting union rallies, and women, long excluded from the ultra-masculine worlds of Brazilian football and public life, were staking a claim on both.

The disastrous state of Brazil's economy in the early 1980s ensured that the military would stay true to their promise and finally depart. Congress, long emasculated, finally found enough nerve to elect Brazil's first civilian president for over twenty years. Tancredo Neves, previously governor of Minas Gerais, was the ultimate centrist, a long-time survivor and pragmatic builder of alliances. He was a known supporter of Atlético Mineiro but made it clear that he also held the other teams of the city of Belo Horizonte in his affections. Neves died, suddenly and painfully, just days before his inauguration, leaving the transition to democracy in the hands of his running-mate José Sarney, an old-school politician of the north-east, who was used to giving orders and dispensing patronage. Managing a complex economic reboot of the Brazilian economy was another matter. In his first year in office Sarney was beset by the unstoppable forces of hyper-inflation that he and his technocrats couldn't bring to heel. In the spring of 1986 Sarney insisted that the Seleção must improve and win the World Cup that year. But Brazilian football had changed. The team that went to the 1986 World Cup was never going to win it and no politician could ordain it.

II

To be fair to the dictatorship there were signs of change and frag-
mentation in Brazilian football before they began their long
occupation of power, but their presence only seemed to magnify
them. The individual players and great clubs of the era were
reaching the inevitable downward turn of their cycle of age and
form; the arrival of television began its transformation of the
game; youth groups challenged the authority of the first generation of *torcidas*; and the propensity of the game for violence and
aggression was on the rise.

The Seleção that went to the 1966 World Cup in England
retained many of the team that had won the previous two World
Cups. Pelé and Garrincha were not on the margins this time but
seasoned champions at their peak. Brazil won their opening game
against Bulgaria but were then soundly beaten by Hungary and
Portugal in rough physical matches, where they were fouled and
harried out of the game. It was Garrincha's last World Cup. He
returned from England already sold on from Botafogo to Corinthians. Both club and player were past their best. Garrincha's
knees, subject to unbelievable levels of torsion, had been held
together with splints and painkillers. When he did have surgery it
was too late. His knees and his game were never the same again.
Worse, after a car crash which he survived but which killed his
mother-in-law, he descended into a deep depression, exacerbated
by his heavy drinking. What little inclination he had for training
and timekeeping collapsed, and he disappeared without a trace for
over a decade.

Brazilian football was used to explosive tempers, fisticuffs and stand-offs, but in the mid-1960s their frequency increased and their mania intensified. In the decisive game of the 1964 Rio–São Paulo tournament Botafogo played Santos. A fight started that quickly spread among all the players on the field. Even the normally unflappable Pelé was involved and sent off with two others. In 1965 Santos's Zezinho punched Vasco's Lima, who hit him back and initiated a fight that saw seven players dismissed. In 1966, in the last match of the Rio Championships, Bangu beat Flamengo 3–0, but not before five of the Flamengo team and four of the Bangu team had been sent off. Finally, in 1967, a game between América and Olaria was abandoned when all twenty-two players were dismissed after eighty minutes; a feat almost matched the same season by Vasco and Fluminense who managed to lose twenty-one. At the same time as the Brazilian security services were conducting huge dragnet operations, pulling in thousands of suspects in their violent attempts to subdue student radicals and urban guerrillas, the football field became increasingly volatile. In 1969 Brazil were 2–1 down to Peru at the Maracanã when Tostão brutally kicked the Peruvian player de la Torre. The ensuing fight lasted forty minutes and required a huge police presence on the pitch; João Havelange was forced to plead with the Peruvians to restart the game.

Santos too were on the slide. The decision of the CBF to withdraw Brazilian clubs from the Copa Libertadores meant there would be no more continental triumphs, and though domestic trophies were won in the late 1960s, the side ceased to be the dominant force in football nationally or even in São Paulo. Instead the club went on tour. In 1967 alone Santos played in Argentina, Chile, Colombia, Uruguay, Peru, Brazil, Gabon, Zaire, Ivory Coast, Germany and Italy. The following year saw them again in

Europe, South, Central and North America. Knowing that Pelé's contract was up in 1972, the management turned on the taps one more time, taking the club to Hong Kong, Bolivia, El Salvador, Martinique, Jamaica, Colombia and Haiti. It was a final payday, but there was precious little evidence of the money earned. The directors did manage to build a fabulous clubhouse for members – the Parque Balneário – but blew a fortune on a failed casino development and left the Vila Belmiro stadium, already ageing, to rot.

Santos may have held Pelé's playing licence, but he had escaped their orbit and established himself as an attraction in his own right. In mid-1969 the press became gripped by the approach of Pelé's 1,000th goal in professional football – a landmark generated by an accounting exercise that remains at best flawed. Statistical precision was not the point. In keeping with the new tenor of the Brazilian media, this was a made-for-TV spectacular. From around goal 990 the Brazilian media worked themselves into a logistical and emotional frenzy. With the tally standing at 998, the number of photographers behind the goal in Salvador reached critical proportions as the mob tumbled on to the pitch. On 999 Vasco's Argentinian goalkeeper, Andrada, was booed for saving a shot from Pelé. The 1,000th goal when it came was a penalty. Pelé made it look easy. After scoring he ran to pick the ball out of the net and in seconds was surrounded, then engulfed, by a horde of photographers and reporters. When he finally emerged from the scrum, it was a schmaltzfest. Pelé dedicated the goal to the children of Brazil and took an endless lap of honour in a specially prepared 1,000 shirt. A senator in Congress wrote a poem to Pelé and read it out on the floor of the house. Everywhere else in the world the newspapers led with the Moon-landing of the

Apollo 12 space mission. In Brazil they split the front page. Pelé was flown to Brasília where he was paraded through the city in an open-topped car. At the presidential palace he was received by the newly installed President Médici, who awarded him the Order of National Merit. Commemorative busts were commissioned, plaques fixed to walls and stamps issued by the Brazilian Post Office. Above all, in a month when guerrillas had kidnapped the American ambassador and the newly sworn-in President Médici was finding his feet, the story dominated every TV news bulletin for days.

From the early 1930s until the mid-1960s, radio had been the main way in which Brazilians had consumed football. Indeed, outside of the small circle of newspaper readers, radio was for most of the country the key source of news, drama and entertainment. The years of the dictatorship, by contrast, were synonymous with the rise of television. In 1960 there were just 600,000 sets in the whole country. By 1986, as the generals withdrew to their barracks, there were 26.5 million, a phenomenal forty-four-fold increase that had been underwritten by government-subsidized instalment plans for buying sets.

Having got the country's attention, the military regime focused theirs on who was allowed to broadcast to it. Through its power to award and revoke channel licences, the government had created a pliant industry in which the most important corporation was Globo, the newspaper and radio empire of Roberto Marinho. Initially a joint venture with US media giant Time-Life, Globo soon outgrew its US partner. The company's access to credit, facilities and buildings, technology imports and broadcast licences was actively supported by the government. In return, the most dynamic, professional and innovative media group in the country was an unfailingly stout ally and friend. Its TV station Rede Globo was launched in 1965, just a year after the coup which had initiated the era of military rule, and for the next twenty years Rede Globo would become the single most powerful cultural institution in Brazil, its mix of news, celebrities, game shows and *telenovelas* dominating the ratings. The football industry, however, remained deeply suspicious of the medium, refusing to sell live broadcast rights for fear of hurting ticket sales. But Globo went ahead and broadcast delayed games and most importantly live transmissions of the Seleção at the World Cup.

Attendance at football matches, especially the big games, held up well through the early years of the dictatorship but the crowd itself was beginning to change. Jaime de Carvalho, for the first time in forty years, began to miss games at Flamengo as his high blood pressure and diabetes kept him at home or in hospital. In the power vacuum created in the stands a group of much younger supporters broke away and would become *Torcida Jovem do Flamengo*. They introduced a whole new style of aggressive and oppositional support, learned in part from studying the games of the 1966 England World Cup on television. In contrast to the old *charanga* and their supporters, the *Torcida Jovem* would boo their own team, gather behind the net and more actively taunt their opponents. Now dying of cancer, Carvalho wrote from his hospital bed to the papers decrying the new turn in fandom and reminding the public that 'Flamengo teaches us to love Brazil above all things.' With his death the original *charanga* retired from the stands and played only at private social functions. A similar generational struggle went on at all of the Rio clubs in the late 1960s, with Dulce Rosalina actually being forced out of the leadership of the TOV at Vasco and her group replaced as the leading *torcida* by *Força Jovem do Vasco*. The same process was at work in São Paulo where similar youth groups broke with the old, like the Hawks and Camisa 12 at Corinthians and Tricolore at São Paulo. In time they would cease to be the breakaways, for they would command the stands.

Cinema Novo which had blossomed in the early 1960s did not fare well under the military, nor did football movies of any genre. The mini-epics of the Canal 100 cinema shorts aside, the only football film made prior to the 1970 World Cup was a stitched-together biography, *Tostão – A Fera de Ouro*. After Mexico 1970, however, there was a flood of money for celebratory football movies. The documentaries that were made about the *tricampeonato* were undistinguished remakes, and in some case literally recuts, of the same films and the same stories made for 1958 and 1962, on to which 1970 was uncritically tagged: Carlos Niemeyer's *Brasil Bom de Bola*, Oswaldo Caldeira's *Futebol Total*, Hugo Schlesinger's *Parabéns, Gigantes da Copa* and Rogério Martins's *Brasil – Tricampeão – Copa 70* all fall into this dismal category. Luiz Carlos Barreto's *Isto é Pelé*, released in 1974 on the eve of the great man's departure to America, was just the latest in the long line of moral biographies of the king, only this time in colour. Meanwhile actor, singer and comedian Grande Otelo was still making a good living, playing the dumb back-country hick, only in *O Barão Otelo no Barato dos Bilhões* the twist was that he won the football lottery. Once a millionaire though, he discovers that fame and wealth are not for the likes of him. It is this kind of dismal racism that makes one almost forgive the 1979 movie *Os Trombadinhas* in which Pelé stars as himself. A thriller with a moral message and characters of the flimsiest cardboard, the film sees Pelé enlisted by a São Paulo tycoon to solve the child-pickpocket problem through football and fighting. Pelé is among the world's worst actors, but he was as comfortable and at ease with fame and money as any member of Brazil's otherwise white elite.

Music's relationship with football fared better than cinema's. Though no World Cup would ever attract the outpouring of musical invention that accompanied 1958 and 1962, and no players would ever garner as many songs as Pelé, the new generation of Brazilian musicians did engage with football. Indeed, as the worlds of literature and poetry began to disengage from the game in the 1970s and 1980s, popular music remained the main cultural tradition in which football as a joyful popular art was still celebrated. The two key figures in the Tropicália movement of the mid-1960s – Caetano Veloso and Gilberto Gil – both recorded a number of football songs. Their fusion of Brazilian and African music with Western pop and rock had seemed so threatening to the authorities that they were forced into exile – a fact that encouraged political readings of their football songs. Gil wrote 'Meio de Campo' in support of the player Afonsinho who was struggling against the feudal control of players by clubs in the early 1970s. Jorge Ben's album *Umbabarauma* was the most pointed reminder since Freyre of the central importance of black Brazil in shaping the nation's game. And as late as 1989, Chico Buarque could compare the art of the musician and the composer to Pelé, and Pelé to the greatest artists and painters:

> A painter measuring exactly
> To hang in a gallery, no
> brushstrokes more perfect
> Than a goal shot
> Crisp
> As an arrow or a dry leaf.

These notions, at least, would survive two decades of the Brazilian military. Not much else about Brazilian football would.

III

For Médici's government money was no object in the preparations of the team for the 1970 World Cup. Army captain Cláudio Coutinho was made the squad's physical fitness trainer and dispatched to NASA to learn the secrets of the US space programme. The coach, João Saldanha, whose communist sympathies had always rankled with the government, was fired after his public criticisms of Pelé and an incident in which he took a loaded gun to a Rio hotel lobby where he was due to meet one of his press critics. The CBF relieved him of his duties on the grounds of emotional instability and installed their own man, Mário Zagallo.

The 1970 World Cup was the first to be broadcast in colour and that gives it, for those who saw it, a kind of chromatic magic. Brazil's yellow shirts shimmered and sparkled in the blistering white sunlight of the Mexican noon – the appointed time of kick-offs to suit European TV schedules. Yet those that saw them in black and white, the vast majority, were no less dazzled. Brazil played six games in the tournament and scored nineteen goals, an unambiguous record of adventure and positive play. They had the decency to keep only one clean sheet, giving the opposition just enough hope to resist – often very entertainingly. To this they added sublime moments of invention: Pelé's attempt on goal from the halfway line and his immaculate layoff to find the only space available in England's otherwise watertight defence. In the final, the Italians held them to 1–1 for two-thirds of the game before a final twenty minutes of exquisite team play brought three goals and victory. Even the most implacable left-wing opponents of the regime, who had sworn not to support the Seleção, melted.

> Critical consciousness failed to resist our first successful attack. Each victory for the *Canarinhos* was a spontaneous carnival in the streets of the big cities and when Brazil became three times world champion the entire country took to revelry, took over the squares, the streets, the alleys, for wild celebrations of the championship.[4]

The squad were flown direct to Brasília from Mexico City and carried from the airport to the presidential palace on a municipal fire engine, just like the one they had travelled on in 1958 through the streets of Rio. The normally empty squares and bleak highways of the federal capital were thronged with people who had gathered to see the team. Outside the palace, tens of thousands assembled to cheer each player individually before they joined President Médici on a public balcony and then joined the cabinet for lunch. For the first and only time in the more than twenty years that they ruled Brazil, the military government opened the palace to the people.

The unambiguously upbeat march 'Pra Frente, Brasil' ('Forward, Brazil') had been the theme tune of the tournament. The song's lyrics imagined 90 million Brazilians all moving together, the national team and everyone else, in harmony. Now it was adopted by the government as their theme tune and combined with football imagery and its own unabashed sloganeering in print and television advertising. Players and coaches were expected to learn their lines. Interviewed by the sports press in Montevideo in

1972, while thousands of the regime's opponents languished in jail or sat in exile, Pelé was reported as saying, 'There is no dictatorship in Brazil. Brazil is a liberal country, a land of happiness. We are a free people. Our leaders know what is best for us and govern us with tolerance and patriotism.'[5] Pelé's image was thrown up on gigantic billboards in the major cities, accompanied by the words '*Ninguém mais segura este país*' – 'Nobody can stop this country now', or 'Brazil, love it or leave it'.

It was the kind of confidence that a third victory in the World Cup can deliver, but the military ebullience was based on more than that. For six years, between 1968 and 1974, the Brazilian economy grew at an incredible 10 per cent a year. The steady migration of the very poor from the north to the south kept wages down and the trade unions were crushed. Brazil's generals increasingly talked not just of Brazil but of *O Grande Brasil* – 'The Great Brazil' – a power of continental proportions and international ambitions. With a solid international credit rating, Brazil's government started borrowing and building, creating a nation and football culture in its own image.

Having left football to administer itself during the 1960s, the military applied a much firmer hand to the sport in the 1970s. João Havelange remained untouchable at the head of the CBF, but with his ascent to the presidency of FIFA in 1974 the regime swiftly installed one of their own. Admiral Heleno Nunes, moonlighting from his job as the head of the Rio state branch of the government political party ARENA, took charge. When not campaigning for the return of Flamengo's Roberto to the national side, he orchestrated the Seleção's qualifying campaign for the 1978 World Cup. Each game was accompanied by the presentation of ARENA politicians on the pitch with the players, much flag waving and generous quantities of political literature, in a thinly disguised campaign rally. Moving in the other direction, Laudo Natel, the president of São Paulo FC and the Bradesco banking cartel, brokered his football connections into political capital and became the ARENA governor of São Paulo state.

After securing control of political institutions, and repressing subversives, the military's greatest energies were reserved for grand infrastructure projects, the steel and concrete sinews of *O Grande Brasil.* In the early 1970s the country embarked on three vast projects: the building of the Trans-Amazonian Highway over 2,000 miles across the continent; the construction of the Itaipu Dam on the Paraguayan border, intended to be the largest hydro-electric complex in South America; and the creation of an atomic energy industry. Part industrial policy, part political spectacular, these projects were matched in the realm of football by a massive burst of government spending on the building of new football stadiums. The aesthetics of the project are best revealed in the closing sequence of the 1970 movie *Tostão – A Fera de Ouro.* The film is for the most part a conventional and rather poorly made hagiography of the great striker, then playing at Cruzeiro, but in the final minutes it seems to switch gear. The camera slowly moves through the empty streets of Belo Horizonte. Not a single car is moving, not a single person is on the pavements. Milton Nascimento's 'Here is the Country of Football' starts to play: 'Brazil is empty on a Sunday afternoon, right? Look, *sambão,* here is the country of football.' The film then cuts to a series of sweeping helicopter shots over and around the recently completed Estádio Mineirão: a deep-angled concrete bowl, set off with a flat roof through which the giant angular cantilevers and buttresses of the stadium walls were set. It was unambiguously large, industrial and brutish – a machine for staging football, the players tiny figures on the vast green swathe, the whole set against a vast flat car park, full to brimming with the Volkswagens and Mercedes coming off the production lines of Brazil's new and explosively growing car industry.

The building of the football wing of *O Grande Brasil* began in the north-east of the country where these immense concrete structures were compensations for the region's enduringly low growth rates and were a political prize for local elites. Estádio Rei Pelé was opened in Maceió, capital of Alagoas, in 1970; the huge Machadão in Natal followed in 1972; and the Castelão in Fortaleza was bigger still. Even Teresina, the tiny state capital of Piauí, acquired the Albertão in 1973, holding a crowd of 60,000. The imposing Estádio Governador João Castelo in São Luís, Maranhão, also known as the Castelão, was the biggest of all, its vast sunken concrete stands holding up to 100,000. All of these stadiums took their architectural cues from the Mineirão – huge circular concrete bowls, ribbed and prefabricated, they nonetheless retained a bulky elegance, though in tropical conditions they did not age well, succumbing to the moisture of the climate and to neglect. The central highlands and the Amazon also built stadiums: the 50,000 capacity Vivaldão in Manaus, deep in the heart of the rainforest, was finally finished in 1970, twelve years after its construction began. In 1975, the Estádio Serra Dourada was opened in Goiânia and the Mangueirão was inaugurated in Belém. Close to the banks of the Amazon itself, it held 70,000, though the state government of Pará had originally planned for 120,000. In a singular act of independence and autonomy, Santa Cruz FC, the smallest and poorest professional team in Recife, opened a stadium that they had built themselves. Estádio do Arruda had been started in 1958; built virtually brick by brick with donations of materials and labour from the club's members and supporters, it opened in 1970.

In the 1960s the long-established but highly illegal numbers games that were played in Brazil's cities were popular – and untaxed. At the end of the decade the military authorities decided to take over the racket by creating their own national lottery. Rather than going just with numbers, they gave the lottery a football theme with competitors guessing the scores of upcoming fixtures in the big cities. It was also intended as an exercise in national consciousness-raising, requiring the huge uneducated pool of Brazilians to think about Brazil's geography. Launched in 1970, the lottery proved to be instantly popular. In his short story 'Opening Act' Edilberto Coutinho depicts the lottery as being at the centre of working life.

> The comments on last week's game will still be made on Tuesday or Wednesday, Thursday is a day of great concentration, every mind in the office working on it, let's fill in the blanks on the Soc-cer Lotto ticket ... Friday and Saturday are the days of great anxiety, for anybody can wake up a millionaire on Sunday.[6]

Encouraged by the nation-building efforts of the national lottery and hungry for more games in the season and therefore more income, the government pressured the football authorities to establish a fully fledged national championship. Extraordinarily, football was still predominantly played at the state level. From 1950 a Rio–São Paulo tournament had been held among the leading clubs and from 1967 clubs from the biggest cities of southern and south-eastern Brazil – Porto Alegre, Belo Horizonte and

Curitiba – were invited to join. Four years later, and with just enough internal air traffic to support the fixture list, the Campeonato Brasileiro was launched. It had twenty teams, including clubs from Recife and Fortaleza for the first time, and it was a marathon. A twenty-team league was followed by two leagues of four for the top eight, and then a final round robin of three teams. This was a taste of things to come. The tendency under the military for projects to balloon out of control, driven by unchecked grandiose ambitions, was exemplified by the football championship. In 1973 there were fifty teams in the competition and the format had already changed twice. In 1975 a new sports law, passed by the government, insisted on equal votes for all state federations in any national-level sporting body. Consequently inside the CBF the votes of Mato Grosso, with a population of 1 million, and São Paulo, with perhaps twenty times that, were electorally equal. This opened the door to vote-buying, politicking and horse-trading, and a place in the national championships was certainly something worth trading. It became a commonplace of political conversation that when 'things are bad for ARENA another team gets in the Brasileiro'. In 1976 there were fifty-four teams and with more added every year the competition peaked in 1979 with ninety-four participants. Formats and rules were changeable and on occasions byzantine. Some years there were relegation and promotion, some years there weren't. One season was played with extra points awarded for victories by two clear goals, in other years ticket sales were included in a team's points total. With an already busy schedule of state championships and cup tournaments, the Brasileiro's relentless expansion filled the calendar. At one point in the mid-1970s Santos, returning from a foreign tour, had less than a week scheduled between the end of one season and the beginning of the next. The strain on players' bodies and well-being was immense, but predictably this was entirely disregarded by the football authorities.

In a deliberate echo of the 1922 South American Football Championship, which had celebrated both a centenary of Brazilian independence and its emergence as the futebol nation, João Havelange and the CBF put on an Independence Cup in 1972 to mark the country's 150th anniversary. The Minicopa, as the tournament was known, was a major event with twenty teams playing in nine venues right across the country and all at the expense of the Brazilian government. It was certainly an impressive demonstration of Havelange's organizational skills and political capital, and it gave him plenty of face time with football officials from all around the world, officials whose votes he would soon be soliciting in his bid for the FIFA presidency. The final was played between Brazil and Portugal, colony and home country, reunited after 150 years, and both ruled by conservative and occasionally violent dictatorships. As they had in 1922, Brazil won the final, but there was none of the celebrations that had marked the centennial game fifty years beforehand.

Pelé had made it clear that he would retire in 1974 and he would not be going to the World Cup that year. Rede Globo ran a nationwide campaign to get him to think again, João Havelange virtually grovelled and President Médici wrote in too, but Pelé was done. Reborn as a global brand, he would surface in America the following year as the star turn of the New York Cosmos during the short boom in American soccer. Havelange himself jumped ship. His long campaign for the presidency of FIFA culminated in victory over the incumbent Englishman, Sir Stanley Rous, on the eve of the 1974 World Cup. He won by mobilizing the votes of Asian and African football associations dissatisfied with the dominance of Europe in the organization and the placation of South Africa's apartheid regime, and once in place he set about revolutionizing FIFA, turning it from a tiny amateurish federation into one of the world's most powerful international organizations.

Left to its own devices the military regime took charge of the Seleção. Cláudio Coutinho, the fitness trainer in 1970, was given overall control. He spoke of his players as light armour and infantry, and their skills as weapons. He festooned the training camps with patriotic slogans and insisted on military discipline among the squad. Drawing on the ideas emerging from the army's physical training schools, he espoused scientific football, a game based on exceptional fitness and cohesive teamwork. He avoided calling up dribblers and individualists, and argued that 'the dribble, our speciality, is a waste of time, and proof of our weakness'. Rebellious characters like Paulo César Caju were out. The 1978 World Cup campaign that followed was defensive and uninspiring. The team scraped their way through the first round in games so disappointing that travelling Brazilian fans in Argentina burnt an effigy of Coutinho in Mar del Plata. When the team was knocked out (albeit without losing a match), he returned home and was fired.

IV

Reinaldo, who had been warned off politics by President Geisel, celebrated his goals for the side with a clenched fist, live on Brazilian television. This was just one of a whole series of challenges to the ruling order expressed through football in the 1970s and early 1980s. The most surprising challenge, and perhaps in the long term the most significant, came from the beaches of Copacabana, Leblon and Ipanema. As early as 1975 there were reports of women, many of them maids in the surrounding duplexes, playing football in their time off. This was an illegal act. In 1941 Vargas's national sports council had banned women's football, and barred them from martial arts and boxing, the pole vault and the triple jump. All were deemed unsuitable. Twenty years later the same arguments were being reproduced through Brazil's coaching and sports administration colleges. Walter Areno, a lecturer in the army's physical education school, wrote in a 1962 paper: 'It is inappropriate for a female to participate in sports where there is physical contact, such as the infamous female soccer or futsal. It is abnormal to watch 20 women (as two are the goalkeepers) running around a ball in ungraceful and rough conditions.'[7] Despite this, women's teams were playing as late as 1949; two women's sides from Pelotas, Vila Hilda FC and Corinthians FC, packed the small stadiums in Rio Grande do Sul and charged entrance money. But with the closure of these clubs in the early 1950s women, who had once been a central element of the Brazilian football crowd, were almost entirely marginalized. Though female fans continued to attend games, Betty Milan's recollections were probably closer to the norm: a world in which women were not included in the football conversation but were expected to serve the coffee.[8]

The ban was revoked in 1979, and at a speed at least the equivalent to the male football mania of the early twentieth century, women's football took off: the sports press were reporting over 3,000 teams by the early 1980s. In 1981 Rio was the first to hold a women's state championship and eleven other states followed in the next couple of years. However, there was almost no money available to support women's football from clubs, the CBF or the lottery. In fact most clubs made the team the responsibility of the social rather than the sporting wing of the institution. In 1984 São Cristóvão and Tomazinho had to cancel a game because both wore white shirts and neither could afford change strips. Equally problematical was the tendency for television and the press to trivialize and sexualize the women's game. Globo, keen to shape the phenomenon, created the Globettes from their roster of TV celebrities. The women's Copa do Brasil, which was meant to help choose the national women's team, was treated like a fashion show. *Gazeta Esportiva* saw it like this:

> Fingernails red polish, shiny lipstick, hairdo, black shorts and yellow jersey: that is Neusa Cavalheiro's look. Braids decorated with colourful beads, the hairdo launched by Stevie Wonder enhanced the beauty of Mocidade Independente's charming samba dancer, Cilda, who was also wearing shorts and jersey in the blue and yellow colours. But the two of them were not part of a samba school rehearsal show, they were on a football pitch.

When on the pitch, many of this generation of women players were subject to sexist abuse. Cenira, a striker with the club Radar, spoke for many: 'Today when I came on to the field, I heard a guy say that I should be at the laundry sink, washing clothes. But I did not bother to reply to him, although I was angry. My reaction came later, with the ball at my feet.'[9]

In the men's game players led the way, challenging the feudal conditions of their employment and the often subservient character of their relationships with coaches, the press, officials and club directors. Initially the challenge came from that small but persistent strain of middle-class, educated footballers in Brazil – a phenomenon stretching back to Botafogo's medical students in the early twentieth century. Tostão, a hero of the 1970 World Cup team, was an eloquent and occasionally outspoken critic of Brazilian football in this era. He retired early in 1973 and became a doctor. Afonsinho and Sócrates, who were among the most well-known rebels, also took that path. Afonsinho played at Botafogo. Already out of favour with conservative coach Zagallo, he had spent the summer of 1970 travelling and watching the World Cup in bars in Europe. He returned to Brazil with his hair long and sporting a small beard, and was banned from training and playing for the team. Most importantly, the club which held his playing licence refused to allow him to move elsewhere. The case went to court and Afonsinho became a cause célèbre, attracting huge support from students, intellectuals and musicians on the left. His fight was the subject of the only serious football film of the decade, Oswaldo Caldeira's *Passe Livre*. Sharply critical of the football authorities and by extension the regime, the film was shown to small groups in a short-lived attempt to create an underground film circuit. Afonsinho won his court case and grew his beard, declaring it 'a symbol of freedom'. He played out the rest of his career in small stints at professional clubs and in his own touring team of bohemians and rebels, the Train of Joy.

In addition to articulating a critique of football's labour relations and cultural conservatism, Afonsinho also criticized the impact of the joyless military style of training, physicality and discipline that was becoming prevalent in football. He was not alone. Reinaldo, the star striker at Atlético Mineiro, had, as we know, crossed swords with President Geisel. He continued to make public statements on political issues, including the amnesty proposals of the late 1970s which would pardon all those charged and convicted during the recent political struggles, and the need for direct elections. It was a stand that saw him garner huge public support. While the CBF threatened his place in the national team, students at the University of Minas Gerais painted a huge wall with the words 'Why shouldn't Reinaldo have a political opinion?'[10]

Rebellious dressing rooms and outspoken players could be dealt with, but the prospect of a truly mass opposition was another thing. The dictatorship's control of political organizations and public spaces had been comprehensive. Thus the Corinthian invasion of 1976, while just a huge football party, had ominous even threatening undertones. Given the huge distance between most Brazilian cities and the ramshackle state of the transport network, away fans were a rare phenomenon in Brazilian football, cross-city derbies aside. In 1976 Corinthians were drawn against Fluminense in the semi-finals of the Campeonato Brasileiro in Rio. Though less than 200 miles apart, the transport connections between Rio and São Paulo were still poor, but there was just enough road capacity and private car ownership to permit a giant caravan of Corinthians fans to be assembled for the trip east. Over two days something in the region of 70,000 Paulistas made their way to Rio. The local press gave the event blanket coverage, reporting that the main avenues were choked with cars bearing São Paulo number plates and that an air of carnival had engulfed the city. The last time a group of people this large had occupied Rio's public spaces they were shot at. The gathering of the crowd at the Maracanã bearing thousands of flags was most impressive of all. In the driving rain a delirious Corinthians crowd saw their side win a waterlogged penalty shoot-out. Later in the year the first signs of a new student movement would emerge and the first tentative protests and occupations would begin.

While the student movement continued to irritate the regime, the most serious challenge to its authority came from the new independent trade union movement that was growing in the ABC industrial suburbs of São Paulo. Once again it was the football stadium that offered the space in which the collective strength of an organized populace could be acknowledged. But rather than deploying it in pursuit of the championship, here it was used to challenge the authoritarian structures of government and industry. The strike wave of 1979 began in the Saab factory, and the union looked to spread it to the other car plants of the region as it stockpiled money and food for the families of its members. In opposition to the government-appointed officials, independent union leaders led by the rising star of the left, Luiz Inácio Lula da Silva, or Lula as he was known, called a mass meeting at the Estádio Vila Euclides in São Bernardo. Over 50,000 people attended and, though without a PA system, relays of speakers conveyed messages of solidarity. The strike then spread to every car manufacturer. As the unions were driven from public spaces with pepper spray and batons, they made Estádio Euclides a citadel. Over the next three weeks, the stadium served as a debating chamber and provided a tangible display of unity.

The final expression of this wave of footballing protest was the emergence of the movement known as Corinthian Democracy in the early 1980s. This combined two forces. On the one hand there was a democratic movement in the Corinthians dressing room where a group of senior players – Sócrates, Casagrande, Wladimir and Juninho – were looking to challenge the authoritarianism of their playing and training regime. On the other hand there was a struggle for control of the club board in elections for directorships. Normally a faction-ridden affair, this time the election took on a wider political significance. Representing the old guard was a slate named 'Order and Truth'. Ranged against them was Corinthian Democracy. The sports magazine *Placar* summed up the choice in an election campaign that was fought on television and in the papers and cost over half a million dollars: 'liberalization or heavy-handedness, efficiency or paternalism, new times or old methods'. The players came out en masse for the democratic slate and Sócrates said he would leave the club if the old guard were to win.

Corinthian Democracy won the vote and for a couple of years the club was engaged in one of the most innovative and important political experiments in the country. The coaches' authority dwindled while the players took on a much bigger role in organizing training and playing. They also allowed for a lot more drinking and smoking and taking it easy. Speaking at the time, Sócrates said, 'I'm struggling for freedom, for respect for human beings, for equality, for ample and unrestricted discussions, for a professional democratization of unforeseen limits, and all of this as a soccer player, preserving the ludic, and the joyous and the pleasurable nature of this activity.' For a short time it worked as the team played with verve and the fans exulted. A banner in the stadium read: 'Win or lose but always with democracy.'

V

The military takeover of 1964 had been justified, at least in part, by the desperate need to control Brazil's unstable inflationary economy; itself a symptom, the military argued, of the country's political polarization and indiscipline. But by 1980 the annual inflation rate was back up to 110 per cent, and in 1985, on the eve of the generals' departure, it had reached 235 per cent and was still heading upwards. The great wave of international borrowing and domestic spending of the 1970s, at what were at the time negligible interest rates, became unserviceable in the early 1980s as interest and inflation rates soared. Brazil was forced to default on its financial obligations in 1982 and was subject to an excruciatingly painful IMF adjustment programme.

Under President Figueiredo the military conducted an orderly retreat from political power, offering amnesties to political prisoners and exiles – and themselves – and opening up the electoral process in 1982. Finally, in 1985 they would permit an indirect congressional election of a civilian president, to whom they would hand a poisoned chalice of problems. The economic miracle of the 1960s and 1970s was truly over and it became apparent that the benefits of the boom had been spread very unevenly. Between 1960 and 1980 the share of national income that went to the richest tenth of Brazilian households rose from 40 per cent to over half. The poorest 50 per cent received less than a fifth of this amount to share among themselves.[11] As public services and employment shrank and the value of what little cash the poor possessed was constantly eaten up by inflation, those inequalities stretched even further. In the north-east, more than 40 per cent of the population remained officially hungry. In the big cities it was at least a quarter. From 1980 onwards the crime rate rose as robberies and homicides increased at a phenomenal rate. High-security measures swept through Brazil as every apartment and office block acquired bars, gates and guard patrols.

Domestic football stumbled its way through the economic crisis, clubs often surviving from week to week by delaying wages and payments long enough for the inflation rate to reduce them to a fraction of their original value. In 1977 stadium advertising was permitted and shirt sponsorship began in 1983. Although the biggest games could still attract crowds approaching 200,000, average attendances had begun a long decline. The debts kept mounting up and after three decades of resistance the club presidents yielded to the inevitable and sold the live rights of Brazilian football to Rede Globo.

On the pitch the character of the game was changing. The *futebol arte* of the past clung on, represented by Zico and the great Flamengo sides of the early 1980s, who won not only the Copa Libertadores but effortlessly dominated the champions of Europe, Liverpool, in their Intercontinental Cup encounter. However, the doctrine of *futebol resultados* and the physicality of *futebol força* had made enormous inroads. Grêmio and Internacional from Porto Alegre in Rio Grande do Sul, the home state of four of Brazil's five general-presidents, played a self-consciously more physical and disciplined European game, and won five national titles between them.

The 1982 World Cup side under Telê Santana was a team that aspired to the artistic and romantic traditions of Brazilian football, and in Zico, Falcão and Sócrates it had players of the requisite skills and dispositions to make it happen. In the early rounds in

Spain they were mesmerizing, scoring ten goals as they beat the Soviet Union, Scotland and New Zealand. Then, in the second round, as the surrender of the Malvinas was being signed, they swept aside a dispirited Argentina. Progress depended on their game with Italy, and as with the 1950 final Brazil needed only a draw to secure this. It proved to be among the most exceptional World Cup games ever played: open, pulsating and unpredictable. But Brazil lost 3–2. Even Carlos Drummond de Andrade had had enough of poetry. In one of his last World Cup *crónicas* he suggested to his readers that they should wipe their tears, roll up their sleeves, and get back to the serious business of making political change happen.

In 1984 the Diretas Já movement gathered all the forces of the opposition in a call for direct presidential elections in 1985 rather than a vote by Congress. A million people demonstrated in Rio, and 1.5 million people gathered in central São Paulo to hear, among others, Sócrates calling on Congress to make the necessary changes to the constitution. He was poised to make a move to Italy, but said he would stay if the measure passed. It did not. Sócrates went to Fiorentina and his club, Corinthians, relinquished their Paulista crown to Santos. They had reached the limits of Brazilian football's democratic uprising. The *abertura* would be on the military's terms.

In 1985 nationwide democratic elections voted in a new Congress and they in turn elected Tancredo Neves as Brazil's first post-military president. But his sudden death before his inauguration left vice-president José Sarney in charge of the country's raging inflation, rising crime rate and unpayable bills. Brazil went to its first World Cup for almost a quarter of a century as a democracy, but neither the team nor the polity felt like winners. The core of the 1982 squad went to Mexico in 1986 and made steady if unspectacular progress to the quarter-finals. In France they met their match. With the score at 1–1 in the seventieth minute, Zico stepped up to take a penalty and made it easy for the goalkeeper to save. The game went all the way to a penalty shoot-out in which Sócrates and Júlio César missed their kicks. Brazil were careless, they were also unlucky, but they were not good enough either. The response of Brazil's football authorities was to rule, without consultation, that all drawn games in the national championship should be decided on penalties – a ruling soon abandoned after some clubs refused and were then forced into replayed shoot-outs in empty stadiums.

Terry Cesar, an American in Brazil for the 1986 World Cup, was a sharp observer of the mood of the nation. Brazil really did close down for the games. The Bolshoi Ballet had to cancel its Rio show when it clashed with a match. Universities and schools closed, business sent employees home, and 'buses just stopped at street corners'.[12] Over the three weeks of the tournament itself, 'Life increasingly took on the character of an interval so utterly engrossing and so ceaselessly represented that it could only be compared to the experience of a nation at war.' For many, the occasion was particularly charged with meaning as this was the first World Cup for a generation where one could cheer and not worry that one was also cheering for a dictatorship. Despite the central role of television in covering the World Cup, Cesar thought that it still mediated an essentially spontaneous and popular festival, rather than taking control of a made-for-TV spectacular.

Even the poorest favelas had lines of green and yellow paper, and richer neighbourhoods were festooned with bunting and streamers dangled above the streets like vines in a tropical forest. Drivers tied green and yellow plastic strips to their aerials, businessmen hung national flags ... in their windows. Children chalked players' names ... on pavements.

In the course of the three weeks Cesar reported that almost every kind of emotion could be observed: delirious pyrotechnic celebrations when Brazil won, a sombre disappointment when they lost. But more complex moods were also present: a sense that a society so divided and disorganized did not deserve to win, and a pervasive nostalgia for the days of Mexico 1970 and for the world that made that moment. That nostalgia had first surfaced three years earlier, in January 1983. After another day of drinking *cachaça* Garrincha was taken to a sanatorium in Botafogo where he had already had a number of episodes in rehab. This time he died in an alcoholic coma. Within hours hundreds were gathering at the hospital. The press, who had not written a word about him for a decade, began to publish a torrent of remembrance. A municipal fire engine, like the one that had carried him through the streets of the city with the 1958 World Cup winners, took his body to the Maracanã. In a deluxe coffin, paid for by Botafogo, he lay in state for three days. On 21 January his body, carried on the same fire engine, wound its way to Pau Grande. Rio's working classes came out to mourn him, packing the pavements and overpasses of Avenida Brasil. Thousands more headed for Pau Grande itself, many forced to abandon their cars outside the town. When the coffin arrived at the church for a hasty blessing, the area was besieged by mourners, some hanging from trees, others balanced on rooftops. The coffin proved too large for the grave that had been dug for it, and after his burial it was barely covered by the earth. A guard of Botafogo *torcida* led the crowd in singing the national anthem. The crowd then departed, leaving the graveyard half destroyed.

Sérgio Leite Lopes argued that 'his death symbolized the end of a certain kind of working-class life' characterized by the political freedoms and rising wages of the 1950s and early 1960s, and by an era of football remembered as a golden age of invention and joy. In the desperate economic circumstances of 1983 its passing was felt all the more keenly. At some point in the late 1970s, the Jules Rimet trophy, then in the possession of the CBF, went missing. It was never recovered, and in an era of hyperinflation, it seems likely that it was melted down for its value as a precious metal. Gold might keep its value, but the golden age was over.

6

Magic and Dreams are Dead: Pragmatism, Politics and Football, 1986–2002

'I have always said that God put the best players here and the worst bosses to compensate' – Juca Kfouri.

Magic and dreams are finished in football.

Carlos Alberto Parreira

In Brazil there is still the ideology of *rouba, mas faz* – it's okay to steal if you get things done. In football this is stretched to the most far-reaching consequences. Everything is forgotten in the light of victory.

Juca Kfouri

I

Magic and dreams looked finished everywhere in Brazilian society in the late 1980s and 1990s. The long-drawn-out process of the *abertura* was not the soil from which utopian visions of the future were going to flourish. In the decade and a half following the end of military rule Brazil began to repair the damage wrought by the dictatorship, but even these gains came at a price. Inflation was finally brought under control, but Brazil endured two decades of slow growth, widespread poverty, rising inequality and a crime wave to match. In the realm of politics, Brazilian democracy was consolidated and the military seemingly neutered, but it was a highly dysfunctional polity in many ways. The fragmented party system made collective decision-making impossible and the whole operation open to vote-buying and old-fashioned embezzlement.

Only pragmatists, it appears, could prosper. Fernando Henrique Cardoso – or FHC as he became known – made the journey from São Paulo sociologist, and Latin America's leading Marxist theorist of underdevelopment, to centrist president implementing IMF-approved monetarist policies. Lula began the era as the leader of the recently founded Partido dos Trabalhadores (PT, the Workers' Party) and called for Brazil to break with the IMF, nationalize key industries and institute real structural change. He lost three elections, steadily moderated his language and economic policies, and then at the fourth attempt won a landslide in 2002.

In 1994, under Carlos Alberto Parreira, twenty-four years after they had last won the World Cup, the futebol nation went to the USA and played neither *futebol força* nor *futebol arte*. As Parreira said, 'We will play in the way modern football demands. Magic and dreams are finished in football. We have to combine technique and efficiency.'[1] It wasn't terribly pretty but it worked: Brazil won. Pragmatism and realism could get one elected, they could even win a World Cup, but these victories came at a cost. In football and politics, legitimacy came to rest on results alone – *rouba, mas faz*. In the 1980s and 1990s the brazen corruption and incompetence of football's administrators were uncovered but went unpunished. The financial gains of the new commercialism were reserved for a tiny minority, and, worst of all, football's fan culture, already perilously poised between a spontaneous popular spectacular and a demonic mob, tilted in favour of the latter as violence at football games became pervasive. This, surely, was passion without dreams. For how long could a football culture nurtured on fantasy and spectacle prosper on a diet of pragmatism?

In the 1990s the cycles of football and politics became closer. From 1994, every four years, July meant the World Cup and October meant Brazil's presidential and state elections. The last presidential race to precede a tournament, rather than be interpreted in its light, was in 1989. Then the contest was between Lula and a hitherto little-known state governor from Alagoas in the north-east, Fernando Collor de Mello. In his youth Collor had dabbled with the populist politics of football, taking on the ceremonial presidency of the leading team in Alagoas, Centro Sportivo Alagoano, but he had registered a shift in the nation's tastes. On television, at any rate, football was gradually being superseded by *telenovelas*, the subtropical revenge tragedies that entranced the country with their heady brew of lust, greed, paternity suits and conspicuous consumption. Collor, rather than pursuing the people through football, lived the life of the small screen's alpha-male patriarchs as an exquisitely groomed playboy-politician. His break in national politics came when the industrial and media elites started to worry about Lula, who was ahead in the polls. As the most plausible candidate to the right of the PT, Collor was supplied with money and unlimited television time. There he adopted a heroic, even messianic tone, promising to clear out corruption, free up markets, reform and shrink the state, and build a new Brazil. He was also telegenic, good-looking and eloquent. Lula was none of these. In the prevailing culture of deference, his fractured Portuguese grammar, rough accent and obvious roots in

Brazil's working classes made him look utterly unpresidential. With the help of some very questionable editing from Globo in the televised debates, Collor sailed into the presidential palace.

Brazil went to the 1990 World Cup, not as a herald of free enterprise, but as a throwback. The team were coached by the dismal Sebastião Lazaroni, a product of the military school of obsessive physical preparation and muscle building. He combined this approach with a rigid commitment to playing a European-style sweeper system. In fact he was so convinced that the system was the solution to Brazil's footballing maladies that he had written a doctoral thesis on the subject. It was not a happy camp in Italy, where the application of military-era discipline could no longer work with players newly enfranchised by wealth and European experience. The Brazilian press feasted on stories of internal rows and huge drinks bills that no one would pay. On the pitch Brazil were lifeless and uninspired. They played four games, scored four goals and went home. Maradona's Argentina put them out of their misery.

Collor could have done with better. His presidency was already faltering. The price stabilization programme was in tatters, and he was ruling by decree over the heads of an uncooperative but paralysed Congress. In early 1992 the stream of rumours about the regime's venality were confirmed. The affairs of Collor's main fixer, Paulo César Farias (known colloquially as PC), became daily news and the subject of a congressional inquiry. Collor denied everything while his brother denounced him on television. Congress established the link between the money in Farias's slush fund, totalling hundreds of millions of dollars, and Collor. In Paris, the Seleção beat France 2–0 in a friendly as Congress voted to accept the damning findings of its own commission of inquiry into Collor. *Gazeta Esportiva* reported that 'The news of the score 16-5 in favour of the Report was celebrated with almost the same joy reserved for the goals from Raí and Luís Henrique.'[2] In a final bid to hang on, the president called for the nation to deck itself in yellow and green, and to show its support on the street. Instead the country dressed in black and demonstrated in their millions for his departure. Collor stood down just in time to prevent his impeachment by Congress.

Into his place stepped Vice-President Itamar Franco, a politician of no known passion or ideological alignment. Provincial, shy and utterly unprepared for the task, he handed the levers of power, in effect, to Fernando Cardoso, first as his foreign minister and then as the minister of finance. Over the next eighteen months, either side of the World Cup, Cardoso and his team of technocrats devised and implemented the Plano Real – a complex anti-inflation programme that would see the shortlived *cruzeiro real* (introduced only in 1993) replaced in 1994 by a new currency, the *real*, and the inflationary expectations and behaviour of Brazilians transformed.

Never before had a World Cup been reported in such detail. Television coverage in Brazil was approaching saturation point. Poor homes were more likely to own a TV set than a fridge. Colour television had become widespread. In addition to the squad of twenty-four players, Brazil sent 440 accredited journalists and hundreds more without press passes. Globo had ten camera crews for every Brazil game. Television viewing figures suggested two-thirds of the nation watched the early rounds and close to the whole population tuned in for the final. The Seleção was on trial before a ball was kicked, the players accused of being dour, boring and unadventurous, even when they were winning. In fact, though the team were neither flamboyant nor adventurous, they were well organized, and nicely balanced in their approach to attack and defence. Brazil squeezed past Holland in the quarter-final, a Branco free kick the difference between them. Then they made heavy weather of beating ten-man Sweden in the semi-final. The final against Italy was billed as a rematch of the legendary 1970 final, an occasion on which to recreate 'the beautiful game'. But the contrast between the two games could not have been starker. Brazil won on penalties after 120 goalless minutes in which neither side appeared to have the energy to break the deadlock. In the end the penalty shoot-out turned on the tragic mistake of one man. Roberto Baggio's skied penalty kick and the despairing droop of his head were perfect symbols for Italian despair, but it was hardly the material from which the futebol nation might be mythologically renewed.

The team returned home to Recife where customs took note of the twelve tons of goods they had accumulated in America; Brazil's collapsing currency had made imported white goods unbelievably expensive even for international footballers. Customs officers insisted that they pay the relevant import duties on the loot and the squad refused. There then ensued a five-hour televised wrangle between Ricardo Teixeira, president of the CBF, the Ministry of Finance and the tax authorities. Finally the CBF agreed to pay the bill, and then promptly deducted it from the players' bonus payments. On the surface, the victory parades could be read as just a modern version of the nationalist celebrations of the past. A typical newspaper column announced, 'The victory inaugurates a new phase in Brazil's history: the return of national self-esteem.' President Franco was hopeful that 'this dignity that the players have achieved should be transferred to Brazil itself'.[3] In the capital Brasília people were exuberant:

> From the second-floor balcony of the presidential palace the team members looked down into a wall of green and yellow. Fans waved green and yellow flags, there were green and yellow hats, green and yellow shirts, green and yellow dogs, green and yellow cars – even green and yellow people.[4]

Cities not on the victory route exploded too. In São Paulo more than 200,000 celebrated on Avenida Paulista under skies filled with fireworks, while in Belo Horizonte thousands danced in the main city square to a large samba band. In Rio, crowds of half a million gathered to welcome the cavalcade which passed all the way from the airport, through the Zona Norte and centre, before heading south through the progressively richer beach neighbourhoods of Flamengo, Copacabana and Ipanema before finishing at the very pinnacle of Carioca super wealth, Leblon.

In the election campaign that followed, Romário backed Lula, and Dunga came out for FHC. Lula argued that Brazil had changed: 'The people know how to distinguish between football and politics. When the festivities are over the people know how to separate fantasy and reality.'[5] Perhaps they did. Lula's large early lead in the polls was steadily whittled away as both rich and poor worried about the implications of his economic policies and the Plano Real began to work. In fact it worked so well that Brazil's annual inflation rate dropped from over 1,000 per cent a year to less than 10 per cent: this was little short of a miracle. Cardoso, architect of the plan and now Lula's main opponent, won the presidency with ease. Over the next four years, his government would maintain strict anti-inflationary policies requiring cuts to social programmes and punitively high interest rates. At the same time it began to implement the neo-liberal agenda that Collor had promised: privatizing state-owned companies, deregulating financial markets and opening up the country to international trade. Nowhere was this agenda more evident than in the sale of Brazilian players overseas. In 1986 Brazil's World Cup squad had just two out of twenty-four players playing in Europe, in 2002 there would be eight and by 2010 the home-based players would number just three. From a handful in the 1980s, there were over 100 Brazilians playing in Portugal alone in 2002.

Brazil approached the World Cup in 1998 with a more impressive roster of talent than in 1994, testament to the capacity of the country to keep turning out players of the highest calibre. To the old guard – Dunga, Bebeto and Leonardo – was added a new generation of players like Rivaldo, Roberto Carlos and the goalscoring *fenomeno* Ronaldo, all of whom were playing in the prime of their careers at Europe's leading clubs. Together they promised something more expansive than the functional football on offer in 1994.

If in the past Brazilian politicians, writers or poets had been the key voices in shaping the meaning of the Seleção and its performances, this was no longer the case. That role had now been contracted out to Nike. France 98 was the company's first World Cup as sponsor and supplier to the Brazilian football team, and it made the most of its investment. Nike's globally shown television advert for the tournament featured the Seleção, bored at the airport, but brought to life by football trickery alongside a fabulously swinging version of Jorge Ben's 'Mas Que Nada' ('More than

Anything'): the sweet ebullient sounds of the golden era, the playful joy of the past and all in globally available branded kit.

Cardoso, who could hardly compete with this kind of image-making, wisely decided to lie low for the tournament. He attended a state dinner in Paris after the opening game, but did not grandstand. By contrast, the PT had decided that football was the perfect metaphor for their presidential campaign. Their advert showed Lula facing the crowd while the Seleção was playing against a team in grey in the background. 'Brazil's team is concentrating on marking inflation, while neglecting the others,' says the voice-over. 'Ah, unemployment and violence are closing in with a dangerous move ... Watch out! ... Goal!! ... Gooooaaaaal against Brazil!!!'[6] In the real tournament Brazil made the final to no one's surprise, though a defeat by Norway in the group stage, and a semi-final victory over Holland on penalties, made them look less than imperious. They went on to lose the final 3–0 to the hosts, France; but it was the manner of the loss that mattered. Brazil's defence was bad, but worse, there was no attacking threat. The day had been rife with rumour as news leaked out of the Brazilian camp that Ronaldo was ill. His name was removed from the team sheet only to reappear just before the game began. Utterly anonymous, he played in a seemingly catatonic trance, detached from the action.

Brazil lost but Cardoso still won and, as the PT predicted, he spent much of the next four years marking inflation – unemployment and violence were given plenty of space in which to operate. The press and politicians conducted the football post-mortem with unaccustomed vigour. Ronaldo's medical condition and the decision-making process that saw him put in, taken out, then put back in the starting eleven were at the centre of their attention: the

Seleção's doctors were cross-examined by the medical establishment, Nike and the CBF came under investigation, and the communist Senator Aldo Rebelo petitioned for a congressional inquiry. All of this came to nothing until, in 2000, the tax authorities decided to take a look at the financial affairs of the national team coach, Vanderlei Luxemburgo, and Renata Alves, who claimed she was his ex-lover. Alves, it turned out, had been purchasing a suspiciously large property portfolio on Luxemburgo's behalf, and under questioning she finally alleged that Luxemburgo had taken a lot of cuts from football deals that needed to be stashed somewhere. While the press slavered over the detail, Luxemburgo's Brazil were beaten by nine-man Cameroon at the Sydney Olympics. He came home to a ritual firing.

At the peak of this scandal there was sufficient pressure for Brazilian politicians to act. Rebelo's CBF–Nike inquiry became a reality, and the Senate created an even more far-reaching commission of inquiry to look into a whole range of problems associated with the nation's game. Both committees sat for over a year and reported in late 2001. The Rebelo commission failed to prove any connection between Nike and the disastrous World Cup final of 1998, but along the way it did uncover detailed evidence of corruption, nepotism and incompetence. The hapless president of the Minas Gerais Football Federation, Elmer Guilherme Ferreira, was found to have employed twenty-seven members of his family at the federation. Ricardo Teixeira, called to give an account of himself and the CBF, went on extended sick leave. The Senate's inquiry concluded by calling for criminal prosecutions to be initiated against seventeen figures. Rebelo himself had called for criminal proceedings to begin against thirty-three football administrators and club directors. But in the years since these reports were published, not one of the serious allegations of fraud, corruption and embezzlement has even gone to court. Brazil's football establishment were saved, as usual, by the timidity of the judiciary, the byzantine complexity of the legal system and the brilliance of the national team.

Luxemburgo's replacement as Brazil's coach was Luiz Felipe. Scolari – known as Felipão or Big Phil – who had pioneered a particularly abrasive style of play and mode of interaction with the press, but had won national and international titles with Grêmio and Palmeiras. His greatest asset was a thick skin. He needed it. The criticism rained relentlessly down upon him as, first, Brazil were knocked out of the Copa América 2001 by Honduras, and then a series of draws and defeats in World Cup qualifying games put the team in danger of not going to the World Cup for the first time since its inauguration in 1930. Cardoso, not given to making statements on the matter, went public, saying that failing to qualify would be a 'bigger disaster' than the looming economic crisis triggered by Argentina's debt default. In the end, Brazil survived the shock waves from the financial disaster on its southern border and a win over Venezuela in the last game of the qualifying round took Brazil to the finals in Korea and Japan in 2002. Once there, they were, for the most part, superb. They were imperious with the minnows Costa Rica and China, beat England despite going down to ten men, and overcame an excellent Turkey side twice. Ronaldo was in extraordinary form and, not to be denied his moments of redemption, scored two goals in twelve minutes against Germany in the final in Tokyo. Brazil had won their fifth World Cup.

Cardoso welcomed the team home, saying, 'The whole world saw the courage of the Brazilian people. They saw we are capable of organizing ourselves and winning . . . and they will see the same thing in the economy. We can organize our domestic affairs and triumph there as well.'[7] But then he had only a few months left of his long period in office and had run out of reforming zeal. The CBF and the football establishment breathed a sigh of collective relief: the commissions of inquiry were closed as World Cup number five came home. As the writer Juca Kfouri said, *rouba, mas faz* – 'It's okay to steal if you get things done.' Teixeira's cheek was undiminished, corralling the team to attend a homecoming ceremony in Fortaleza to support his favoured presidential candidate, Ciro Gomes. Yet Lula's claim that Brazil now understood the gap between sporting fantasy and political reality proved true. That October Gomes came in third as Lula, finally, was elected president of Brazil.

II

Juca Kfouri's assessment of Brazilian football – 'I have always said that God put the best players here and the worst bosses to compensate' – was confirmed by the president of the Senate's commission of inquiry into Brazilian football. Senator Álvaro Dias presented the commission's 1,600-page report, saying, 'The Brazilian Football Confederation is truly a den of crime, revealing disorganization, anarchy, incompetence and dishonesty.'[8] It was a fitting summary of the first decade in office of CBF president Ricardo Teixeira, and an accurate predictor of the decade still to come. The governance of Brazilian football was no longer shaped by the armed forces, but it was rotten and the rot was at its most virulent at the top.

Ricardo Teixeira was born to a banking family in Minas Gerais, grew up in Rio, dabbled in law, finance and volleyball, and then struck the mother lode: he married Lucía Havelange, daughter of CBF and then FIFA president João Havelange. Under Havelange's tutelage Teixeira was groomed for a life in football, and in 1989 he was manoeuvred into the presidency of the CBF. In his long years in the post, he came to think of the institution, indeed the Seleção itself, as both his personal property and a public incarnation of his own unquenchable ego. As he said when discussing the CBF's finances, 'I have $75 million in the bank', and looking back to the draw for the World Cup in Germany, 'I didn't want to play the opening match of the 2006 World Cup.'[9]

In keeping with the neo-liberal agenda of the Cardoso years, Teixeira removed the CBF from the public sphere altogether. His decision to stop taking government grants or lottery monies absolved the organization from any external scrutiny or social obligations, and freed it up to pursue more inviting commercial opportunities. In 1996 he signed off a ten-year sponsorship and kit deal between the CBF and Nike. Reputed to be worth $300 million over ten years, its details were kept secret, though a congressional investigation later revealed that Nike had a significant say in the location and timing of Brazil's friendlies. Liberated by this huge injection of cash from any need to engage with domestic football, the CBF went on a spending spree. Between 1997 and 2000 its income quadrupled, directors received 300 per cent pay rises, the money spent on hotels increased five times over, yet the percentage of the budget devoted to football fell. Expenditure on the football lobby, as it was known, was maintained though. The organization took five Rio High Court judges on all-expenses-paid trips to the 1994 World Cup and all were sitting on at least one of the forty cases then lodged against the

CBF in the Brazilian legal system. In Brasília a discreet CBF house was maintained from which favour and money were dispensed to a network of politicians who could be called upon when necessary. There was still change left for the CBF to commit to buying the milk production of Teixeira's own ranch and to rent his string of nightclubs at exorbitant rates.

The CBF, at least, made money. Brazil's football clubs stumbled through the 1990s losing money. Despite raising considerable sums from player transfers to Europe and Asia, clubs were notorious debtors and late payers to their players, the taxman and everyone else. In part this was a product of incompetence and infighting: Flamengo reached a point in 2001 when it had seven coaches' contracts on its books, having sacked six in a year. Not content with a single warring board, a few years earlier the club had managed to have two boards of directors at each other's throats.

The dire situation among the clubs was also a consequence of football's dysfunctional relationship with television. Globo had acquired the domestic monopoly over football on television in 1987 and they held on to it tenaciously. While this ensured a steady supply of money to the clubs, the lack of any serious competitors meant that the rights boom enjoyed in Europe was not replicated in Brazil. Equally importantly, football held a subservient position in Globo's scheduling strategies. *Telenovelas* were, from the late 1980s, the real ratings winners and the source of the most valuable advertising income. To ensure that these programmes occupied prime time the football schedule was determined by Globo, forcing fans to attend inconveniently early or very late kick-offs, with changes often announced at the last moment. In 1999 the third and decisive game of the final of the Brasileiro, between Corinthians and Atlético Mineiro, was scheduled by Globo and the CBF for the Wednesday afternoon before Christmas – a ludicrous time. The mayor of São Paulo actually went to court in an effort to move the start of the game, leaving fans unsure as to when it would be played. At lunchtime on match day an injunction was granted shifting the kick-off to 9 p.m. Those who actually made it to the game saw Corinthians creep to the title through a miserable goalless draw beneath a torrential downpour. Average attendances for the national championship, over 20,000 in 1987, had fallen to 10,000 by the end of the century. Most infuriatingly for the majority of football fans, Globo pandered to a small number of the largest clubs, giving them much greater and much more sympathetic coverage, whatever their form, than smaller teams. TV was like the absentee landlord of a crumbling property: it put a roof over Brazilian football's head but let its assets waste away.

A third reason the clubs were in such financial trouble is that a lot of money just went missing. The Senate's 2001 investigation into football made clear the kinds of things that had become entirely commonplace over the previous decade. Eduardo José Farah, president of the São Paulo Football Federation, was asked to account for very large transfers of money from the organization to his own account. Whatever the payments were for, they weren't showing up in his income tax statements. Samir Jorge Abdul-Hak, president at Santos for five years from 1994, had similar difficulties explaining the disappearance of over 30 million *reais* from the club's accounts on his watch. Edmundo dos Santos Silva, president of Flamengo for two spells between 1999 and 2002, was all at sea tackling the details of the club's transfer dealings. He had somehow forgotten about the existence of an offshore Flamengo bank account in the Cayman Islands, an account that the Bank of Brazil should have been notified of but wasn't. Eurico Miranda, the pugnacious president of Vasco da Gama and a federal deputy for a party of his own invention, simply couldn't understand why the committee would be interested in how he had acquired property in Florida and a fabulous yacht despite drawing no salary at Vasco or indeed anywhere else. Didn't they know how business was meant to be conducted? 'What the court has to understand,' Miranda told them, 'is that the best Brazilians have their own laws.'

Foreign investors, who against all known reason had been persuaded to invest in Brazil's leading clubs, found their business model equally lopsided. Between 1999 and 2001, Parmalat, the Italian dairy company, invested in Palmeiras; ISL, the global sports marketers, put money into Flamengo and Grêmio; the US venture capital firm Hicks, Muse, Tate & Furst bought slices of Corinthians and Cruzeiro; the Bank of America, for its sins, found its way to Vasco da Gama. Within two years all of these deals had been terminated. Parmalat went bust for reasons of their own back in Italy, but the rest were simply taken to the cleaners with no discernible returns. ISL put $13 million into Flamengo's ancient training facilities, but after the money had been spent the Gávea stadium was still infested with cockroaches, its pitch covered in cat shit.

Perhaps the most telling feature of football governance in Brazil was the attitude of leading clubs to relegation. In 1996 Fluminense were relegated but in a classic *virada de mesa* – a turning of the tables in which the rules are suddenly changed in favour of the powerful and to the detriment of the weak – they retained their place in the top flight. For no plausible reason, the top division expanded by four teams. This kind of manoeuvre just delayed the inevitable as the big clubs kept on losing. A two-year points-averaging system was used to calculate relegation places, which allowed them the luxury of having an off season. Nonetheless, in 1999, Botafogo and Internacional still managed to get themselves relegated from the national championship. They were saved by a post-season decision at the CBF to award extra points to the teams for games they had played against São Paulo, who had fielded the ineligible Sandro Hiroshi. Interestingly, of the twelve games that Hiroshi played in, only these two triggered any alteration of the record, and São Paulo themselves were not penalized with the usual five-point deduction for this kind of misdemeanour. The net result of all this intricate maths was that Botafogo and Internacional would stay up and the small provincial team Gama were going to take the drop. Gama and their congressman took the CBF to court, which ruled that Gama should stay up and Botafogo go down. The CBF responded with scorched-earth tactics. They abolished their championship, to which the ruling applied, and handed the operation of the league to a cartel of leading clubs. They in turn created the monstrous 116-team João Havelange Cup, including virtually every professional side in Brazil but for Gama. Gama went back to the Brazilian courts, which ruled that their exclusion from the new tournament was illegal, which then became a 117-team competition. Even by Brazilian standards this was chaos. Some teams played just one game in a month, others had four in a week; a third of games had to be rescheduled, and Fluminense, who had been relegated to the third division at this point, were allowed to miraculously resurface at the top.

The need for some kind of reform of football governance

exercised both the Collor and Cardoso administrations. President Collor appointed Zico as sports minister in 1990 and he fashioned a limited set of reforms designed to bring a minimum of order to the legal status of Brazilian football clubs; to remove the state from direct interference in sporting institutions of all kinds; and to abolish the pernicious player-licensing system. In 1993 the Zico Law made its way through Congress with little rancour, but then it merely tinkered with the system.

A more serious effort was made to address football governance in 1998 when President Cardoso appointed Pelé as Extraordinary Minister of Sport. Pelé's four years in office were spent drawing up a set of regulations that would make two key changes: first, football clubs would be converted into private limited companies, extracting them and their accounts from the utterly opaque legal world of charities and social clubs; and second, the murky world of player contracts would be reformed. Even such a minimalist programme was subject to the furious attentions of the CBF's football lobby, who rewrote key provisions and forced whole sections of the law to be dropped. Despite a restive press and widespread public recognition of the laughable state of affairs into which football governance had descended, this was as far as reform could go. But then the reality of Brazil's post-dictatorship democracy was a polity in which public opinion, if it could be formed and aired, counted for very little. As Eduardo Viana, president of the Rio Football Federation through this era and entirely typical of Brazil's football establishment, said, 'I detest public opinion. The people could all be shot by machine guns for all I care. I'm the son of a factory owner, the elite and I'm a right-winger.'[10] And for the moment they were all still in post.

III

Football, which had continued to be a component of elite and popular cultures through the dictatorship, proved a less attractive subject under democracy. Its adoption by the military and the collusion of much of its establishment with them had, for some artists, tainted the game. More importantly, the game's abandonment of flamboyance and spectacle in pursuit of victory made for more World Cup wins but less material out of which to construct mythologies and heroes. No poet or writer of the calibre of the Andrades or Lins do Rego took on the football *crónica* in the 1990s, nor did the game feature in the new writers' poems and plots. Juca Kfouri, the pre-eminent football journalist of the era, was distinguished by his unrelenting attacks on the probity and competence of the football authorities rather than fantastical accounts of football triumphs. In the visual arts, the pop encounters of the 1960s were not repeated, nor did the generation of minimalist and conceptual artists that followed find football a useful trope out of which to construct their installations and performances. The huge street-art scene that emerged in the 1990s included the odd football reference or image, but these were just a few of the thousands of sources of glyphs, icons and imagery that appeared on the nation's underpasses, bridges and walls. Football was left to naïve or outsider artists, now given more recognition in Brazil's art world, who continued to paint football matches as dreamscapes and high colour cartoons.

Economics also played its part. The harsh conditions of the era squeezed the market for most books, films and music. The Brazilian film industry was, perhaps, the sector most harshly affected by these economic circumstances. The withdrawal of federal subsidies and competition from Hollywood reduced its output in the early 1990s to a small core of local comedy and domestic pornography. Certainly there were no football films of note. In fact until the very late 1990s there were no football films at all. Only towards the end of the decade did the industry begin to revive. Among its successes were two football movies, both released in 1998. They stood out as popular and accomplished pieces of film-making but also as weathervanes of Brazil's changing attitudes to football.

Boleiros – Era Uma Vez o Futebol ('Football, Once upon a Time'), directed by Ugo Giorgetti, was set in a bar in São Paulo. A group of friends, ex-players and coaches as well as fans, reminisce about football times past, their stories told in flashback: a referee who took bribes to fix a match and has to get a penalty retaken three times to make it happen; a short-sighted player of the past forced to sell his glasses to pay his debts; an injured player who is relentlessly pursued by fans who want him to get better – or else; a star striker who escapes from his team's training camp to attend a romantic tryst. The tone is gentle, humorous and humane. Unquestionably the film has a nostalgic and melancholy quality, but not for a golden age that didn't exist or is known only through myth. These are not the stories and settings of exceptional football, but of the quotidian game; its characters are neither demons nor angels, but complex and flawed people. Their stories do not speak to great moments of nation-making but to the everyday grind of working life in an industry that enriched so few of its participants.

That everyday grind was the central concern of Arthur Fontes and João Moreira Salles's three-part film *Futebol*. In its open-eyed look at the realities of life as a professional football player, it reached back to the Cinema Novo films of the early 1960s like *Subterrâneos do Futebol* and *Garrincha: Alegria do Povo*. However, a quarter of a century later there had been a huge growth in Brazil's football industry, with nationwide networks of scouts, agents and middlemen, a phenomenon of such a scale that it required something more ambitious and wide-ranging than the films of the 1960s. *Futebol* rises to the challenge, covering the whole trajectory of a player's career: from hopeful youngsters trying to break in, via new professionals making their way, to the retirees of an earlier generation struggling to survive. Part one begins with 1,500 boys showing up at Flamengo for its annual open trial, many travelling across the country to attend, families borrowing money for the coach fare. The film makes clear that in an era of declining living standards for the poor, football remains an absolutely central escape route for individuals and their extended families. The odds of success, though fantastically long, look better than in the lower reaches of the labour market and the lottery. A pair of teenagers from inland Goiás spend the last of their savings to go to Rio. Here they end up living with an agent who scans the beach with binoculars from the window of his cramped flat in Copacabana. He schemes on the phone to sell them to Grêmio, a deal which turns out, when they make the long journey south, to be a mirage. Part two focuses on two players – Lúcio and Iraldo – from similar backgrounds who have made it into Flamengo's squad. Both struggle with the huge emotional and psychological pressures of the life, pressures for which they are almost entirely unequipped. Part three is a brilliant profile of Paulo César Caju, a great star of the late 1960s and early 1970s, remembered for his exquisite playful football, his flamboyant public demeanour and the wildest wardrobe in the country. The late 1990s finds him, bald but raff-ish, making a living from his network of high-end private football games and society parties. This was Brazilian football without much joy and precious little magic. There were dreams aplenty but they were dreams of survival rather than flights of fancy.

Boleiros announced the turn from magic and mythology to a more sober reckoning with Brazil's fabulous football past. *Futebol* took a long hard look at dreams, and found them increasingly quantified by the rule of money. Nostalgia and the cash nexus will get you so far, but for some this was thin emotional and spiritual gruel to help explain their engagement with football. Religion, long a component of the Brazilian game, was the most important cultural response to this secular vacuum. Prior to the 1980s Catholicism mainly appeared in Brazilian football as a form of popular religiosity: crossing oneself before running on the field, a goalkeeper uttering a blessing as he tapped the crossbar, a striker kneeling after scoring or pointing to the sky. Many clubs built chapels within the confines of their grounds. Vasco's is no more than thirty metres from the pitch and houses holy soil from the grounds of the three great Portuguese clubs: Porto, Sporting and Benfica. The national shrine of Our Lady of Aparecida has side rooms storing the innumerable football shirts and other memora-bilia that are taken there as offerings. African religious and belief systems, both the rural syncretic *candomblé* and its urbanized magical form *macumba*, have been present in Brazilian football since the 1930s when the first reports of fans bringing charms to the stadium appear. It was certainly common currency in Rio that Vasco da Gama's long wait for a championship through the 1940s was a consequence of a curse laid on them by Arubinha, a player with a small team called Andrari who had been humiliated 12–0 by Vasco in 1937.

While both Catholic and African traditions persisted in Brazilian football, the spiritual landscape of the game underwent the same massive shift as the rest of Brazilian society. From being an almost totally Catholic society, Brazil's evangelical Protestants now make up nearly a quarter of the population. Although they had a small presence in Brazil from before the First World War and started to grow in the 1950s, their explosive growth began in the late 1970s and early 1980s. Traditional evangelical practice had demanded the strictest of lifestyles: no alcohol, no non-religious music, no TV and no sex before marriage. Even in this hairshirt version it was attractive to the lost and hungry souls of the urban peripheries of Brazil who were prey to crime and drugs and misery. It also offered football players a framework within which they could survive the rigours and temptations of professional life. This was the impetus behind the creation of *Atletas de Cristo*, Athletes for Christ, by evangelical pastor and 'God's goalkeeper' João Leite of Atlético Mineiro. Using a small group, even cellular structure, key proselytizing individuals spread the word through their squads via prayer groups and Bible-reading sessions. They preached a model of Protestantism that encouraged players to acquire an individual relationship with God, to take control of their lives, monitor their behaviour and battle their devils – a theology particularly suited to the emotional demands of professional football with all its uncertainties, rivalries and fluctuations of form. Under the leadership of ex-Formula 1 driver Alex Dias Ribeiro, the organization recruited across all sports, but especially football, and by the late 1990s it had a membership of 7,000. There were enough former members of the Seleção for them to play as an *Atletas de Cristo* exhibition team. At the 1994 World Cup alone there were six members: Jorginho, Taffarel, Paulo Sérgio, Müller, Zinho and Mazinho. Ribeiro served as chaplain to that World Cup squad and the next two.

Some traditional evangelicals continued to view football and indeed all sports with suspicion, referring to the ball as the devil's egg. But the influence of this kind of Protestantism was swept away by the arrival of the theology of prosperity in the 1970s. The many neo-Pentecostalist churches founded in this era preached a gospel that drew on the language of self-help and positive thinking, and asked congregations to channel their religious energies into making money and enjoying their bounty. This volte-face opened up the churches to a whole new constituency and provided the revenue streams for the remarkable profits they would make and assets they would accrue. Austerity and poverty were out; paying, consuming and spending were in. Indeed in a bizarre twist on Calvinism, consumption became the outward sign of one's piety.

Football players have been part of this evangelical constituency. In the last decade hundreds more Brazilian footballers have become evangelical Christians, particularly in the huge diaspora of players working overseas for whom the churches are a powerful connection to home in otherwise very alien environments. Prominent evangelicals playing for the national side over the last fifteen years have included Lúcio, Edu, Edmílson and Kaká. Jorginho, while playing for Bayer Leverkusen, worked as a pastor and opened a church. The donations have been rolling in. Estevam and Sônia Hernandes, founders of the Reborn in Christ Church, which counted Kaká as one of its members, were reputedly worth over $50 million and the Brazilian midfielder apparently made donations of 2 million *reais* from Milan – though he left it in 2010 after allegations of the leadership's mishandling of its finances. The Seleção prayed standing in a circle at the 1994 World Cup; in 2002 they were kneeling, though Cafu, the captain, dedicated his victory to his family and the poor, not to Jesus. After winning the 2009 Confederations Cup in South Africa captain Lúcio and five other players celebrated wearing 'I belong to Jesus' T-shirts.

In the 1990s these player narratives of miraculous but perilous social mobility, personal piety and spiritual transformation, while present in the mainstream coverage of football, were really mere subplots. Poets, novelists and artists may have abandoned football, but television and the popular press remained true. The increasing wages for the playing and managerial elite and their often erratic behaviour combined with the aesthetics of Brazil's media conglomerates to turn many players' private lives into their own personal *telenovelas*: scandal, rivalry, paternity suits and conspicuous consumption were at the heart of football's mediascape. Modern celebrity culture, with its intrusive photographers, relentless hype and cynical invention, had arrived.

Among the cast of characters that football offered Brazil none was more extraordinary than Edmundo. Born in 1971, he made his debut with Vasco da Gama in 1992 and with the national team later that year. Though there were fallow periods, especially when he played in Italy, he consistently scored a lot of goals. For this, he was much forgiven – and there was much to forgive. Over the eighteen years of his career he changed club seventeen times, breaking up and getting back together with Vasco five times. He fell out, often violently, with teammates, opponents, officials, coaches, journalists, fans and administrators. Soon nicknamed 'the Animal', he received five red cards in his first full season and was famously attacked by three Corinthians players he had taunted, sparking a mass brawl. After smashing a camera at a Copa Libertadores game he was put under house arrest in Ecuador. In 1997, his record goalscoring season with Vasco as champions, he received seven red cards. In 1995 he was accused of drink-driving in a car crash in Rio in which three other people were killed. Edmundo spent much of the next ten years eluding trial and sentencing, appealing decisions, and after just a few nights of actual incarceration, exhausting the legal system entirely. His career, alongside a lot of fabulous goals, was filled with splenetic anger, ill-disciplined emotions, immaturity and violence, all of which were covered in microscopic detail in the press – as on the occasion he was supposed to have got an ape drunk at his son's birthday party.

In the stories the futebol nation told itself most often we do not find the struggles of the poor or the pious professional, but the tales of the rich and famous who enjoyed not only their wealth but their immunity too.

IV

The *torcidas organizadas* that had first emerged in Rio and São Paulo in the late 1960s and 1970s as breakaway youth groups from the more conservative *charangas* of the 1950s had the stands to themselves in the 1980s. In 1997 Juventude from Rio Grande do Sul played Portuguesa of São Paulo in the quarter-finals of the national championships – fifty-five people paid on the door. Crowds as laughably small as this were not uncommon in Brazil. In a poll in *Lance!* – a leading football daily – three-quarters of their readers said violence was keeping them away from the game. Average attendances at matches in the Brasileiro were half that of their peak in the early 1980s.

For the very grandest occasions Brazilian football could still summon huge crowds. The state championship of Bahia would regularly overfill the 80,000-plus capacity of the Fonte Nova in Salvador. As late as 1992 Flamengo could draw 120,000 to the Maracanã. But people went at their peril. The policing of football was exemplified by the special Rio Football Units, established in 1991. As well as providing escorts for match officials, these highly militarized and armed units were responsible for dealing with stadium disorder mainly by using higher levels of violence than the organized fans. Clubs and their officials had long abandoned any attempt to steward or control the *torcidas*.

While the rest of the crowd often stayed away, the *torcidas* remained in place and were responsible for maintaining the carnivalesque dimension of the game, organizing flags, fireworks and chanting. Over the next two decades they spread right across the country, to every professional club. Their leaders established informal working relationships with club directors and boards, getting access to free tickets and subsidized transport, and in places shaded into the organized crime and gang culture of the urban peripheries. Always more oppositional in style than their predecessors, the new *torcidas* of the 1980s ended up at war with each other and the police in a nationwide wave of disorder and violence. In this regard they only slightly lagged behind the wave of violence against people of and property crimes that engulfed Brazil in the early 1980s. Under the most extreme conditions of hyperinflation and hunger, crime rates doubled between 1980 and 1985, and continued to climb thereafter. In São Paulo the rate of homicides tripled between 1980 and 1996, a collective psychological brutalizing to add to the still unresolved wounds of the dictatorship. Under such conditions, the intense protective solidarity and communality of the *torcidas* was easily converted into rage and violence.

Brazilian football had seen deaths before of course. Stadium crushes and panics at Fortaleza in 1971, and Teresina in 1973, had resulted in a dozen deaths and many injuries. Lima Barreto, back in the 1920s, had recorded the first gunfire in the stands, but 1988 saw the first football murder. Cléo Dantas, the president of the Palmeiras *torcida* Mancha Verde, was shot dead in front of their clubhouse, in a killing widely attributed to Corinthians fans. In 1992 São Paulo fans threw a home-made bomb into the Corinthians crowd at a cup match between their youth sides, killing a thirteen-year-old boy. In 1993 a Palmeiras supporter shot a sixteen-year-old São Paulo fan in the stands of the Morumbi.

If the crowd didn't get you, the stadium might. By the 1990s Brazil's football infrastructure was creaking. Twenty years of economic stagnation and neglect had prematurely aged the raw concrete bowls of the military era. The Maracanã, approaching half a century old, was crumbling. Some of the concourse's concrete walls were stained and worn from serving as open-air urinals. During a Flamengo–Botafogo game in 1992 a fence on the upper tier gave way before a huge crowd. Fifty people, together with metal railings and concrete debris, plunged into the stands below. Three died of their injuries and many were hospitalized.

Behaviour on the pitch was little better. The 1993 season opened with a red card per game. During their match with Santos, Grêmio players and officials attacked a referee when he awarded a penalty against them. In their furious Supercopa match with

Peñarol in Porto Alegre, four players from each team were sent off and the match finished with the home side fighting the police on the pitch. These were just the most explosive moments of a football culture where both feigning injury and violent tackling were on the rise, and where ballboys were encouraged, when required, to waste time and distract opponents. Encroachment on free kicks by the defending side was so out of control that the São Paulo State Federation introduced disappearing paint sprays for referees to mark the ten-yard line: the paint burnt a hole in the turf. In 1994 the carnage spread to smaller cities. A Corinthians fan was trampled during a brawl in the stands in Campinas and died in hospital eight days later. In São Caetano a young São Paulo supporter was chased through the streets by a gang of Corinthians fans demanding his club shirt. He died, hit by a train, as he fled across a railway line. Back in São Paulo later in the year a Palmeiras fan died after being struck on the head while running away from a post-game fight with Corinthians supporters; a Corinthians fan was then shot in the back of the head by a Palmeiras fan. The disorder reached a new peak in 1995 at what became known as 'The Battle of the Pacaembu'. Hundreds of *torcidas* from São Paulo and Palmeiras invaded the pitch at the end of a youth team game. Live on television, they fought wildly with sticks and iron bars, leaving one dead and over 100 injured. Both clubs' *torcidas organizadas* were closed down by the São Paulo police, only for them to mutate into samba schools or re-form under new names – Palmeiras's Mancha Verde becoming Mancha Alvi Verde in 1997.

The risks involved in trying to exclude the *torcidas* were made clear in 1999 when Palmeiras won the Copa Libertadores at home, beating Deportivo Cali on penalties. Many members of the reformed Mancha Verde, along with other ticketless fans, gathered outside the stadium and tried to storm the turnstiles during the match. Scuffling and fighting between police and *torcidas* turned into a full-scale battle when they were joined by the delirious Palmeiras crowd leaving the stadium. Riot police were called in and volleys of tear gas were fired ahead of massed baton-and-shield charges down Avenida Paulista, the corridor of skyscrapers at the heart of the city's business district. The Palmeiras *torcidas* tore up the paving stones and erected impromptu barricades.

Not content with fighting each other and the police, the *torcidas* began to attack their own players. In 1997 the Corinthians team bus was returning to São Paulo after being beaten by Santos 1–0. Once their police escort had departed the squad found itself chased and harassed by cars with blacked-out windows, a wayward lorry and finally another coach that forced them to pull up on the road. This coach was packed with *torcidas* from *Gaviões da Fiel* ('The Hawks of the Faithful') who proceeded to stone the bus, then storm it, physically and verbally abusing the players.

At the turn of the century the numbers of dead and injured in Brazilian football continued to rise with another eight killings in the next four years. The prevalence of guns and, it seemed, the increased willingness to use them saw more football-related shootings in São Paulo. A fan in Porto Alegre was killed when the home-made bomb he had brought to the stadium exploded in his hands. Thus by the end of the twentieth century the atmosphere inside Brazil's dilapidated and increasingly empty football stadiums, the heart of the futebol nation, was increasingly determined by the aggression and violence of the *torcidas* and the police.

At least one of Brazil's World Cup victories should perhaps

be the defining moment of this era. But a strong case can also be made for the final of the Campeonato Brasileiro in late 2000. Eurico Miranda's Vasco da Gama played São Caetano, a small team from the industrial heartlands of São Paulo. The first leg finished 1–1 in São Paulo. The deciding game would be played at Vasco. In a typical act of spite the tickets promised to São Caetano were all sold to home fans, and as was often the case, the club had sold 5,000 tickets more than there were safe places in the stadium. After about twenty minutes, the game was brought to a halt by the referee who had noticed a huge crush of people behind one goal. A twisted mass of bodies and wire fencing had tumbled on to the field; 168 people were injured, two very seriously. A dozen ambulances came on to the pitch, a helicopter landed beside them to take the most critical casualties to hospital and the military police surrounded the players on the touchline. Miranda, incandescent, informed the cameras, 'Nothing serious happened. But something could if the game doesn't continue. I want these fucking ambulances out of here!'[11] São Caetano's president thought it common sense to abandon the match. An hour after he had stopped the match the referee announced it was all over. The governor of Rio state, Anthony Garotinho, watching the fiasco on television, had called in to insist that the game be abandoned. A little later, Miranda and the Vasco players reappeared on the pitch, grabbed the national trophy that was still sitting on a table by the halfway line, and took a lap of dishonour. The following day *Lance!*'s front-page editorial was genuinely shocked: 'Eurico Miranda ... has always been praised for putting his club's interests above everything else. No one imagined that he was capable of taking this obsession to the limit of not respecting human lives.'[12] Now Brazil didn't have to imagine – he did, and he would get away with it. Vasco won the replay and Miranda won the next election as Vasco's president: *rouba, mas faz*. In a society where the rule of law was weak, where elites were so rarely called to account, and where winning and efficiency had become the sole measures of progress, this too was the price of pragmatism.

7

Futebol Nation Redux: The Game in Lula's Brazil, 2002–2013

Be careful what you wish for: Brazil wins the right to stage the 2014 World Cup. Left to right: Dunga, Lula, Romario, Blatter.

I am among those who think that God has crooked hand-
writing. I think that if we could not win in 2010, it is because
God knows that we cannot fail in 2014.

Lula

I

In 2002 Luiz Inácio Lula da Silva, or Lula as he is known, and his
Workers' Party won the Brazilian presidency at the fourth attempt,
Brazil's first unambiguously social democratic and popular government. This, in itself, was a remarkable achievement, but Lula
was also the first president to truly hail from Brazil's lower classes
and to establish a deep emotional and political link with them
while in office. As he put it in a speech in São Luis, 'I want to
know if the people are in the shit and I want to take the people
out of the shit in which they are.' It was an earthiness that most
of Brazil, his most implacable enemies apart, came to find endear-
ing. His charm, his cunning and his strategic capacity for
compromise were essential elements of his government's success.
He went on to win a second term, leaving office at the end of
2010 with higher approval ratings than when he arrived, and

handed on the presidency, in effect, to his chosen successor, Dilma Rousseff.

Football was one strand of Lula's popular persona and vocabulary. Certainly his relationship with football was far closer to that of the average Brazilian football fan than any of his predecessors' had been. He was unambiguously a supporter of Corinthians, often commenting on the team and its performances, and helping ensure that the club would receive a new stadium in time for the 2014 World Cup. The social kickabouts he held at the presidential palace were well attended and keenly contested, as evidenced by the finance minister Antonio Palocci entering Congress on crutches after a crunching game between the president's team and the Ministry of Fisheries. When speaking to the Seleção by video link before the 2006 World Cup, he asked whether Ronaldo was still fat. Innumerable state occasions and audiences involved the exchange of football shirts with diplomats and meetings with players and coaches; the press had fun with the curse of Lula that seemed to follow so many of these encounters, as teams tumbled out of cup tournaments or their form collapsed. His language was peppered with football metaphors: justifying a cabinet reshuffle he argued, 'Pelé was the best player in the world and he was replaced.'

Cordiality and an easy intimacy with the Brazilian people and the game of football would only get one so far. Lula's success rested on the economic, social and political changes his governments helped bring about. The state of the Brazilian economy was perhaps the most significant of these. While never achieving the relentlessly high growth rates of the Far East or China, Brazil experienced a decade of unbroken growth and historically low levels of inflation which delivered across-the-board increases in wages and living standards. This was driven by the breakneck growth of China and the widespread industrialization of the global South which together created a huge demand for Brazilian agricultural products like soya beans and sugar. Lower interest rates and access to consumer credit saw the newly enriched working and lower-middle classes splash out on white goods and cars, in turn fuelling growth in Brazil's manufacturing centres.

Emboldened by Brazil's increasing importance in the global economy, Lula's government pursued a more independent foreign policy than any previous administration. The United States, engrossed in its involvement in the Middle East and Afghanistan, was a minimal presence in the politics of the region, leaving space for Brazil to develop new relationships and commercial alliances with China, India, Cuba and the rest of Latin America. Alongside India, Japan and Germany, Brazil was arguing for a permanent seat on the UN Security Council. And alongside China, India and Russia, it was part of the BRIC bloc, a notion coined by the investment banking firm Goldman Sachs but made political reality when the four states began to arrange their own summits.

At home, social policy was in many ways constrained by the regime's conservative approach to macroeconomics. Public health care and education, in particular, remained woefully underfunded. But in one area, Lula brought decisive change: consolidating a whole series of poverty- and hunger-reduction programmes into the *Bolsa Família* ('Family Allowance') and then massively extending it across the country. Thus the government presided over the biggest fall in hunger and absolute poverty that the country had ever seen. This was of enormous symbolic importance, as it was one of the only occasions in which the Brazilian state had truly attended to the needs of its most vulnerable citizens, but its practical political import was immense too. While the poor of Brazil had often voted in the past for conservative parties, afraid that the left would make inflation worse and destroy what little remaining purchasing power they had, the combination of Lula's macroeconomic conservatism, the *Bolsa Família* and big increases in the minimum wage, all cemented by Lula's charisma, saw them shift their votes overwhelmingly to the PT. Prior to this the PT had tried to rule without a majority in Congress, where the fragmented party system made it hard to create a working government coalition. Key figures in the leadership of the PT, from which Lula was able to distance himself, decided to remedy the problem by piecing together an ad hoc coalition in Congress from the PT and the 'votes for sale' caucus. Indeed the whole matter was regularized through various safe houses in Brasília, where congressmen would receive, in cash, the *mensalão* – the big monthly pay-off. The *mensalão* scandal came to public attention in 2007 and dragged on throughout the rest of Lula's time in office. What small energies had been devoted to rooting out the country's systemic forms of corruption and unaccountable zones of power were consistently undermined by the government's own disgrace.

If football had helped define Lula's style of governance and public image, he did not enter office measuring the state of the nation by the metrics of the Seleção. On the contrary, he came to power on the promise to measure the progress of the nation by how many Brazilians ate three square meals a day, and how many participated in the huge changes required: 'Brazil has rediscovered itself, and this rediscovery is being expressed in its people's enthusiasm and their desire to mobilize to face the huge problems that lie ahead of us.' But the disenchantment with Brazilian football that Lula had announced back in 1994, when he faced an election in the wake of Brazil's fourth World Cup victory, did not survive his term in office. By the end of his second term, as he opened a new stadium for the 2014 World Cup, the fate of the nation had passed to the Seleção and the Lord. Yet how else could Brazil mark and celebrate the Lula years? It had been a period of tremendous economic growth, rising international prestige and progressive social change. From the moment in 2007 that Brazil acquired the hosting rights to the 2014 World Cup it was almost inevitable that the staging and winning of the tournament would, once again, be defined as the conclusive proof of Brazil's transformation and modernity.

As in 1950, this was a double-edged sword, for the futebol nation displayed both the successes of the era and its limits. The commodity-export model of growth was paralleled in Brazilian football. During the global boom in demand for football players Brazil proved to be the leading exporter. In fact, this became the key revenue stream for many Brazilian football clubs, but it didn't bring the crowds back to the stands. The *Bolsa Família* may have banished hunger from Brazil but it has yet to blunt the keen edge of poverty that continues to spur such an enormous pool of footballing talent. Brazil's more adventurous and assertive foreign policy, which began by using the Seleção as an instrument of soft power, mutated into the altogether grander strategy of using sporting mega-events to the same end. The binge of infrastructural spending that followed became emblematic of all the most problematic elements of Brazil's political economy: corruption, clientelism, inequality and injustices. The Lula government's policies on racism and gender discrimination found echoes in the world of football where both remained endemic, but for the first time some small advances could be registered. Similarly, small steps were taken in the direction of transparency and openness, and the detection and prosecution of corruption, but as in other areas of political life the Lula government's direct interventions in the game were often blunted by the resistance of entrenched powers. Nowhere were the limits of the Lula years more starkly demonstrated than in the problem of football violence, itself a mere echo of an enduringly violent society.

II

In the last year of the Cardoso government, following the congressional investigations into football governance, the football lobby and the CBF were *personae non gratae* at the presidential palace. Away from their baleful influence, the sports ministry laboured to craft reforming legislation that would force clubs to take the interests of their fans, or rather their customers, more seriously. Lula and his sports minister, Agnelo Queiroz, inherited the legislation that would become the Supporters' Charter and pushed it through Congress against the wishes of the football lobby. In 2003, a week after the charter was signed into law, the flag of revolt was raised by the presidents of eight clubs, three state federations and the president of the CBF, Ricardo Teixeira, who in an act of unabashed blackmail suspended the national championship, claiming that their stadiums did not match up to the new requirements. The idea of the football establishment suddenly posing as the guardians of the public interest was so laughable that after virulent nationwide criticism by President Lula and the press they backed off.

Yet, at the same time, the government reopened personal

relationships with the CBF. In its early months in office Lula's administration had persuaded many clubs to back its domestic policy programmes by wearing government-approved shirts – particularly in support of the *Fome Zero* ('Zero Hunger') campaign that was a precursor to the *Bolsa Família*. However, to make a really big impact at home and abroad the government needed access to the Seleção, and that access lay with the CBF. The CBF in turn needed access to the corridors of power in Brasília, made more urgent by the up-and-coming prospect of a bid to host the 2014 World Cup. A discreet dinner between Queiroz and João Havelange smoothed the way for a rapprochement, though in classic Brazilian style Lula and Teixeira never held an official audience, preferring Friday afternoon informal meetings over glasses of whisky.

In early 2003 the Seleção played a friendly against China in shirts bearing the words *Fome Zero* and then against Ireland later in the year. The relationship between the government and the CBF was close enough that by the following year, sports minister Queiroz was able to grandstand with the team after they had won the Copa América 2004, while on visits to poorer nations the Brazilian squad handed out sports equipment manufactured as part of a rehabilitation programme in Brazilian prisons. Later the team would play in Haiti, where the Brazilian armed forces comprised the majority of the UN peacekeeping mission.

With solid government support Brazil won the right to host the 2014 World Cup. Ricardo Teixeira may have been prepared to concede some space on the Seleção's shirts and on its timetable to the government but he certainly didn't intend to concede any power. Teixeira formed an organizing committee for the World Cup without a single government representative, elected or unelected. By contrast, the organizing committees for the three previous World Cups, in South Korea and Japan, Germany and South Africa, had all had serious representation from national and local government. Instead Teixeira appointed himself as the chair, his daughter Joana Havelange to the number two spot, and added his lawyer, his press secretary, his personal secretary and factotum, and the man who had advised him during the 2001 congressional investigation into football. He then garlanded the team with Carlos Langoni, a right-wing economist who had served as president of the Bank of Brazil in the last days of the military dictatorship. The football paper *Lance!* commissioned a poll asking the Brazilian public how they felt about this: one-third wanted a tripartite organizing committee with representation from civil society as well as elected politicians on the board but the vast majority didn't care. The political disengagement and apathy of the majority have often been the elite's most powerful resource.[1]

The 2003 Supporters' Charter had many components, but perhaps the most important was to give football fans the same legal status and rights as any other kind of consumer. While the most basic forms of consumer protection had been established in Brazilian law in 1990, they had hitherto not applied to people who bought match tickets. This in itself was an advance, as was the insistence that all football stadiums must be equipped with an adequate number of functioning toilets for both genders, as well as drinking fountains and medical care – none of which had been the norm. More substantially, the law made the clubs themselves responsible for the health and safety of the fans, an obligation that had not occurred to most of them before. A football ombudsman was established to whom fans could take their grievances. As part of the quid pro quo for having to take on these responsibilities, and acknowledging the gigantic levels of unpaid debts that the football clubs owed to the Brazilian tax office, in 2007 Lula's government introduced a new football-based lottery, Timemania. With the backing of the clubs, whose results formed the basis of the competition, Timemania would deliver 22 per cent of its profits to them, which were in turn earmarked for the repayment of their government debts. In addition, participation required clubs to open their books to a level of scrutiny that neither the Zico nor Pelé laws had ever managed.

Lula's Brazil proved better at passing reforming legislation than implementing it. In 2013, looking back on ten years of the Supporters' Charter, *Lance!* concluded that there had been real improvement for Brazilian football fans, but many elements of the original charter remained unrealized. Whether it was a consequence of political apathy or the widespread disregard in which judicial procedures were held, the football ombudsman was barely used over the ten years of its existence. Supporters were still treated with contempt by some clubs, especially away fans who would continue to be deliberately delayed or denied entrance to grounds. Above all, the insistence of the charter that the relevant authorities draw up a plan of action covering security and safety for every game was simply not put into action, with the consequence that many games were blighted by chaotic logistics. The police continued to treat football more as an exercise in controlling public disorder than securing the safety of citizens in public spaces. Worse, what the charter and the other reforms of the Lula years did not do was halt the violence associated with Brazilian football, inside and outside the stadiums. Indeed the problem became so serious that in 2010 the government updated and amended the charter with a whole series of highly draconian measures designed to crack down on the *torcidas organizadas*.

The record of reform, in the end, was mixed. The Seleção had been mobilized in pursuit of progressive social policy but the centres of football power remained totally unaccountable. The Supporters' Charter sought to empower fans, but it could not corral the police or the clubs. The political coda to the Lula years came in 2011 under his successor, Dilma Rousseff. In the first twelve months of her administration four cabinet ministers were lost to accusations of corruption and embezzlement. Late in 2011, Orlando Silva, the communist sports minister, made it five. *Veja* magazine published a series of allegations, accusing him of embezzling money from the operation of the government programme *Segundo Tempo* ('Second Half'), which supported participation in sport for underprivileged children. A police officer, João Dias Ferreira, who ran a small youth sports project, reported having to pay back, in cash, a good chunk of his organization's grant from *Segundo Tempo*. The method was a personal delivery to Silva in the garage underneath the Ministry of Sport and the money was split between his own pocket and the electoral funds of the PCB. Silva denied the claims but quit his post.

III

In the first decade of the twenty-first century Brazil became the leading supplier of playing talent to the global football economy – an export drive that rested on a nationwide network of scouting, recruiting and training that was at best exploitative and at worst murderous. While transfers kept many football clubs afloat, this diminished the appeal of domestic football, which now faced global competition for its TV audience as well as its players. After many years of effective isolation, Brazilian television stations, especially the cable challengers to Globo like ESPN, began to show a lot more foreign football: by 2006 there were over 400 games shown a year and at weekends a dozen from the biggest leagues in Europe. The European Champions League, in which so many of Brazil's best players participated, was immensely popular. For the first time one could see on the streets of the country, alongside local strips, the colours of teams from the English Premier League and Spain's La Liga.

The football-wage differentials between Brazil and Europe, and increasingly between Brazil and the richer parts of Asia, had been driving an exodus of players since the late 1980s. As recently as 2010, 60 per cent of Brazilian professional football players earned the minimum wage. Even those that were being paid a more substantial salary didn't always see it – throughout this period Brazilian clubs were notoriously late payers, and sometimes non-payers, of wages. The Bosman ruling in European football, the classification of all European Union players as home players and the arrival of transcontinental scouting networks all contributed to the creation of a large and liquid global labour market. Official data includes only players over the age of sixteen – there is considerable evidence of players being bought and sold much younger than that – but even so the figures are huge. In the late 1990s annual player exports were running at about 200 a year with a significant number returning. The CBF's figures show that around 800 players made the trip abroad in 2005 with a net exodus of over 500 players. In 2008, the peak year for football exports before the European economic crisis put the brake on the football boom, just under 1,200 players were exported from Brazil with a net loss of over 700. According to the Bank of Brazil, this brought in nearly a quarter of a billion dollars to the sellers.

The geography of this exodus was complex and multilayered. The majority of players headed for Europe, but there were also significant numbers in Asia, especially South Korea and Japan, and in Latin America. Within Europe, the largest contingent by far, over 100 players a season, were going to Portugal. While some settled there, for many it was a waystation, either upwards into the top European leagues or downwards into the small leagues of Cyprus, Azerbaijan and Moldova, whose wages, though lower, were still far higher than could be expected at home. In fact Brazilians were tempted to the very furthest reaches of the football world, with players going to Qatar, Vietnam, the Faroe Islands and Australia.

The very best Brazilian players were concentrated in the top five leagues in Europe and, within those leagues, at the top clubs. On a regular basis there were more Brazilians playing in European Champions League squads than there were any nationalities other than Italians and most of them were playing for the Italian clubs. Almost none of them stayed and settled in Europe – Leonardo, who became a director at Milan, was a rare exception. However, some Brazilians took up foreign citizenship to allow them to play for other national teams. Marco became Mehmet Aurélio and played for Turkey, Alex and Eduardo became Japanese and Croatian respectively, Pepe and Deco became Portuguese. Roger Guerreiro was a Pole, Egmar Gonçalves was Singaporean, Emerson a Qatari and Lúcio Wagner a Bulgarian.

In the 1980s and 1990s the complex web of transfers was arranged by clubs and agents, but in the twenty-first century a number of outsiders came into the market. Traffic began as a small company in the 1980s selling advertising space in Brazilian football stadiums. In the 1990s it progressed to buying and selling media rights and offering sports marketing services. In the 2000s it began buying and selling players with a mix of its own money and that of outside investors. As the company's president put it, 'Instead of investing in the stock market or real estate these people are investing in buying the economic rights to football players.'[2] What that meant in practice was that the company bought up the contracts of Brazilian players they were interested in and then lent them to clubs who would both pay their salary and showcase them to the world. Palmeiras were Traffic's main partners, with up to twelve of the company's players in the squad at any one time. In the event that the players were sold on, Traffic and its investors received the lion's share of the fee. FIFA banned third-party ownership of players in 2007 but Traffic and the other companies got round this by creating or buying their own clubs – like Desportivo Brasil and Ituano – and signing their players to them. This made their subsequent loan periods and sales a notional club-to-club deal. It also meant that an increasing number of teams playing in the lower divisions and in the state championships were in effect ghost clubs, without fans or any intention of winning championships, but hugely effective shop windows. Traffic was not alone. Grupo Sonda, one of Brazil's largest supermarket chains, created its own football investment department, spending up to $10 million a year and in the late 2000s delivering rates of return of up to 150 per cent.

While Traffic and Sonda have been pioneering a relatively high-investment, high-profit model of player development and commodification, some of Brazil's football clubs have been pursuing an alternative sweatshop model. The many reports of poor conditions in the training camps established by clubs all over the country were confirmed in 2012 by the death of fourteen-year-old Wendel Venâncio da Silva while on a five-day trial at Vasco da Gama's Itaguai youth training centre. The investigation that followed revealed that boys were being kept in dangerously insanitary conditions in buildings with broken toilets and leaking roofs. Players who lived outside of the state were only covered for one journey home a year and had to use their own phones exclusively. Those who wanted water found it rationed. Those who wanted medical treatment had to pay for it, if in fact there were any medical staff around. On the day Venâncio collapsed there were none present. The judge, who ordered the closure of the facility, described the conditions which the children were exposed to as slave-like.[3] With depressing familiarity, the CBF's response to the scandal, and the outstanding allegations against Flamengo, Fluminense and Botafogo, was to remain completely silent.

Given the long-term weakness of the Brazilian football economy as well as the contemporary pressures the clubs were under, it was clear that their finances were in a parlous state, but so opaque and arcane were the accounting practices of the game that no one knew quite how bad they were. This changed in 2007 with the arrival of the Timemania lottery and its insistence on the publication of transparent accounts by participating clubs. The new data showed that in terms of revenues, and even attendances, Brazilian football was in a reasonably healthy state; certainly revenues were increasing and average gates had crept upwards from their nadir at the turn of the century. But these signs of growth needed to be set against the fact that all of the leading clubs were mired in huge accumulated debts and remained, for the most part, loss-making institutions. In 2007 eleven out of the fifteen top clubs lost money, the largest of which were losses of €22.7 million (£18m) at Flamengo and €53 million (£42.5m) at Fluminense. The following year twelve out of fifteen were in the red.

Brazilian football clubs were locked into an impossible business model. Up to a third of their income came from profits from player sales. This money kept sides afloat, but led to the diminishing quality of football on offer. Match-day sales were bringing in only 10 per cent of the clubs' income, and they were reluctant to deal with the problems of crumbling stadiums, pervasive violence and disastrous scheduling. For the first they lacked money or access to credit; the second would require them to take on both the police and their own *torcidas*, neither of which they wished to do; the third would have required them to take on Globo. Despite the emergence of new stations and serious competitors, like the evangelical network TV Record, and the efforts of the clubs to extricate themselves from the company's clutches, Globo retained a monopoly over televised Brazilian football. The channel's trump card was that many of the clubs were in debt to them, as advance TV payments covered their immediate cash-flow problems. In such a compromised situation they were unlikely to start voting for an alternative.

One way in which the clubs have tried to respond to their predicament is to make better use of returnees, devising innovative sponsorship packages to cover the cost of homesick but expensive players. Some, with a reasonably well-heeled fan base, went down the route of gentrification, significantly raising the cost of tickets in an effort to price out the troublemakers and bring in a bigger slice of income. Across the country the cost of going to watch football rose by around 300 per cent. There is no sign as yet though that these strategies can staunch the flow. São Paulo remains the only club in the country that consistently breaks even. In 2009 the cumulative debt of the leading fifteen clubs stood at €1.15 billion (£920m), half of which was owed to the government, and the debt mountain was growing. Vasco da Gama, at €145 million (£116m), were the most indebted, though Flamengo's €128 million and Fluminense's €123 million (£103m and £98m) ran them close. Flamengo's president exclaimed, 'Even if we sold our boats and even the photographs of former presidents, we would still owe money.'[4] Yet none of them ceased to operate nor were they threatened with bankruptcy. Brazil remained enough of a futebol nation that its football clubs could continue to defy economic reality.

IV

Brazilian football may have been broke and badly governed, but it retained its enduring place in Brazilian cultural life; an encounter that sometimes suggested the emergence of more plural and even critical artistic intelligentsia. The leading football clubs continued to be markers of regional and urban identities, and the game as a whole served as a well-calibrated barometer of the state of social relationships, from the prevalence of corruption to the position of women. The often circuitous revival in interest in the late 1990s in football as a subject for other art forms continued through the Lula years. Novelist João Ubaldo Ribeiro wrote on the game; José Miguel Wisnik, musician and composer, published widely on football, both in *crônica* format and in his 2008 book

Veneno Remédio ('Poison Remedy'), a renewal of Gilberto Freyre's interpretation of Brazilian football. Yet these were voices forged in an earlier era; among the pieces by the twenty new Brazilian writers selected by *Granta* magazine in 2012, there was barely a mention of the game.

Football continued to play its part in the wider samba culture. *Torcidas organizadas* supported samba schools, carnivals took occasional football themes, and bacchanalian players like Ronaldinho lent their presence to the parades. However, the most popular football songs of the era were not samba tunes at all, but the rock-reggae of Skank's 'It's a Football Match', the Brazilian metal of Dr Sin's 'Football, Women and Rock 'n' Roll' or the work of the *mangue* beat artists from Recife. Mundo Livre's 'Meu Esquema' ('My Scheme'), compared a lover's presence to the ecstasy of scoring: 'She's what the doctor ordered, a fabulous Rivaldo goal', and then in the notes accompanying the CD issued a call for a football- and music-based uprising; even if made in jest it was an almost unique popular call to link the solidarities of football with radical leftist politics:

> The recently founded AR-28 – the Revolutionary Alliance of October 28th – has the objective of creating a National Football and Samba Conference . . . The NFSC aims to bring together as members and activists all Brazilians who really believe in the power of Brazil. Supporters of Palmeiras, São Paulo, Vasco, Cruzeiro, Atlético, Sport, Bahia and in the end all clubs . . . We will expel the leeches from power . . . the consortia and the international and multinational financial institutions who for almost four decades have done nothing but lie and conspire, and take our sweat to pay immoral, illegitimate and unpayable debts.[5]

There was also room for nostalgia. From the north-eastern state of Maranhão, singer Zeca Baleiro teamed up with the noted poet Celso Borges to write a sweet ode to Canhoteiro – an unsung hero of the golden era, born in Maranhão too, but like so many forced to make his career in exile in São Paulo. The decline of samba was confirmed in 2004 when *Placar* magazine released a CD of the leading clubs' official hymns, as they are known, re-recorded by major musical artists who were also fans of the teams. Only two out of the seventeen – Zeca Pagodinho for Botafogo and Paulinho da Viola for Vasco – could be considered samba versions. The other fifteen featured an eclectic array of rock, punk, reggae, funk, mainstream MPB, backcountry *sertanejo* and inner-city hip-hop, reflecting the increasing diversity of Brazil's musical culture. More recently Brazilian hip-hop artists like Rashid located football in the grinding life of the poor urban peripheries, while the funk star MC Guimê released 'País do Futebol' ('Country of Football'), a song of praise for striker Neymar.

A more critical sensibility was on display in the sculptures of Nelson Leirner, who produced a series of football pitches populated by neatly arranged crowds of plastic figures, from *Star Wars* troopers to massed ranks of toy soldiers and Disney characters. These strange static tableaux evoked an air of regimented ritual and deracinated play. However, for a really critical voice, Brazilian football could turn to Juca Kfouri, a product of the '68 generation of Brazilian student politics and an active Trotskyist in his youth. His columns and his show on ESPN rained down articulate and informed criticism on the Brazilian football establishment. He coined the term 'House of Bandits' for the CBF and Ricardo Teixeira's near-fifty law suits against him were not enough to staunch the flow of comment. In this enterprise he was joined by others, as ESPN was one of several that provided a platform for more reflective thinking on the state of the game; Daniela Pinheiro's portrait of Teixeira in the leftist monthly *Piauí* was simply the most devastating piece of reporting on football politics of the era. These were of course marginal voices, accessed by a tiny fragment of the public and drowned in the great oceans of hysteria and hair-splitting that occupied much of the football press, but they represented progress nonetheless.

Eduardo Campos, governor of Pernambuco, like many in the *nordeste*, worried about the region's economic and sporting progress. Reflecting on the poor condition of football in the region outside his own state, he said, 'We know that football is an important part of our culture. This means the presence of our supporters in the stadium. In the *nordeste*, only Pernambuco continues to mount strong resistance. We are in a trench and need to be an example.' On the pitch it continued to be an uphill battle for the clubs of the north-east, with Sport Recife's win in the Copa do Brasil in 2008 the region's first national title since Bahia won the national championship in 1988. The long-standing structural economic inequalities between north and south in Brazil meant teams from the north had less private and public money to draw upon: poorer fans, sponsors, directors and state governments. They suffered the constant talent drain of players to the big clubs of the south who made all the money when selling them on to Europe. Television monies were inequitably distributed, with small teams in the richer states able to win large media deals even while playing in a lower division than north-eastern teams. When the north's best teams have made it to Série A of the Brasileiro, their stays have been short. All of Recife's teams – Santa Cruz, Sport and

Náutico – as well as Fortaleza, Ceará and América from Rio Grande do Norte, have suffered repeated relegations.

On the other hand, the north-east does have soul. As Governor Campos suggested, the state's clubs were ensuring the region's presence in the game. At Santa Cruz in particular but also at Sampaio Corrêa, from São Luís in Maranhão, a fan culture has been created which is truly loyal through thick and thin. While many of Brazil's biggest clubs have a very fickle fan base, even after three relegations Santa Cruz were able to count on home crowds of more than 50,000 – making them the best-supported fourth-divison team in the world – and away support almost as large on occasions.

If a decade of the PT in government had left the balance of football power between north and south unchanged, in the south itself there were recent signs of it tilting away from the central Rio–São Paulo axis. In 2013 the two leading teams in Belo Horizonte, capital of Minas Gerais, Cruzeiro and Atlético Mineiro, were the stars of the season. Cruzeiro dominated the Brasileiro, claiming the title with over a month of the season still to go, while Atlético Mineiro, having attracted Ronaldinho for a final season or two, won the Copa Libertadores.

For the most part, however, the Lula years were dominated by teams from his political hometown – São Paulo. Santos, who had never quite recovered from Pelé's departure in the 1970s, were reborn in 2002 with a young squad starring teenage sensation Robinho which won the national championship. It was a short-lived revival though, as Robinho, inevitably, was sold on to Real Madrid and the promised retooling of the team and the renovation of their dilapidated stadium never quite happened. The same process was repeated between 2009 and 2011 as the latest Brazilian star Neymar was paired with a repatriated Robinho in a team that won the 2011 Copa Libertadores before he was flogged off to Barcelona. São Paulo FC turned their unique financial strength and stability into an equally solid, unadventurous, but successful team in the mid-2000s that won the Copa Libertadores and the Club World Cup. Under coach Muricy Ramalho they won three consecutive Brasileiros between 2006 and 2008. Ramalho defended his team's pedestrian qualities in a distinct Paulista dialect: 'If you want to see a spectacle go to the theatre.' Corinthians, long the symbolic representatives of the city's working classes and the team of outsiders, now became the team of the insiders. The early Lula years saw them winning titles, including the national championships, before an ill-fated relationship with the enigmatic international sports company MSI turned so sour that the team were relegated to the second division. In the last years of Lula's administration they returned to the top division under the presidency of Andrés Sánchez, a businessman and PT insider. They went on to win the 2011 Brasileiro, followed by the Copa Libertadores and Club World Cup in 2012. A mark of the changing nature and wealth of the team's support was that a self-conscious reprise of the Corinthians invasion of Rio in 1976 could now be conducted in Tokyo.

Rio's football clubs fared less well than São Paulo's. Vasco won almost nothing in the years after the infamous São Januário final of 2000. Eurico Miranda was forced out of Congress and then out of the presidency of the club. His successor, Vasco's much-loved striker Roberto Dinamite, has proved a well-tanned but hopeless replacement. Fluminense and especially Flamengo have remained the most publicly fractious, disputatious and chaotically run of all clubs. Fluminense managed to win the Brasileiro twice – 2010 and 2012 – only to decline so badly afterwards that they were relegated in 2013; but their status as the most politically connected club in the country was secured when they got their relegation overturned by post-season decision-making at the CBF. Portuguesa were punished for fielding an ineligible player for fifteen minutes in a game of no importance. Their punishment, although permissible, was the severest possible, ensuring their relegation and Fluminense's survival. Flamengo, who managed a single national title in 2009, sacked the successful coach and have won nothing of consequence since.

Although corruption in Brazilian football had been widespread, it was mainly confined to financial matters – self-enrichment, embezzlement, tax-dodging. Match-fixing and cheating, although not unknown, were relatively rare. Whereas in some football cultures, like Italy, relegation was avoided by ensuring that results on the last day of the season went a team's way, in Brazil it was traditionally avoided by post-season adjustments to points totals or league structures. However, the creation of online betting in the twenty-first century meant that a new breed of match-fixer emerged. In 2005 the *Escândalo do Apito* ('Whistle Scandal') broke. Two São Paulo referees, Edílson Pereira de Carvalho and José Danelon, were accused of fixing at least seventeen matches earlier in the season – eleven in the Brasileiro, two in the Paulistas, and four in the second division of the national championships. It transpired that an organized group of São Paulo criminals, aware of Pereira's large personal debts, were paying him around $5,000 a game to ensure the right results – results that were winning them millions of *reais* from bets with online bookmakers. Brazil's

Supreme Sports Court insisted that the eleven Brasileiro games be replayed, despite endless challenges in other courts from affected clubs. The replayed games saw Internacional lose the title they thought they had won and Corinthians claim a title they thought they had lost.

In 2009 the problem surfaced again when referee Gutenberg Paula Fonseca accused Sérgio Corrêa, head of the CBF's refereeing panel, of running a system of rewards and punishments for referees (like access to prestigious domestic and international games, demotion to lower league football) which he used to favour some teams over others when required. Corrêa himself was not dislodged by this accusation, but previously invulnerable administrators were finally displaced. Eduardo Viana, nicknamed 'the Water Tank', had run the Rio State Football Federation with an iron fist for eighteen years. He had been indicted on corruption charges three times in his football career and on each occasion managed to elude conviction. In 2004 he and five others working for the Rio Federation were arrested and charged with embezzlement, specifically the disappearance of nearly $300,000 of Maracanã ticket receipts. The court dismissed his defence and he went on immediate sick leave, dying of a heart attack before the case could be concluded.

Racism is another issue football – and the country generally – has had to face. The Cardoso governments had, to their credit, called time on any official notion that Brazil was a racial democracy. They and the Lula governments acknowledged the deep-rooted and pervasive racism of Brazilian society, appointed Afro-Brazilians to important state positions (under Lula this included the first black judge at the Supreme Court) and introduced affirmative action policies in the foreign ministry, in the wider civil service and in university entrance procedures. Significant progress in these realms must be set against the country's enduring racial inequalities that leave Afro-Brazilians – at least half the population – overwhelmingly concentrated in the poorest classes, and underrepresented in the ranks of nearly all elite occupations. Precisely who is black, or Afro-Brazilian, remains an open question in the country's unspoken and complex racial codes where one's position is only partly determined by skin colour or genetics. When Ronaldo, clearly a man of mixed African and European heritage, was asked what he thought of racism in Brazilian football, he acknowledged its existence but replied, 'I'm white, so I am really ignorant of these matters.' This was the same Ronaldo whose black mother was denied access to the residents' lift and directed to the service lift in her son's exclusive apartment block.

Brazilian football and its media have long been sensitive to racist abuse by foreigners against Brazilians, dating back to the infamous Brazil–Argentina game of 1937 when the Argentinian crowd howled racist insults. Similarly, the press has been quick to cover the many incidents of racism in contemporary European football towards Afro-Brazilians. It has, however, been rather slower off the mark in exposing the same kind of behaviour at home. In this regard at least there has been progress recently. The long-standing use of racial epithets by players and racial abuse from the crowd were exposed by a number of incidents in which the authorities actually prosecuted perpetrators: Juventude supporters were barred from their ground after racially abusing Internacional's Tinga in 2005; the club's defender Zago was given a long suspension after being caught on camera making monkey gestures to Grêmio's Jeovânio; Danilo of Palmeiras was actually sentenced to a year in prison for abusing Atlético Paranaense's defender Manoel – though this was later reduced to a fine.

Despite the massive presence of Afro-Brazilian players, and the game's long association with the struggle against social and racial exclusion, there have been precious few black coaches and even fewer club directors or football administrators. Didi, star of the 1958 and 1962 World Cup sides, prospered as a coach only when he left the country for Peru. Of the black players in the great 1970 World Cup team just Carlos Alberto went into management. Again, the Lula years have seen advances and retreats. In 2009 Flamengo won their first national championship for seventeen years and they did it under a black coach, Jorge Luís Andrade. Television pundit Telmo Zanini said, 'Hopefully this will become a symbolic day for Brazilian football and help to open doors for black coaches.' Andrade's reward, for what was a footballing miracle, was to be made the scapegoat for the next season's disappointments and fired, leaving the Brasileiro without a single black coach.[6]

The collapse of organized women's football in Brazil in the late 1980s and early 1990s began to be repaired in the 2000s. Football clubs started up women's teams and the CBF, against its own instincts, found itself locked into global and regional women's international tournaments that necessitated creating a minimal programme of national women's teams. There was no shortage of players to staff them. A whole generation of dedicated and talented women had emerged, scrapping it out in the male worlds of the street, the *pelada*, and the five-a-side pickup game. What there was, however, was a simply remarkable level of sexism, in which the women's game was consistently framed in terms of men's erotic interests and TV advertising revenue. This was all clearly expressed in 2001 when the São Paulo Football Federation put on its own women's competition – the Paulistina – promising a 'good and beautiful championship' that would unite 'femininity and football'. Rather than recruiting from existing clubs and sides, the federation chose the participants at huge trials. In practice players with cropped hair were banned, blonde players were given preference and all had to be less than twenty-three years old. One player who had attended the try-outs recalled, 'Everything is because they wanted to sell the image of the championship on TV; they didn't want to see a toothless girl on TV, they wanted to see the blonde girl . . . It was an appearance championship and this made me very mad.'[7]

Despite the unrepentant sexism of Brazilian men's football and the callous disregard of the women's game by the CBF, the number and quality of women football players grew and they were good enough to take two silvers at the Athens and Beijing Olympics, and to win the Pan-American games in Rio in 2007. Marta, the team's leading striker, was FIFA's female player of the year five times in a row, a feat no man has correspondingly managed. Brazil rewarded her prowess by making Marta one of the official ambassadors for the 2014 World Cup, but typically among the leading women players, it was Sweden and the United States that allowed her to earn a small living from the game. No one was expecting parity with the men's game, but having finally established themselves as part of the futebol nation, women players were asking, like so many of Brazil's citizens, not just for membership, but for dignity. As one international, who continued to play club football in Brazil, pointed out: 'I know that men's soccer is involved in a network of corruption that it is hard to understand or escape from, we don't want that, we simply want to play our soccer with dignity. We don't want to earn millions, but we also can't live earning so little, in poverty, like so many players who continue to work as cleaning women to be able to support themselves.'[8]

V

In May 2006, in a string of incidents orchestrated by the leaders of the criminal gangs who ran São Paulo's bursting prisons, thirteen banks were attacked, fifty-six buses torched and revolts broke out in seventy-three of the 144 prisons in the state. The police counter-attack saw over 100 people killed on the streets of the city and in the jails. Among the demands of the Primeiro Comando da Capital, the leading criminal gang, was one for sixty televisions to ensure that they could watch the Seleção at the upcoming World Cup in Germany. The football nation now included almost half a million in prisons designed for half or a third of this capacity, most in connection with organized crime and drug trafficking. Kidnapping was one of the main growth industries and 2004 saw four high-profile footballers' families targeted. The mother of Santos star Robinho drove her new Mercedes to a barbecue with old friends in a notoriously troublesome district. She was held for forty days. Campinas, a small and wealthy town north-west of São Paulo, became the centre of a small crime wave with the kidnapping of the mothers of São Paulo forward Grafite and Portugal-based Luís Fabiano and Rogério. All were resolved by paying the ransom rather than bloodshed. In 2008 Pelé was robbed at gunpoint. He told the gang who he was but they took his phone and his jewellery anyway. Although there were falls in the statistics for violent crime and murder at the peak of the Lula boom, crime rates remained worrying, harsh narcotics laws ensured that the already high level of incarceration was unchanged, and much of the day-to-day policing of Brazil's cities was still brutal in its execution.

The incidence of violence in Brazilian football itself, already high in the 1990s, took another step upwards. More than 100 people died in football-related incidents in the decade that followed. *Lance!* estimated that the total number of deaths in Brazilian football since 1988 had risen to 234. Between May 2011 and May 2012 at least eleven fans were killed in a gang war between Goiás and Vila Nova in the western city of Goiânia. Multiple incidents of disorder would break out on many weekends, particularly towards the end of the season. In December 2004 Botafogo fans stormed the pitch and attacked the referee as their team were defeated by Corinthians. The match was concluded while truncheon-wielding police fought their way into the stands and *torcidas* attempted to tear down the fences and netting behind the goals. Ticket-holding Atlético Paranaense fans were denied entry to Vasco da Gama's stadium after a twelve-hour journey; they were reported to have fought police with bottles and stones. Palmeiras players were spared humiliation when police confiscated thousands of flip-flops that the Mancha Verde planned to pelt them with during their game against Criciúma. Guarani, relegated after being beaten by Paysandu, had their clubhouse stoned so badly that the last home game of the season was rescheduled to an out-of-town venue.

Alongside the run-of-the-mill disturbances there were

exceptional moments of mass disorder. In 2006 at the Porto Alegre derby between Grêmio and Internacional fans threw dozens of portable toilets into the stadium moat, set them ablaze and pelted the firefighters attempting to put out the conflagration. In March 2012 about 500 Palmeiras and Corinthians fans took part in a prearranged brawl on São Paulo's Avenida Inajar de Souza, leaving two Palmeiras fans dead. Violence also spilled over into the previously tranquil world of futsal, the indoor game. In 2008 a Palmeiras versus Corinthians match descended into on-court brawling which led to nine arrests.

Fans were not the only protagonists in these disturbances. On one occasion Vasco's coach Antônio Lopes threw a ball at an injured player sparking a pitch-wide fight among coaches, officials, players and police. In 2012 Fluminense's kitman received a twelve-match ban for running on to the pitch and attacking a linesman so violently that he had to be restrained by the police. In 2013 the club masseur of Série D side Tupi ran on to the field to make a last-minute goal-line save before being chased by the enraged opposition and grabbed by the police for his own protection. Meanwhile, attacks by *torcidas* on their own players and directors intensified. In 2012, after a defeat to Botafogo, fighting broke out amongst Palmeiras fans and players, death threats were issued to the club president and a director's restaurant attacked. Hernán Barcos, the club's Argentinian striker, despaired: 'If it is to live like this, driving an armoured car and with a gun in hand, I would rather go home.'[9] The following year the players were attacked by fans at the airport in Buenos Aires after losing a game to Tigre 1–0. The trend towards exporting violence had begun a month beforehand when Corinthians were playing San José in Oruro, Bolivia, in the Copa Libertadores. A naval flare launched at the Bolivian crowd struck and killed a fourteen-year-old boy, and a seventeen-year-old scapegoat was offered to the police by the organized *torcidas* who were responsible.

On the 30 June 2013, in the small town of Pio XII in the state of Maranhão, referee Otávio Jordão da Silva Cantanhede showed a player and sometime friend, Josemir Santos Abreu, a red card. Abreu refused to leave the pitch and in the ensuing argument Cantanhede pulled out a knife and stabbed him twice. Abreu died before reaching hospital. An angry and intoxicated mob then stormed the field, beat Cantanhede with a wooden pole, smashed a bottle of *cachaça* in his face, and drove a motorcycle repeatedly over his body, before he was finally decapitated and quartered.[10]

Football provides the stage on which the desperate conditions and self-destructive energies of Brazil's poor can be played out. Accustomed to a world in which violence is pervasive, life is cheap and the public authorities – police and judiciary – cannot be relied upon to keep the peace or administer justice, many of Brazil's young men go armed and ready to use their weapons. Moreover, in a world that constantly strips them of economic dignity and offers them little but enduring marginalization, humiliation in public becomes simply intolerable. It is the same rage and embarrassment that fuel pitch invasions when a team is losing or attacks on players who have let them down. From acts of grotesque rural revenge to the urban riots of the national championships, unchecked by the police and ignored by the sport's authorities, Brazilian football has been a conduit for the mental and emotional pathologies of a still brutalized society.

8

Copa das Manifestações: Civil War in the Futebol Nation, 2013–2014

The spectacle and the counter-spectacle – Brasília, June 2013.

Let's forget all this commotion happening in Brazil, all these protests, and let's remember how the Seleção is our country and our blood.

Pelé

If Pelé is the King, then I am a Jacobin.

Protestors' placard, Rio de Janeiro

I

Pelé, like the rest of the Brazilian establishment, simply could not believe his eyes: the citizens of the futebol nation were in revolt, and football, long a source of unity, had come to be at the heart of the country's intersecting problems. The events of June 2013 in Brazil constituted one of the largest waves of social protest the country had ever seen. Easily bigger than the crowd of 100,000 students that took to the streets of Rio in 1968, they were also cumulatively larger than the two key demonstrations of the mid-1980s at the end of military rule, and the crowds that demanded Collor's impeachment in 1992. At least six of the marches that took place in São Paulo, Rio, Belo Horizonte and

Fortaleza in 2013 were 100,000 strong. The very largest gathered somewhere between 300,000 and half a million. While the earlier protests had a backbone of predictable political organization and singular focus, and were concentrated as one-offs in a few big cities, these newer protests were protean, complex and diverse. Consequently they had a much bigger geographical spread than their predecessors. On the night of 20 June protestors gathered in over 120 Brazilian cities – testament to the explosive wave of urbanization that the country had undergone in the last two decades and the new digital connectedness of the previously isolated provinces.

The protestors' demands were remarkably heterogeneous. From what appeared to begin as a protest over a rise in bus fares in São Paulo in early June, the demonstrators, with their tens of thousands of handmade placards, were concerned with a huge range of grievances: the state of the public-health and the public-education systems; the passage of federal legislation, sponsored by Protestant evangelical groups, that would make homosexuality a treatable psychological disease; legislation that would reduce the powers of the federal police to investigate politicians; and a more general revulsion against the systematic corruption of business and political elites and the brutality of many police forces.

The forces that lay behind these events derived from the tremendous economic boom that Brazil had enjoyed. This had principally benefited two key groups. The very rich and powerful had enjoyed a massive surge in their wealth. The very poor, especially in the most undeveloped zones of the north-east and the interior, had benefited from the *Bolsa Família* – the centrepiece of Lula's eight-year presidency. Neither of these groups was present in any number at the demonstrations. A few organized bodies from the favelas who were actively opposing housing relocation were present, youths from the peripheries took part in some demonstrations, and a few tiny right-wing groups and evangelicals tried to join the protests, but the crowds were overwhelmingly made up of the urban middle classes, a category that stretches from downtown junior office workers to university professors. As a class they had swelled under Lula and then Rousseff, especially as enrolment in higher education had expanded, but their circumstances only inched forward. They were paying, in their own words, 'European taxes to get Mozambican services'. They took their own toilet paper and blankets to public hospitals and went into debt to get some private health cover. Deep-seated resentments were multiplied by the contemptuous manner in which Brazil's elites treated the rule of law and indeed the other classes.

This had all been the case for some time. The question, then, is why the protest should have erupted in June 2013. Significantly perhaps, participants and observers struggled to name the events. The Vinegar Revolution was tried out – a reference to its use as a tear-gas antidote and the arrest of a number of protestors merely for carrying vinegar in their bags. Others opted for the Brazilian Spring. The comparisons with the Middle East were real but limited: the events' reliance on social-media networks and the collective disbelief of rulers and ruled alike that this was happening had shades of Egypt. However, Brazil had been booming economically, it had no really problematic foreign entanglements and it was not under military rule. Perhaps the best option was *Copa das Manifestações* – the Demonstrations Cup. For what gave rhythm and focus to the protests was the simultaneous staging of the 2013 FIFA Confederations Cup; and what allowed the many grievances of the Brazilian public to coalesce into this wave of outrage were the economic costs and the social impact of staging the 2014 World Cup to come.

Protestors chanted, 'Hey hey, FIFA, pay my bus fare' or held placards that contrasted the shiny new football temples with the peeling paint of the average Brazilian school classroom and called for 'Education – FIFA quality'. FIFA may have come in for a mauling, but the crowd did not spare its own elites, sporting and political, for their institutionalized corruption and unaccountability to the public. Even FIFA, whose own probity was profoundly compromised, had recognized these traits. The organization's report into the ISL scandal, in which members of the FIFA executive committee had received considerable kickbacks from the sale of World Cup media rights in the 1990s, described the behaviour of both João Havelange and Ricardo Teixeira as 'morally and ethically reproachable', and went on to say:

> It is certain that not inconsiderable amounts were channelled to former FIFA president Havelange and to his son-in-law Ricardo Teixeira . . . there is no indication that any form of service was given in return by them . . . These payments were apparently made via front companies in order to cover up the true recipient and are to be qualified as 'commissions', known today as 'bribes'.[1]

The extraordinary fact that until very recently Swiss law did not recognize the crime of bribery or corruption in international organizations like FIFA saved the pair from criminal proceedings. Teixeira, who must have seen the writing on the wall, turned a period of sick leave into retirement in early 2012, standing down from the CBF, the World Cup organizing committee and his positions at FIFA. Havelange stood down from the IOC but hung on as honorary life president at FIFA – only to resign in early 2013. Teixeira's farewell speech was read out by his deputy and successor, José Maria Marin. Rather like George W. Bush's take on Iraq, Teixeira believed that it was 'mission accomplished'. Marin ended by saying, 'The stupendous work that was being done by Ricardo Teixeira will continue.'[2]

The CBF was certainly passing to the right person for that to happen. Marin had made his first career in politics, as a member of the party descended from Salgado's 1930s fascists and then as a willing stooge of the military dictatorship's pet party ARENA serving as governor of São Paulo. Two months earlier he had been handing out the winners' medals at the final of a São Paulo youth tournament. Captured live on television and endlessly repeated on ESPN, Marin clearly takes one of the medals, carefully folds the ribbon around it and then slips it into his trouser pocket. Corinthians' goalkeeper Mateus, for whom the medal was meant, shuffled down the line and got nothing. Marin first denied the incident, and then tried to laugh it off as 'a real joke'.

No one expected the *Copa das Manifestações*, and it is not clear that anyone can fully explain it now. What is certain is that there was plenty of tinder ready to burn and plenty of sparks to light the conflagration.

II

'This is the chronicle of a mess foretold,' wrote Juca Kfouri in the final months before Rio staged the Pan American Games in 2007. 'Everyone knew when Brazil won the right to host the

Games that the moment would arrive when the organizers were going to blackmail the government and that all the normal regulations on bids and oversight would be thrown out the window in the name of haste and avoiding a stain on Brazil's reputation.'[3] Exactly how much the Games cost is a matter of some dispute but it was at least 5 billion *reais*, which was roughly six times the original budget. This might not have been so bad had any of that money been spent on desperately needed transportation infrastructure, but the new highways and light-rail projects that were part of the package never materialized. Similarly, the planned clean-up of Guanabara Bay, now a toxic pool of sewage and industrial effluent, never started. There was, however, money for security, with an extra $300 million made available for 18,000 additional police to be on duty and 1,700 CCTV cameras to be installed.

The athletes' village was located in the wetlands to the west of the city, in Barra da Tijuca. The ground here was so unstable and waterlogged that the builders had to sink forty-five-metre concrete pylons into the earth, making the seventeen apartment blocks enormously more expensive than planned. The project was bankrolled by the Workers' Support Fund, which had been established by the federal government to provide loans and unemployment insurance to its low-paid workforce. Needless to say, the kind of leverage available to the fund was not used to ensure some element of social housing in the project and so the whole shoddily built edifice was flogged off to upper-middle-class buyers. The government ended up suing the contractors for systematic malfeasance, grotesquely and falsely inflating wage bills and unfinished work.

The Marina da Glória in Parque do Flamengo was the intended

location of the sailing competitions at the Games and plans were laid to build a gigantic fortified complex there, including a convention centre, shopping malls and a huge car park. Together with the space required to host the various sporting events of the Games, all of this would have necessitated a massive transfer of public space and parkland to the private sector and the creation of buildings so high that they would steal the view of Guanabara Bay from everyone else. This flagrant act of theft was eventually stopped by local protests and the courts. Three major complexes that did get built included the Estádio Olimpico João Havelange, known as the Engenhão, the Maria Lenk swimming complex and the Arena Multiuso. All came in many times over budget. The Engenhão, which was intended to be the centrepiece of the Rio Olympics bid, was so shoddily built that the roof let in the rain, and it was closed in March 2013 by the city's mayor for safety reasons. The swimming complex, though functional, was not built to Olympic specifications and has been neither adapted nor made available for public use. Exactly the same was true of the velodrome. All of them, during and after the Games, functioned as highly fortified and protected enclaves in the city rather than as a part of the public urban fabric. Teresa Caldeira's description of this central element of modern Brazilian urbanism captures them perfectly.

> They are physically demarcated and isolated by walls, fences, empty spaces and design devices. They are turned inward, away from the street, whose public life they explicitly reject. They are controlled by armed guards and security systems, which enforce rules of inclusion and exclusion . . . They are private property for collective use and they emphasize the value of what is private and

restricted at the same time they devalue what is public and open in the city.[4]

The Games themselves were attended almost exclusively by Rio's middle and upper-middle classes, who had the internet access necessary to buy the tickets and the money to pay their very high prices. All the venues and their management corresponded to Caldeira's description. In this regard the Pan American Games in Rio were not greatly different from other sporting mega-events in the rest of the world which have become increasingly security-conscious, but for one important fact: the police and the military were conducting massive operations in the city's favelas before and during the Games themselves. The security operation began in May, and two weeks before the Games started 1,350 heavily armed police stormed the Complexo do Alemão in the north of the city, taking on the drug-trafficking gangs (*traficantes*) who were the de facto authorities in the area. *Veja* referred to it as 'a necessary war', *Época* praised it as 'an innovative attack'.[5] Nineteen people died and nine were injured on the first day of the operation. Over the next month, as the Games took place, the entire zone was in a state of military lockdown, with residents unable to attend schools or health clinics, while rubbish and sewage piled up. By late July the death toll had climbed to forty-four. While some of these were the results of gun battles and stray bullets, both federal government and human rights groups concluded that there had been many executions as well.[6] In the years since, these operations have been formalized in Rio as the process of pacification, where military-level assaults have been used to clear the traffickers from the favelas, after which the Brazilian flag is hoisted and the regular police move in.

Thus the 2007 Pan American Games became the template for the way in which Brazil planned for, built and staged sporting mega-events. The country could put on a slick spectacular for a privileged local audience and the TV cameras in fortified enclaves, secured by a mixture of flagrant media boosterism and harshly authoritarian political and policing practice. Financially the show rested on a huge transfer of resources and land from the public to the private sector. There was no meaningful democratic consultation or planning, helping ensure that money was lost, embezzled and wasted, and almost no thought was given to post-Games planning and legacies. None of this, not even the slaughter at the Complexo do Alemão, gave FIFA or the IOC pause for thought as they handed the hosting rights for the 2014 World Cup and the 2016 Olympics to Brazil and Rio respectively.

Brazil had known it would be getting the World Cup long before it was made official. In the wake of the controversial decision to give the 2006 World Cup to Germany rather than the favourites, South Africa, FIFA make a knee-jerk decision that future World Cups would be rotated around the continents (a practice they would later abandon). The 2010 World Cup would be held in Africa, ensuring South Africa got the tournament, and 2014 would be in South America. Colombia toyed with the idea of bidding for the tournament, but in a classic behind-closed-doors stitch-up the rest of the continent's football associations had long thrown their weight behind Brazil. Colombia withdrew from the fray and in 2007 Brazil was duly awarded the games.

The choice of World Cup host cities provides an insight into the politics of the tournament. FIFA required a minimum of eight cities and a maximum of ten for the competition, but Brazil insisted on twelve. This would create innumerable logistical problems in a continent-sized country, as would the decision to send teams around the country rather than geographically grouping their games. But advocates argued, not unreasonably, that it would allow more of the country to be shown off, and it also allowed more patronage to be handed out in the right political places. In São Paulo the obvious choice for a World Cup stadium was to renovate São Paulo FC's Morumbi, but the long-standing political feud between the club's president, Juvenal Juvêncio, and Ricardo Teixeira at the CBF meant that a vastly more expensive new stadium would be built for Corinthians instead. The *nordeste*, Lula's political stronghold, got four host cities and Fortaleza was given the privilege of holding six games, including a quarter-final; but the then state governor of Ceará, Cid Gomes, was a well-known ally of Lula and Dilma Rousseff and a useful regional counterweight to the presidential ambitions of Eduardo Campos, governor of Pernambuco. In the north both Manaus and Belém were in contention. Eduardo Braga, former governor of Amazonas, was on the rise, and seen as a future leader of the Senate, while Ana Júlia Carepa, governor of Pará where Belém is situated, was heading for electoral defeat. Manaus won over Belém. Brasília, the capital, was always going to get a stadium, but the initial plans to build a reasonably sized 40,000-seat arena, given the tiny crowds for the local football teams who would inherit the facility, were overtaken by the desire of local politicians to secure a quarter-final of the World Cup for their city. For this they required a much more expensive 70,000-seat stadium, which was duly agreed. Most contentious of all was the choice of Cuiabá, the capital of the central state of Mato Grosso and a city without any professional football at all. However, the long-standing governor of the state was Blairo Maggi, the country's biggest soya-bean producer and a major funder of the PT.

Brazil's relationship with FIFA also proved to be a highly politically charged affair. The *Lei Geral da Copa* – the general law of the cup – is the legislation that FIFA requires all of its hosts to sign up to. The law, which is meant to stand above all national laws, makes special provisions for FIFA itself, like generous tax provisions, but also specifies a whole series of legal requirements that must be adhered to during the tournament: for example, ensuring the protection of FIFA sponsors' brands from ambush marketing and local competition. Two issues proved to be particularly contentious: FIFA's insistence that alcohol, specifically sponsor Budweiser's beer, be available for sale in World Cup stadiums in contradiction of Brazil's 2003 law which banned this; and Brazil's desire to preserve reduced-price seats for seniors and students. In addition, FIFA and President Rousseff clashed over changes to Brazil's visa regulations and immigration law. On all these issues Congress, after much huffing and puffing, just had to play ball.

Perhaps the most pernicious of all FIFA's micro-regulations was their decision, following the vuvuzela experience in South Africa in 2010, to ban musical instruments from the stadiums. Brazilian efforts to devise more melodious instrumentation than the vuvuzela, though equally cheap and easy to play, were rejected, and thus in the society where football and music are most closely correlated in the global imagination there will only be the dire offerings of the official PA. If the Confederations Cup is anything to go by, samba football will be played to the sledgehammer rhythms of AC/DC's 'Hell's Bells' and whatever curious mutant emerges from the Sony Corporation's competition for a new

World Cup song – to be recorded by the Puerto Rican Ricky Martin.

Agreeing the host cities and passing the laws was the easy bit. Then the new stadiums had to be funded and built. Alongside this the government proposed the largest programme of new infrastructure ever associated with a World Cup, including a complete renovation of the country's antiquated airports and air-traffic-control technologies; new monorails in Rio and Manaus; and high-speed bus routes everywhere, as well as light-rail projects, bridges and highways. An agenda of this level of ambition required some degree of haste, but as a representative of Brazil's construction industry put it, 'We won the right to host the World Cup in October 2007 but we didn't decide what needed to be done until January 2010. In 2008 and 2009 we did little or nothing. You can call it lack of money, or will, or competence, but there was definitely a lack of something.'[7] Some transport projects were cancelled because the initial plans were so badly put together that they couldn't go ahead. Others were halted by judicial interventions that disclosed corruption and incompetence, or tried to defend the rights of the thousands of families whose homes were under threat from these projects.

Those that did go ahead were often achingly slow. By mid-2013 it was obvious that neither São Paulo nor Rio would have any working rail links to either of their two airports by the time of the World Cup. The airport-renovation programme was so behind schedule that most of the extra capacity would have to be handled by temporary hangars and shelters that would disappear after the tournament. In Brasília, work started on tramlines to the airport but was then halted in 2011 when a judge ruled the contractors had massively overpriced the job. Manaus cancelled its monorail and bus lanes. A year before the World Cup kicked off it was clear that none of Salvador's planned new roads or rail links would be ready for the tournament, while in Fortaleza no work had even started.

The story of the stadium-building programme was not dissimilar but without the luxury of cancellation, prompting FIFA president Sepp Blatter to tell a Swiss newspaper in January 2014 that Brazil was further behind in its preparations at this stage than any other country during his time with FIFA. Four were still unfinished, and Curitiba, in the state of Paraná, looked like it might be completed so late that crowds could expect to be using portable toilets. The later the stadiums and the transport projects were finished and the more maniacal the timetable, the more expensive they became: the stadiums alone were going to cost $3.5 billion. According to Brazil's National Court of Auditors, public expenditure on the World Cup was expected to reach $13.5 billion, making 2014 the most expensive World Cup ever – enough money to pay the entire country's annual *Bolsa Família* bill twice over.

The single infrastructure project that best illustrated the preparations for the 2014 World Cup, and certainly the most publicly symbolic, was the reconstruction of the Maracanã in Rio. It was first renovated in the late 1990s in preparation for the inaugural FIFA Club World Championship in 2000. A large, ugly glass box was fixed to one side to ensure that the elite wouldn't have to mingle, at any point, with the riff-raff and could enjoy their own dedicated entrance and secure facilities. A whole series of executive boxes were installed on the upper level, which aside from their ugliness also served to reduce the air circulation in the stadium, making it unpleasantly hot and humid. The upper-level terraces were filled with plastic seats, reducing the stadium's capacity from 175,000 to 103,000. The stadium was closed again in 2005 and underwent a two-year refit for the Pan American Games. This time the changes were more than merely cosmetic. Despite the high water table in the area, the pitch was sunk by over a metre, leading to endless problems with the playing surface. More significantly the *geral*, the open area in the lower stands where fans could enter the stadium for less than a single *real* and stand, was obliterated. Despite promises from the stadium authorities to provide cheap seats, the newly configured Maracanã made only a tiny number of low-price tickets available and these were sold at more than ten times the cost of the entrance to the *geral*. A vast investment of public money had been used to exclude the public.

The Maracanã was always more than just a stadium. In its original incarnation it was part of a larger integrated collection of public facilities conceived of and used as a genuinely public space. Alongside the football stadium, the complex included a beautiful mini-arena – the Maracazinho; a small athletics stadium and swimming complex, both of which were used by schools and the public for decades; a public primary school, which was considered among the very best in the city; and a superb if dilapidated nineteenth-century colonial mansion, the Aldeia Maracanã, which served as the Museum of the Indian. More than just concrete and plazas, the Maracanã was, for Cariocas and the futebol nation as a whole, a repository of historical memory, a site of national identity, a source of immense pride and, for all its faults, a continuing statement of Brazil's rare moments of utopian, democratic populism. In 2009 the stadium was closed for a third renovation in anticipation of the World Cup, and this time there would be no mistakes: the football and architectural authorities intended to wipe out every last progressive element of that complex, every trace of its original generous aesthetic and political vision.

Rebuilding the complex began in 2009 without a proper licence and was thus in contravention of the architectural preservation orders that had been placed on the stadium and the other buildings around it. The process was, from start to finish, entirely illegal under Brazilian law, a systematic transgression for which no one has been held accountable. The school, the athletics stadium and the swimming complex were all slated for demolition, with no plans to relocate or replace these vital public facilities. Massive public protest managed to save the school, but both sports facilities were closed and the athletics track demolished. A last-minute court injunction in 2013 saved the magnificent angular concrete stand that stood next to it. It now looks down on to a temporary car park and rubble, and no amount of screening will disguise it when the World Cup is held.

The Museu do Índio had actually moved to Botafogo in the late 1970s, and the Aldeia Maracanã had stood empty, ruined and uncared for, for over two decades until it was squatted and renovated by indigenous Brazilians in 2006. Over a number of years they built a small functioning community. Needless to say, the authorities were determined to remove them, claiming erroneously that FIFA wanted them out, that the space was needed for emergency exits from the Maracanã and that it should be the site of a new Brazilian Olympic museum. All of this can be taken with a pinch of salt. As an ex-member of Brazil's Olympic Committee put it, 'Rio's governor wants to polish the city, and the Indians are no good for this purpose. It is racial segregation and cruelty coming from an elite that harms Brazil.'[8] In early 2013, as civic officials negotiated with the occupants, the military police stormed the building, using pepper spray, tear gas and rubber bullets against its unarmed occupiers. Rio's mayor for sport and leisure caustically responded to critics by saying, 'Real Indians live in the rainforest, right?'[9] As of January 2014, a new preservation order on the building has been issued by the courts, preventing its destruction, and a small number of activists have reoccupied it.

Appalling as all of these changes were, nothing compares to the act of architectural vandalism and cultural desecration that has been perpetrated on the Maracanã itself. Once the largest and most beautiful football stadium on the planet, it has been reduced to a parody of its former self. The internal two-level structure was gutted and an anodyne off-the-shelf single-tier stand rammed into the space. The once fabulous views of Rio's skyline, clearly visible between the top of the stands and the roof, were obliterated. The roof itself, the crowning glory of the stadium, was, entirely illegally, demolished and replaced with a pathetic concoction of scaffolding and canopies. Where once the quadruple ellipses of pitch, stands and roof created an uninterrupted 360-degree panorama of simple but beautiful symmetries, the eyeline is now dominated by ugly gantries from which hang four gigantic television screens. These serve to distract the observer and, through carefully edited filming of the crowd, create the illusion that the stadium is full.

The *coup de grâce* was delivered by the plan to privatize the Maracanã. After more than 1 billion *reais* of public money had been spent on it, the government intended to hand the complex over to private operators, who on a thirty-year lease would only be required to pay a small fraction of the costs of renovation (less than 20 per cent). Though they would also be required to spend money on completing the complex renovation for the 2016 Rio Olympics, there was little to suggest that this would be rigidly enforced. To no one's amazement a committee of one awarded the contract to a consortium of IMX, Odebrecht and AEG: IMX was the main holding company of Eike Batista, then one of Brazil's richest men, whose organization had done the original economic feasibility study on privatizing the stadium; Odebrecht, a huge construction firm with major links to the PT; and AEG, a US-based 'entertainment' conglomerate that administered over a hundred soulless arenas around the world. When the completed stadium was opened up to the press and public in April 2013, in anticipation of the Confederations Cup to be played later that year, campaigners against privatization protested from the stands and were, once outside, treated to plumes of tear gas. The global media didn't seem to notice. Had they or indeed Brazil's elites done so the events of June 2013 would have seemed less surprising and incomprehensible.

III

The Confederations Cup began life as a PR exercise for the House of Saud. Having built one of the most opulent but underused stadiums in the world – the King Fahd – the Saudis created the tournament in 1992 to fill up the schedule and play soft-power football politics. The cup pitted their own national side against a selection of leading international teams, invited on an all-expenses-paid jaunt. The King Fahd Cup was held again in 1995 and 1997, with the Saudis attempting to invite all the sides that had won their continental competitions (like the European Championships and the Asian Cup). In 2001 the tournament passed into the hands of FIFA, who have since staged it on a four-year basis as a warm-up and dress rehearsal for the World Cup. Korea-Japan 2001, Germany 2005 and South Africa 2009 all passed without comment or much incident. Brazil 2013 was meant to be the same.

Through the autumn of 2012 and into early 2013 there were small but visible signs of discontent. The *Comitê Popular da Copa e Olimpíadas*, which had cut its teeth as the main opposition to the Pan American Games, maintained its regular protests in Rio and other cities over the wastefulness and corruption of the World Cup infrastructure programme, attracting 3–4,000 people to their anti-privatization marches on the Maracanã. At the same time increases in bus fares were attracting protests, led by the *Movimento Passe Livre*, most notably in Natal in late 2012 where buses were burned and police violently dispersed the crowds. In March 2013 the same pattern of events was seen in Porto Alegre when fare increases were announced, and in May much larger and fiercer confrontations took place in the inland city of Goiânia – a fact barely noted by the Brazilian media, let alone the rest of the world.

Then on 6 June, just nine days before the Confederations Cup was due to begin, the *Movimento Passe Livre* began to demonstrate against bus-fare rises in São Paulo, blocking Avenida Paulista and other major thoroughfares. This could not be ignored. The police, as ever, reacted with the use of maximum force, and although the media were depicting the protest as an antisocial nuisance, the demonstrators' bravery in the face of police brutality began to bring more supporters on to the streets. Organized through a complex mixture of social movements, personal connections and massive use of social media, demonstrations took place every day in São Paulo and were supported by marches in Rio, Brasília and Belo Horizonte of between 1,000 and 5,000 people. Almost immediately the protestors began to talk about more than just fare increases. Chants and placards soon made reference to the hopeless state of the nation's public-education and health-care systems; the pervasiveness of political corruption; the unaccountability and brutality of the police. Yet for all this, the protests remained small and only partially connected acts of defiance. What turned these smouldering embers into a conflagration was the football.

On 15 June the Confederations Cup opened in Brasília with the host nation playing Japan. Riot police used pepper spray and rubber bullets on a small demonstration close to the stadium where protestors carried signs like 'Health? Education? No! Here everything is for the World Cup.' FIFA president Sepp Blatter stood to give his speech and was roundly booed throughout. Blatter attempted to respond by asking the audience, 'Where was the fair play in all of this?', but he was booed even more loudly. President Rousseff was next up, and she too was booed while protestors unfurled a variety of banners inside the stadium. The disparate demands of the street were suddenly given a theme around which its many concerns could crystallize; the protean spasm of activism acquired a focus and a rhythm. The commercial sporting spectacular had brought the world's cameras to Brazil; now a political and popular anti-spectacular would meet it head on. Hitherto the mainstream press had systematically tried to portray the protestors as extremists and marginal, and the football establishment had called for the futebol nation to go home and rally behind the

Seleção. Now they would have to eat their words. The scale and range of protest, the existence of alternative media sources and the widespread public recognition that football, rather than just a source of unity and pride, now also exposed Brazil's ugliest sides, rendered all of their arguments untenable.

Two days later major demonstrations were held in twenty cities, 65,000 strong in São Paulo and more than 100,000 in Rio. A very small number of protestors attacked the state legislature where evidence emerged that the police were resorting to *agents provocateurs* as a way of justifying the use of violence against the protestors. In Brasília protestors climbed on to the roof of the Congress building. In Porto Alegre demonstrators set fire to a bus, and in Curitiba they attempted to force their way into the office of the state governor, but these were overwhelmingly peaceful protests policed as if they were an armed uprising. On 19 June, as Brazil faced Italy in Fortaleza, 25,000 people marched directly to the stadium, where they were met by the usual combination of armed brutality and incompetence.

The following day was the occasion of the biggest demonstrations yet, as Brazilians took to the streets of 120 cities, including every state capital in the country from Rio Branco, deep in the Amazon on the Peruvian border, to Porto Alegre, 2,000 miles to the south. At least 300,000 people gathered in Rio alone and were once again met by chaotic and violent policing. The carnivalesque front of the march along Avenida Presidente Vargas was bombarded by tear gas and percussion bombs, destroying the bonhomie and internal order of the crowd. In the ensuing chaos looting broke out on some side streets, and as one eyewitness noted, the military police 'roamed the streets like rabid dogs, guns pointed in everyone's faces. Worse, they threw tear gas into restaurants.'[10] Everywhere the crowds carried thousands of hand-made, hand-drawn placards and banners. Truly a thousand voices were set free: from the instructional 'This is about more than just bus fares, it's a scream by people who cannot take corruption any more' to the exasperated 'Too many reasons to fit on here'; from the crude 'Fuck off International Football Association' and 'FIFA the bitch' to the entirely reasonable 'Brazil, wake up! A teacher is worth more than Neymar'; and everywhere, sprayed on the bus shelters and in the underpasses, 'The Cup kills the poor.'

On 21 June President Rousseff made her move, going on television, accepting the right of the nation to protest and promising to address the people's concerns by holding down bus fares, importing extra doctors from Cuba to fill the gaping holes in Brazil's health service, reserving oil revenues for education, but defending spending on the World Cup. It wasn't much, but it was enough to take the sting out of the movement. With truly remarkable haste Congress passed the necessary legislation, and the contentious laws on corruption and homosexuality as a treatable disease were withdrawn.

Protest, though still widespread, thinned. In a final flourish 120,000 people marched from the centre of Belo Horizonte to the Mineirão as Brazil beat Uruguay in their semi-final. Activists occupied the state legislature and in the Sete de Setembro Square, the traditional place in which the Seleção's victories were celebrated, the night ended with a fusillade of tear gas so vast that the huge obelisk in the centre, over thirty metres high, was completely obscured. Five days later, on the night of the final in Rio, a crowd of 5,000 marched on the Maracanã and was met by an enormous deployment of the Rio police department's riot squads. The military police and the army were on standby, though as ever there was no medical care available to anyone but for the six volunteer medical students and their plant sprays full of milk of magnesia. Half a dozen helicopters swooped and hovered above the narrow canyon-like streets through which the crowds moved. While those inside the stadium sang the Brazilian national anthem, those outside took in the harsh symphony of tear-gas grenades, batons beating on riot shields and the relentless thudding and whirring of helicopter blades. Brazil won the match 3–0 as the crowd was charged, gassed and dispersed.

Coda: February 2014

In the months following the *Copa das Manifestações* the spirit of protest remained alive: strikes in July affected ten states and brought Brazil's busiest port, Santos, to a halt. Public transport was at a standstill in most cities. Teachers and doctors continued to take to the streets, the *Mídia Ninja* activists – a media collective born of the *Copa* – filmed and live-streamed them, while small anarchist groups, notably the Black Bloc, generally made trouble. Buses were torched in São Paulo, while protest and disruption brought the city's metro to a halt. The *Comitê Popular* and other social movements kept up the pressure. Brazil's friendly with Australia in Brasília in September saw a protest march that was repelled with multiple volleys of tear gas. Jérôme Valcke, FIFA's general secretary, was met by protestors while on a visit to the calamitously late Arena Pantanal in Cuiabá in October. A series of small victories were won by threatened favela communities resisting eviction, and the privatization plans for the Maracanã were put on hold.

More widely, there were reasons for some optimism that change was coming. The trial of the leading PT politicians who had orchestrated the *mensalão*, the vote-buying scandal which had almost brought down Lula in 2005, finally reached a conclusion with the Supreme Court imposing immediate prison sentences on some senior figures including José Dirceu, Lula's chief of staff.

The most widely reported resistance came, unusually, from within football itself. Towards the end of the season, many championship games began with an act of defiance from the players.

On some occasions they simply sat down when the whistle blew to start the game and remained there for a minute. Sometimes they would aimlessly pass the ball among themselves or all twenty-two would form a circle in the centre of the pitch with their backs to the crowd. This was *FC Bom Senso*, 'FC Common Sense', an organization formed by a number of the more senior players in the league, which quickly attracted over 1,000 members. Their central grievance was the football timetable. Already clogged in 2013, 2014 was due to be even worse as space was cleared for the World Cup. The practical implication of this was that players would have less than a week's holiday between the end of the 2013 season and the beginning of the next. The toll on players' physical and mental well-being would be immense. In addition *Bom Senso* threatened a nationwide players' strike unless the squad at Náutico, who had not seen their salary for months, were paid. As with the protest movement in June, the gathering sense of confidence and organization among the players led them to make bolder demands, insisting on financial transparency in Brazilian football and a players' representative on the CBF. The CBF didn't even refuse to negotiate, it simply tried to ignore them.

If the *mensalão* trial and the emergence of *Bom Senso* suggested that some change had occurred in the futebol nation, there were many indications to the contrary. 100 Corinthian *torcidas* broke into their club's training ground, using bolt cutters on the huge wire fences. Once inside they physically attacked the squad and the coaching staff, berating them for their poor performances. Flamengo, the club of the people, were happy to set ticket prices for their Copa do Brasil final at more than twenty times the minimum wage. The prices being set for hotels and internal flights during the World Cup took on such astronomical proportions that the government convened a meeting of the airline and tourist industries in an effort to stop the rampant price gouging. Fluminense once again escaped relegation by pulling the right strings and getting lowly Portuguesa demoted instead.

The World Cup construction programme remained desperately behind schedule with real concerns as to whether the stadiums in Curitiba, São Paulo and Manaus could be finished in time. The pace of work quickened at these sites and with it the death rate. In late November a giant construction crane was lifting the final part of the roof of the Estádio Itaquerão in São Paulo into place when it fell to the ground, dropping the 420-ton roof panel which sliced through a perimeter wall, damaging the roof and killing two people. Later it would be revealed that the crane driver had been working for weeks without a day off. In Manaus, where the long rainy season had delayed the completion of the stadium roof, Marcleudo de Melo Ferreira fell over thirty metres to his death while installing lights. The Ministry of Labour revealed that construction at the Manaus site had violated sixty-three of sixty-four health and safety labour codes. Sports minister Aldo Rebelo remained blithely optimistic though: 'There is always a bride and a groom at a wedding and 100 per cent of the time the bride is always late but I have never known a wedding not to happen because of it.'[1]

On the final day of the 2013 season Vasco da Gama played Atlético Paranaense. Atlético's stadium in Curitiba was being rebuilt for the World Cup and, with the work hopelessly behind schedule, it was unavailable for the game. Instead it was played in Joinville, in Santa Catarina state. Vasco's *torcidas* had been among the most violent in 2013, invading their players' dressing rooms after defeats and conducting pitch invasions. Given that Vasco needed to win in order to avoid relegation, and given that their threadbare squad made a win the most unlikely outcome, the authorities decided not to have any police in the stadium, nor did they effectively segregate the crowd. When Vasco went 1–0 down, the inevitable fight broke out in the stands as Vasco *torcidas* charged their opponents. Live on TV, the nation was treated to Atlético and Vasco supporters brawling and trampling on their opponents. The police eventually arrived and restored some kind of order after firing tear gas. Vasco went on to lose the restarted game 5–1, but had the temerity to appeal the result, claiming that the long delay had adversely affected them. It is hard to know what the worst element of this dismal story is: the engrained and systemic violence of the *torcidas*; the complete failure of any level of Brazilian football administration to properly acknowledge let alone tackle the problem; the contemptible behaviour of Vasco's board; the pathetic punishments meted out to the clubs; the platitudes that emerge from the mouths of politicians who have presided over all of this, but who have barely mentioned the torrent of disorder and violence inside or outside the stadiums. The iron fist appears to be the first and only policy option.

Just a few weeks later, the government announced that the prospect of protests at the World Cup would be met with a budget for security of over $1 billion and the formation of a national police force 10,000 strong, deployable anywhere in the country. Reassuringly the government said they would be trained to the same standards as UN peacekeepers. Perhaps they will be taking courses with the Brazilian forces who served in this capacity in Haiti, and who treated the exercise as a cross between a military occupation and a favela pacification programme, and who were repeatedly accused of summary executions and human rights abuses. Perhaps they will be needed to quell the gun battles and protests that have been emerging in Rio's 'pacified' favelas, where the rule of the *traficantes* has yet to be replaced by the rule of law. Perhaps they will take their lead from the São Paulo police who, at an anti-World Cup demonstration, just 2,000-strong, in early February, kept order by shooting one protestor dead. This death barely made a ripple in Brazil, let alone the rest of the world. Come 12 June 2014 we shall see.

Brazil might still be, as Milton Nascimento had sung, 'the country of football', but when the Seleção plays, Brazil is no longer just at the stadium and its streets are no longer empty. There might still be victories to be won on the field, but it is hard to imagine that they could unite the futebol nation the way they have done in the past, for they have been bought at the cost of making Brazil's divisions and its injustices starker than ever. In the long run, we can hope that this is its triumph rather than its tragedy.

Notes

Introduction: The Curious Rise of the Futebol Nation

1 This line of thinking was inspired by P. Anderson (1994), 'The Dark Side of Brazilian Conviviality', *London Review of Books* 16(22), 24 November. I have also been guided throughout in my understanding of the politics of Brazil by P. Anderson (2002), 'The Cardoso Legacy: Lula's Inheritance', *London Review of Books* 24(24), 12 December; P. Anderson (2011), 'Lula's Brazil', *London Review of Books* 33(7), 31 March; T. Skidmore (1967), *Politics in Brazil*, Oxford: Oxford University Press; T. Skidmore (1988), *Politics of Military Rule in Brazil*, Oxford: Oxford University Press; T. Skidmore (2010), *Brazil: Five Centuries of Change*, 2nd edn, Oxford: Oxford University Press.

2 The phrase was popularly credited to Pelé after he published his memoirs with the title *My Life and the Beautiful Game* in 1977. Others with a prior claim include H. E. Bates, Didi and Stuart Hall.

3 H. McIlvanney (1994), *McIlvanney on Football*, Edinburgh: Mainstream, p. 168.

4 J. M. Wisnik (2008), *Veneno Remédio: O Futebol e o Brasil*, Rio de Janeiro: Companhia das Letras.

5 R. DaMatta (1986), *Explorações: Ensaios de Sociologia Interpretativa*, Rio de Janeiro: Rocca, p. 130, cited in T. Mason (1995), *Passion of the People: Football in South America*, London: Verso.

1. Champagne Football: The Game of the Belle Époque, 1889–1922

1 M. de Andrade (1984), *Macunaíma*, New York: Random House.
2 Quoted in Paulo Mendes Campos (1981), 'Passes de letra', in *Diário da Tarde*, Rio de Janeiro: Civilização Brasileira, p. 92.
3 See José Moraes dos Santos Neto (2007), *Visão do Jogo – Primórdios do Futebol no Brasil*, São Paulo: Cosac Naify.
4 This section draws extensively on V. de Melo and J. Mangan (1997), 'A web of the wealthy: modern sport in the nineteenth-century culture of Rio de Janeiro', *International Journal of the History of Sport* 14(1), 168–73.
5 Cited in ibid., p. 170.
6 Quoted in A. Hamilton (1998), *An Entirely Different Game: The British Influence on Brazilian Football*, Edinburgh: Mainstream.
7 Ibid., p. 44.
8 Quoted in ibid., p. 40.
9 Letter from Charles Miller to *Bannister Court School Magazine* III(31), March 1904, repr. in Hamilton (1998), p. 42.
10 See T. Mason (1995), *Passion of the People: Football in South America*, London: Verso, p. 12.
11 Quoted in T. Mazzoni (1950), *História do Futebol no Brasil 1894–1950*, Rio de Janeiro: Edições Leia, p. 69 and Mason (1995), p. 12.
12 Quoted in B. Buarque, J. Malaia, L. Henrique, V. Andrade (2012), *A Torcida Brasileira*, Rio de Janeiro: 7Letras.
13 Quoted in Mason (1995), p. 14.
14 João do Rio (pseudonym of João Paulo Coelho Barreto), 'Pall Mall Rio – Foot-ball', *O Paiz*, 4 September 1916.
15 Buarque et al. (2012).
16 A. Torelly, 'Match de foot-ball', in M. Pedrosa (ed.) (1967), *Gol de Letra: O Futebol na Literatura Brasileira*, Rio de Janeiro: Gol, p. 112.
17 Quoted in A. Bellos (2002), *Futebol: The Brazilian Way of Life*, London: Bloomsbury, p. 31.

18 L. Barreto (1922), 'O nosso esporte', *A.B.C.*, 26 August 1922.

19 Quoted in G. Bocketti (2008), 'Italian immigrants, Brazilian football, and the dilemmas of national identity', *Journal of Latin American Studies* 40 (2), 275–302.

20 Quoted in L. Pereira (1998), 'O jogo dos sentidos: os literatos e a popularização do futebol no Rio de Janeiro', in S. Chaloub and L. Pereira (eds.), *A História Contada: Capítulos de História Social da Literatura no Brasil*, Rio de Janeiro: Editora Nova Fronteira, p. 201.

21 Afrânio Peixoto (1916), 'Para vencer no futebol', *Jornal do Commércio*, 25 October 1916.

22 Ibid.

23 Carlos Sussekind de Mendonça quoted in L. Pereira (2000), *Footballmania: Uma História Social do Futebol no Rio de Janeiro, 1902–1938*, Rio de Janeiro: Editora Nova Fronteira.

24 L. Barreto (1919), 'Liga contra o futebol', *Rio Jornal*, 12 March.

25 G. Ramos under the pseudonym J. Calisto (1921), 'Índio', *Palmeira dos Índios*.

26 On Friedenreich see M. Curi (2013), 'Arthur Friedenreich (1892–1969): a Brazilian Biography', *Soccer and Society*, 18 November.

27 L. Barreto (1921), 'Bendito football', *Careta*, 1 October.

2. Modern Times? Football and the Death of the Old Republic, 1922–1932

Epigraph. Extract from Antônio de Alcântara Machado (1927), 'Corinthians (2) vs. Palestra (1)', in *Brás, Bexiga e Barra Funda*, Rio de Janeiro: Imago, pp. 36–41.

1 Quoted in K. Jackson (2012), *Constellation of Genius, 1922: Modernism Year One*, New York: Farrar, Straus and Giroux.

2 Mário de Andrade (2008), 'Brasil – Argentina', in *Os Filhos da Candinha*, Rio de Janeiro: Agir, pp. 65–8; Mário de Andrade (1922), *De Paulicéia Desvairada a Café (Poesias Completas)*, São

Paulo: Círculo do Livro; Mário de Andrade (2001), *Macunaíma, o Herói sem Nenhum Caráter*, Belo Horizonte/Rio de Janeiro: Garnier.

3 Oswald de Andrade, *Memórias Sentimentais de João Miramar*, São Paulo: Globo, 1991.

4 Machado (1997), 'Corinthians (2) vs. Palestra (1)'.

5 *New York Times*, 28 January 1917, quoted in C. Gaffney (2010), 'Mega-Events and Socio-Spatial Dynamics in Rio de Janeiro, 1919–2016', *Journal of Latin American Geography* 9(1), 7–29.

6 The football fragments of *Terra Encantada* can be seen at http://www.youtube.com/watch?v=5cYyVmLhiWs.

7 J. Manuel, C. Malaia Santos, V. Melo (eds.) (2012), *1922: Celebrações Esportivas do Centenário*, Rio de Janeiro: 7Letras.

8 Ibid.

9 T. Mason (1995), *Passion of the People: Football in South America*, London: Verso, p. 56. Fausto compared himself to an orange which would be squeezed and pulped by football's bosses.

10 W. Caldas (1990), *O Pontapé Inicial: Memória do Futebol Brasileiro*, p. 88.

11 Amílcar quoted in ibid., p. 62.

12 *Folha da Manhã*, 10 July 1931, quoted in G. Bocketti (2008), 'Italian immigrants, Brazilian football, and the dilemmas of national identity', *Journal of Latin American Studies* 40(2).

3. Brasilidade: *Football and the New Order, 1932–1950*

Epigraph. José Lins do Rego quoted in E. Coutinho (1991), *Zelins – Flamengo Até Morrer*, Rio de Janeiro: Ed. Fundação de Amparo à Pesquisa do RJ.

1 Quoted in M. Maia (2002), *Villa-Lobos, Alma Brasileira*, São Paulo: Ed. Contraponto, pp. 48–9.

2 'Inaugurado o Estádio Municipal do Pacaembu', *O Estado de São Paulo*, 28 April 1940, p. 8.

3 Ibid.

4 *Jornal dos Sports*, 13 March 1937, quoted in Renato Soares Coutinho (2009), *Pelo Brasil e pelo Flamengo: José Bastos Padilha e o Projeto de Construção de uma Nação*, paper given at International History Congress, Maringá, Paraná, September 2009: see http://www.pph.uem.br/cih/anais/trabalhos/273.pdf.

5 *Jornal dos Sports*, 19 February 1937, quoted in ibid.

6 See R. Levine (1984), 'Elite interventions in urban popular culture in modern Brazil', *Luso-Brazilian Review* 21(2).

7 See L. Shaw (1998), 'São coisas nossas: samba and identity in the Vargas era (1930–1945)', *Portuguese Studies* 14, 152–69; L. Shaw (2002), 'Samba and "Brasilidade": notions of national identity in the lyrics of Noel Rosa (1910–1937)', *Lusotopie* 2, 81–96.

8 Lamartine Babo actually composed hymns (supposedly in less than a week) for eleven of Rio's teams, all of which were released as records, testament to the depth of football support in the city. See http://globoesporte.globo.com/futebol/noticia/2012/02/lamartine-babo-o-compositor-dos-hinos-dos-clubes-do-rio-de-janeiro.html.

9 *Correio da Manhã*, 15 June 1938.

10 G. Freyre (1964), *The Masters and the Slaves: A Study in the Development of Brazilian Civilization*, New York: Random House.

11 P. Robb (2004), *A Death in Brazil*, London: Bloomsbury, pp. 24–5.

12 Mário de Andrade (2008), 'Brasil – Argentina' in *Os Filhos da Candinha*, Rio de Janeiro: Agir, quoted in B. Buarque de Hollanda (2011), 'In praise of improvisation in Brazilian soccer: Modernism, popular music, and a Brasilidade of sports', *Critical Studies in Improvisation/Études critiques en improvisation* 7(1).

13 Domingos da Guia, vídeo Núcleo /UERJ, 1995, cited in M. Murad (2007), *A Violência e o Futebol: Dos Estudos Clássicos aos Dias de Hoje*, Rio de Janeiro: Editora FGV.

14 Quoted in R. Levine (1980), 'Sport and society: the case of Brazilian futebol', *Luso-Brazilian Review* 17(2).

15 *Jornal dos Sports*, 10 June 1947.

16 Quoted in A. Bellos (2002), *Futebol: The Brazilian Way of Life*, London: Bloomsbury, p. 48.

17 Ibid.

18 Quoted in T. Mason (1995), *Passion of the People: Football in South America*, London: Verso, p. 89.

19 N. Rodrigues (1994), 'O drama das sete copas' [June 1966], in *A Pátria em Chuteiras: Novas Crônicas de Futebol*, São Paulo: Companhia das Letras, pp. 112–19.

4. Brasília and the Ball: Inventing the Beautiful Game, 1950–1964

Epigraph. O. Niemeyer (2000), *The Curves of Time: The Memoirs of Oscar Niemeyer*, London: Phaidon Press, p. 62.

1 Quoted in Geoffrey Green, *The Times*, 30 June 1958.

2 J. Leite Lopes (2000), 'The People's Joy vanishes: considerations on the death of a soccer player', *Journal of Latin American Anthropology* 4(2).

3 Cited in *The Pelé Albums* (1990), vols. 1 and 2, Sydney: Weldon Publishing.

4 J. Lever (1995), *Soccer Madness: Brazil's Passion for the World's Most Popular Sport*, 2nd edn, Prospect Heights, IL: Waveland Press.

5 Ibid., p. 74.

6 Ibid., p. 72.

7 J. de Ryswick (1962), *100,000 Heures de Football*, Paris: La Table Ronde, pp. 224–5.

8 Cited in T. Mason (1995), *Passion of the People: Football in South America*, London: Verso, p. 123.

9 Rodrigues quoted in A. Bellos (2002), *Futebol: The Brazilian Way of Life*, London: Bloomsbury, p. 249.

10 The whole of João de Cabral Melo Neto's letter can be seen at http://www.literaturanaarquibancada.com/2011/11/joao-cabral-de-melo-neto-e-o-futebol.html.

11 Carlos Drummond de Andrade (2002), *Quando é Dia de Futebol*, Rio de Janeiro: Editora Record.

5. Playing the Hard Line: Football under the Dictatorship, 1964–1986

Epigraphs. *Jornal do Brasil* and Telê Santana quoted in T. Mason (1995), *Passion of the People: Football in South America*, London: Verso.

1 As reported in *Jornal do Brasil*, 22 June 1970, translated by and cited in Lever (1995), *Soccer Madness: Brazil's Passion for the World's Most Popular Sport*, 2nd edn, Prospect Heights, IL: Waveland Press, p. 69.

2 *Jornal do Brasil*, 19 June 1973, translated by and cited in Lever (1995), p. 64.

3 The conversation between the two may be apocryphal, reported by someone in their presence over twenty years later and widely reported in the Brazilian press; see for example http://www.jornaldapaulista.com.br/site/page.php?key=3985.

4 B. Milan (1989), *Brasil: O País do Futebol*, Rio de Janeiro: Best Editora, p. 12.

5 Cited in R. Levine (1980), 'Sport and society: the case of Brazilian futebol', *Luso-Brazilian Review* 17(2).

6 E. Coutinho (1994), *Bye-Bye, Soccer*, trans. Wilson Louria, Austin, TX: Host Publications, p. 6.

7 Walter Areno, 'Os desportos femininos: aspectos médicos (Female sports: medical aspects)', *Physical Education* 62, 63, 1942,

p. 57, cited in G. Knijknik (2011), 'From the cradle to Athens: the silver-coated story of a warrior in Brazilian soccer', *Sporting Traditions* 28(1), 63–83.

8 B. Milan (1989), *Brasil: O País do Futebol*, Rio de Janeiro: Best Editora.

9 Quoted in S. Votre and L. Mourão (2003), 'Women's football in Brazil: progress and problems', *Soccer and Society* 4(2–3), 254–67.

10 Cited in E. Couto (2010), 'A esquerda contra-ataca: rebeldia e contestação política no futebol Brasileiro (1970–1978)', *Revista de História do Esporte* 3(1).

11 See T. Skidmore (2010), *Brazil: Five Centuries of Change*, 2nd edn, Oxford: Oxford University Press, pp. 188–91.

12 T. Caesar (1988), 'Bringing it all down: the 1986 World Cup in Brazil', *Massachusetts Review* 29(2), Summer, 77–86.

6. Magic and Dreams are Dead:
Pragmatism, Politics and Football, 1986–2002

Epigraph. Carlos Alberto Parreira quoted in the *New York Times*, 1 July 1994.

1 *New York Times*, 1 July 1994.

2 *Gazeta Sportiva*, 27 August 1992.

3 Quoted in J. Brooke (1994), 'Rio Journal; Brazilians say their World Cup runneth over', *New York Times*, 19 July.

4 T. Caesar (1988), 'Bringing it all down: the 1986 World Cup in Brazil', *Massachusetts Review* 29(2), Summer, 78.

5 Quoted in T. Mason (1995), *Passion of the People: Football in South America*, London: Verso, p. 145.

6 Quoted in ibid., p. 150.

7 Quoted in H. Tobar (2002), 'Brazil gets "Biggest Happiness"', *Los Angeles Times*, 1 July.

8 Quoted in A. Bellos (2001), 'Crime, anarchy, incompetence: how the blazers betrayed Brazil', *Guardian*, 6 December.

9 Quoted in D. Pinheiro (2011), 'The President', *Piauí* 58.

10 *Guardian*, 6 January 1994, cited in Mason (1995), p. 145.

11 Quoted in Bellos (2002), *Futebol: The Brazilian Way of Life*, London: Bloomsbury, p. 302.

12 Ibid., p. 303.

7. Futebol Nation Redux: The Game in Lula's Brazil, 2002–2013

Epigraph. Lula quoted in Terra.com report, 29 July 2010: 'Deus sabe que o Brasil não pode perder a Copa de 2014, diz Lula', see http://esportes.terra.com.br/futebol/brasil2014/noticias/0,,OI4594075-EI10545,00-Deus+sabe+que+o+Brasil+nao+pode+perder+a+Copa+de+diz+Lula.html.

1 *Lance!*, 19 August 2010, see http://www.lancenet.com.br/info-graficos/organizacao-da-copa-2014/.

2 Júlio Mariz quoted in A. Downie (2008), 'Trading in soccer talent', *New York Times*, 19 July.

3 Quoted in Leonardo Sakamoto, 'Após morte de jovem, MPT quer processar Vasco por trabalho infantil', 25 February 2012, see http://blogdosakamoto.blogosfera.uol.com.br/2012/02/25/apos-morte -de-jovem-mpt-quer-processar-vasco-por-trabalho-infantil/.

4 Quoted in M. Proni and F. Zaia (2013), 'Financial condition of Brazilian soccer clubs: an overview', *Soccer and Society*, 12 November. All the above financial data on Brazilian football clubs is drawn from this article.

5 See the notes to the Mundo Livre S/A CD *Por Pouco*, 2000.

6 R. Shaw (2009), 'Brazilian football's race problem', *WSC Daily*, 10 December, see http://www.wsc.co.uk/wsc-daily/978-December-2009/4194-brazilian-footballs-race-problem.

7 J. Knijnik and P. Horton (2013), ' "Only beautiful women need apply": human rights and gender in Brazilian football', *Creative Approaches to Research* 6(1), June, pp. 60–70.

8 Quoted in J. Knijnik (2013), 'Visions of gender justice: untested feasibility on the football fields of Brazil', *Journal of Sport & Social Issues*, 37(1), 8–30.

9 Quoted in T. Azzoni (2012), 'Fans turn threatening as Brazilian team struggles', Associated Press, 9 November, see http://bigstory. ap.org/article/fans-turn-threatening-brazilian-team- struggles.

10 J. Longman and T. Barnes (2013), 'A Yellow Card, Then Unfathomable Violence, in Brazil', *New York Times*, 31 October.

8. Copa das Manifestações: *Civil War in the Futebol Nation, 2013–2014*

Epigraph. Pelé's remarks were made during an interview with TV Tribuna de Santos, a Brazilian television station, and widely reported.

1 *Statement of the Chairman of the FIFA Adjudicatory Chamber, Hans-Joachim Eckert, on the examination of the ISL case*, 29 April 2013, p. 3.

2 Quoted in D. Conn (2012), 'Fifa corruption intrigue deepens as Brazil's Ricardo Teixeira resigns', *Guardian*, 12 March.

3 Quoted in L. Rother (2007), 'For Pan-Am Games, the big race is to the starting line', *New York Times*, 22 May.

4 T. P. R. Caldeira (2000), *City of Walls: Segregation and Citizenship in São Paulo*, Berkeley, CA: University of California Press, p. 258.

5 Quoted in R. de Almeida (2007), 'Brazil: the shadow of urban war', *Open Democracy*, 18 July, see http://www.opendemocracy. net/article/brazil_shadow_urban_war.

6 That's certainly how the UN General Assembly sees it. See *Report of the Special Rapporteur on extrajudicial, summary or arbitrary executions, Philip Alston, A/HRC/14/24/Add.*8

7 José Roberto Bernasconi quoted in A. Downie (2013), 'As Brazil World Cup nears, public transport worries mount', Reuters, 5 March, see http://uk.reuters.com/article/2013/03/05/soccer-world-brazil-idUKL1N0BW1DL20130305.

8 Alberto Murray Neto quoted in J. Andersen (2013), 'The battle of Maracaña', 10 May, see http://www.playthegame.org/knowledge-bank/articles/the-battle-of-maracana-5598.html.

9 Ibid.

10 C. Gaffney (2013), 'Chega de bullying', 21 June, see http://www.geostadia.com/2013/06/chega-de-bullying.html.

Coda

1 Quoted in BBC News (2013), 'Brazil World Cup: opening match venue "ready mid-April"', 5 December 2013, see http://www.bbc.co.uk/news/world-latin-america-25244199.

Select Bibliography

This list includes a number of books already cited in the notes as well as many books and articles that have not been cited but that I have drawn on heavily in both constructing the book's narrative and fleshing out key issues or incidents.

Alvito, M. (2007), 'Our piece of the pie: Brazilian football and globalization', *Soccer & Society*, 8(4), 524–44.

Anderson, P. (1994), 'The dark side of Brazilian conviviality', *London Review of Books* 16(22), 24 November.

—— (2002), 'The Cardoso legacy: Lula's inheritance', *London Review of Books* 24(24), 12 December.

—— (2011), 'Lula's Brazil', *London Review of Books* 33(7), 31 March.

Bellos, A. (2002), *Futebol: The Brazilian Way of Life*, London: Bloomsbury.

Castro, R. (2004), *Garrincha: The Triumph and Tragedy of Brazil's Forgotten Footballing Hero*, London: Bloomsbury.

Curi, M. (2008), 'Samba, girls and party: who were the Brazilian soccer fans at a World Cup? An ethnography of the 2006 World Cup in Germany', *Soccer & Society*, 9(1), 111–34.

Curi, M., J. Knijnik and G. Mascarenhas (2011), 'The Pan American Games in Rio de Janeiro 2007: consequences of a sport megaevent on a BRIC country', *International Review for the Sociology of Sport*, 46(2), 140–56.

Gaffney, C. (12/2013), 'Virando o jogo: the challenges and possibilities for social mobilization in Brazilian football', *Journal of Sport & Social Issues* (0193–7235).

Gaffney, C. T. (2008), *Temples of the Earthbound Gods: Stadiums in the Cultural Landscapes of Rio de Janeiro and Buenos Aires*, Austin, TX: University of Texas Press.

Gordon, C. and R. Helal (2001), 'The crisis of Brazilian football: perspectives for the twenty-first century', *International Journal of the History of Sport*, 18(3), 139–58.

Hamilton, A. (1998), *An Entirely Different Game: The British Influence on Brazilian Football*, Edinburgh: Mainstream.

Hollanda, B. B. Buarque de (2003), 'O descobrimento do futebol: modernismo, regionalismo e paixão esportiva em José Lins do Rego', Masters thesis, Programa de Pós-Graduação em História Social da Cultura, Pontifícia Universidade Católica do Rio de Janeiro.

Knijnik, J. (2013), 'Visions of gender justice: untested feasibility on the football fields of Brazil', *Journal of Sport & Social Issues*, 37(1), 8–30.

Knijnik, J. and P. Horton (2013), '"Only beautiful women need apply": human rights and gender in Brazilian football', *Creative Approaches to Research* 6, 60–70.

Leite Lopes, J. S. (1997), 'Successes and contradictions in "multi-racial" Brazilian football', in G. Armstrong and R. Giulianotti (eds.), *Entering the Field: New Perspectives on World Football*, Oxford: Berg, pp. 53–86.

—— (1999), 'The Brazilian style of football and its dilemmas', in G. Armstrong and R. Giulianotti (eds.), *Football Cultures and Identities*, London: Macmillan, pp. 86–98.

—— (2000), 'The People's Joy vanishes: considerations on the death of a soccer player', *Journal of Latin-American Anthropology* 4(2).

see also Lopes, J. S. L.

Lever, J. (1995), *Soccer Madness: Brazil's Passion for the World's Most Popular Sport*, 2nd edn, Prospect Heights, IL: Waveland Press.

Levine, R. (1980), 'Sport and society: the case of Brazilian futebol', *Luso-Brazilian Review* 17(2).

Lopes, J. S. L. (2000), 'Class, ethnicity, and color in the making of Brazilian football', *Daedalus* 129(2), 239–70.

—— (2007), 'Transformations in national identity through football in Brazil: lessons from two historical defeats', in R. Miller and L. Crolley (eds.), *Football in the Americas: Fútbol, Futebol, Soccer,* London: Institute for the Study of the Americas, pp. 75–93.

Manco, T. and C. Neelon (2005), *Graffiti Brasil,* London: Thames and Hudson.

Mason, T. (1995), *Passion of the People: Football in South America,* London: Verso.

Melo, V. de and J. Mangan (1997), 'A web of the wealthy: modern sport in the nineteenth-century culture of Rio de Janeiro', *International Journal of the History of Sport* 14(1), 168–73.

Pereira, L. (2000), *Footballmania: Uma História Social do Futebol no Rio de Janeiro, 1902–1938,* Rio de Janeiro: Editora Nova Fronteira.

Rodrigues Filho, M. (1964 [1947]), *O Negro no Futebol Brasileiro,* Rio de Janeiro: Civilização Brasileira [Preface by Gilberto Freyre]

Shirts, M. (1988), 'Sócrates, Corinthians, and questions of democracy and citizenship', in J. Arbena (ed.), *Sport and Society in Latin America: Diffusion, Dependency, and the Rise of Mass Culture,* Westport, CT: Praeger, pp. 97–112.

—— (1989), 'Playing soccer in Brazil: Socrates, Corinthians, and democracy', *The Wilson Quarterly* 13(2), 119–23.

Skidmore, T. (1967), *Politics in Brazil,* Oxford: Oxford University Press.

—— (1988), *Politics of Military Rule in Brazil,* Oxford: Oxford University Press.

—— (2010), *Brazil: Five Centuries of Change,* 2nd edn, Oxford: Oxford University Press.

Taylor, C. (1998), *The Beautiful Game: A Journey through Latin American Football*, London: Victor Gollancz.

Votre, S. and L. Mourão (2003), 'Women's football in Brazil: progress and problems', *Soccer and Society* 4(2–3), 254–67.

Young, J. (2012), '"The Far Corner": how football in the north-east of Brazil struggles to keep up with the giants of the south', *The Blizzard* 6, September.

Acknowledgements

This book ought to have been written by someone else, preferably someone Brazilian, at the very least a person with a good command of the Portuguese language, at best someone coming to the task after a long period of study in the field. I could claim none of these. In fact, I feel like one of the least Brazilian people in the world, my Portuguese is poor and, though I have been thinking and writing about the history of football for over a decade, I was hardly an expert in Brazilian football history. My best defence, I think, is that someone had to write it. There is no single social and political account of Brazilian football history available in the English language. Tony Mason's *Passion of the People* has the spine of such a book within, but it is predominantly concerned with Argentina and Uruguay and almost twenty years old. Alex Bellos's *Futebol: The Brazilian Way of Life* opened up a lot of new historical and cultural territory for English readers, but for those who require a serious political reading of the sport, it is too journalistic and episodic. Although Brazilian football historians and social scientists are producing more and better research than ever before, no one has synthesized this new work into a single, considered social and political narrative.

It was out of these resources that I created my own thin narrative spine of Brazilian football history in *The Ball is Round: A Global History of Football*. In some ways *Futebol Nation* fills out the details of that book's arguments, and in places I have used some of its words. There were paragraphs that I knew I would never write so well again and I have used some of them in this book. Forgive me, I could have rewritten them badly, but I'm not sure how that helps anyone. In other ways, the process of researching and writing *Futebol Nation* has made me take those arguments apart and refashion them.

My time in Brazil, notable for the warmth with which I was received and the forbearance shown to my relentless questioning, made me appreciate its charms, its generosity and the joys of its flexible and circuitous way of being. As a witness to the demonstrations in Belo Horizonte and Rio in June 2013 my hopes for a new Brazilian civil society and my worst suspicions of the old Brazilian state were confirmed. This book is hardly the last word on the subject. It feels to me like an exploratory essay, but one that has convinced me that Brazilian football's cultural and political significance demands that its history be written.

Above all what has made this book possible has been the time and generosity, the memory banks and intellects, of dozens of people. So it's a very big thank you to: Alex Koch for getting me out to Brazil in the first place and igniting my imagination; Bruna Bastos for being a guardian angel; Luíz Gustavo Leitão Vieira and Élcio Loureiro in Belo Horizonte for a lovely evening of drinks and conversation that turned into a lot of reading; the Paul Weller of South American football, Tim Vickery, who says he won't write a book but knows enough to fill a dozen. In Rio, thank you to Juliana Barbassa, Misha Glenny, James Young, Rodrigo Ferrari, Leonardo Perreira and Martin Curi. In São Paulo, thank you to José Paulo Florenzano, Newton César de Oliveira Santos, Enrico Spaggiari, Sérgio Settani Giglio, Matthew Cowley, Andrew Downie and Tom Hennigan, and Daniela Alfonsi, Bernardo Buarque de Hollanda and all the staff at the Museu do Futebol – unquestionably the best institution in all of Brazilian football. In Durham, North Carolina, thank you to Laurent Dubois for having me over and giving me a place to think, Joshua Nadel for sorting me out in so many ways, and John French for stern unbrazilian words. Back in the UK, the thanks go out to Sally Holloway, Tony Lacey, John English, Ben Brusey, David Wood, David Brookshire, Luciana Martins, Tristan Manco, Matthew Brown, Jean Williams and the ICSHC at De Montfort University. And to Gregg Bocketti in Transylvania and Jorge Knijnik in Australia.

Special thanks to Chris Gaffney; my guide to the protests was also a generous host and an endless source of information and ideas. His blog Hunting White Elephants (www.geostadia.com) is the place to get informed about Brazil's sporting mega-events. And, of course, the biggest thanks and the most love to the people who lived with me while I wrote this: Sarah, who has shown me the way of the lark, Molly and Luke.

Photo credits

Index

He just wanted a decent book to read ...

Not too much to ask, is it? It was in 1935 when Allen Lane, Managing Director of Bodley Head Publishers, stood on a platform at Exeter railway station looking for something good to read on his journey back to London. His choice was limited to popular magazines and poor-quality paperbacks – the same choice faced every day by the vast majority of readers, few of whom could afford hardbacks. Lane's disappointment and subsequent anger at the range of books generally available led him to found a company – and change the world.

'We believed in the existence in this country of a vast reading public for intelligent books at a low price, and staked everything on it'
Sir Allen Lane, 1902–1970, founder of Penguin Books

The quality paperback had arrived – and not just in bookshops. Lane was adamant that his Penguins should appear in chain stores and tobacconists, and should cost no more than a packet of cigarettes.

Reading habits (and cigarette prices) have changed since 1935, but Penguin still believes in publishing the best books for everybody to enjoy. We still believe that good design costs no more than bad design, and we still believe that quality books published passionately and responsibly make the world a better place.

So wherever you see the little bird – whether it's on a piece of prize-winning literary fiction or a celebrity autobiography, political tour de force or historical masterpiece, a serial-killer thriller, reference book, world classic or a piece of pure escapism – you can bet that it represents the very best that the genre has to offer.

Whatever you like to read – trust Penguin.